Greenough White

Outline of the Philosophy of English Literature

Part I

Greenough White

Outline of the Philosophy of English Literature
Part I

ISBN/EAN: 9783337072926

Printed in Europe, USA, Canada, Australia, Japan

Cover: Foto ©Thomas Meinert / pixelio.de

More available books at **www.hansebooks.com**

OUTLINE

OF

THE PHILOSOPHY

OF

ENGLISH LITERATURE

BY

GREENOUGH WHITE A.M. B.D.

PART I

THE MIDDLE AGES

BOSTON U.S.A. AND LONDON
GINN & COMPANY PUBLISHERS
1895

TO

HARVARD UNIVERSITY

IN TOKEN OF GRATITUDE
FOR THE LIBERALLY ACCORDED USE
OF THE TREASURES OF ITS LIBRARY
WITHOUT WHICH THIS COULD NOT HAVE BEEN WRITTEN
AND FOR THOSE EARLIER INTELLECTUAL OPPORTUNITIES .
THAT FURNISHED ITS FIRST SUBSTANCE
THIS WORK IS PRESENTED
BY A LOYAL ALUMNUS

PREFACE.

In view of the excellent treatises upon English literature that have multiplied of late years until they form by themselves a veritable library, the only excuse that the present work can allege for being is that in it the great subject is considered under a somewhat new light. To describe the process of mental development; to determine the limits and character of literary ages; to get at the basal principle of each successive age and trace its derivation from that which preceded it, — such has been the motive of the work. The lives of authors, therefore, have not been a primary concern, yet it is hoped that the personal element in literary history has not been unduly depressed and that the leading characteristics of men of commanding and formative genius have been firmly grasped and forcibly presented.

It is best to explain at the outset that in prosecuting his endeavor the author has welcomed any light that contemporary history, literature or art seemed to afford; he has refused to regard any event in the progress of European civilization as not germane to the subject and has selected many facts that may at first sight seem remote from it to illustrate his theme. The result may prove to have a reflective value; for in laying European history under contribution in order to interpret English literature, that literature in its turn may make the course of contemporary history more perspicuous.

In this First Part of the work in particular, which treats of the ages known as mediaeval, the author will never regret any pains he has taken if he be deemed to have been successful in breaking up the stark unity which those great and misunderstood ages — so often dismissed as Feudal and Catholic — present to many minds; in unfolding the mighty movement that went on in them and discovering in some measure the source of their subtle attraction; and in showing how great is the value they possess for culture — a value, indeed, which nothing that preceded them can supply.

It is right to add that the above was written in Cambridge the last day of the year 1892, when the work, since subjected to repeated revision, seemed to be approaching completion.

CHARLESTON
February 1895.

OUTLINE OF THE PHILOSOPHY OF ENGLISH LITERATURE.

———◆———

INTRODUCTION.

IT is customary to begin treatises upon English literature
with an account of Anglo-Saxon, or as some of late prefer to
say, Old English writings. Without detracting in the least
from the value of the study of the Anglo-Saxon language as an
intellectual discipline, from its necessity for a complete knowledge of English, from the importance and interest of some of
its literary remains, one may question whether it is truly scientific thus to identify Anglo-Saxon with English literature;
whether it conduces to clearness, or tends to obscure differences and cause confusion; whether without affectation a work
can be included in English literature which an intelligent Englishman of the present day can enjoy only in translation, unless
he would take all the pains necessary for learning a foreign
language. Acquaintance with Latin is necessary for a thorough
knowledge of Italian, — but histories of Italian literature do not
therefore begin with Ennius. And yet the connection between
Latin and Italian literature is exceedingly close, and the influence of the ancient upon the modern authors has been over-
whelming, — while the influence of Anglo-Saxon upon English
literature has been just nothing. It was as late as the year
1832 that the treasures of the Vercelli book, among them
Cynewulf's best work, were first made known to the world;
the same year Benjamin Thorpe edited and translated Cædmon's Scripture paraphrase; the year following J. M. Kemble

brought out the first English edition of Beowulf, and thus at last made that noble epic, the most precious relic of Anglo-Saxon poetry, accessible to students, and by a prose translation of it in 1837 first unfolded its beauties to the general reader. In 1842 Thorpe edited the collection known as the Exeter book. Thus at last the body of that old poetry was brought to the light of day, and yet, a full generation later, an Anglo-Saxon scholar could complain of the slow awakening of interest in the subject, and the unaccountable neglect of that ancient literature in its native land.

That neglect is sufficiently explained by the lack of originality which, with the brilliant exception of Beowulf, pervades the whole mass of Anglo-Saxon composition. There are passages of power and beauty in Cædmon and Cynewulf, — but on the whole one cannot fail to be struck by the absence of native energy and invention, which leaves to the body of that composition a purely antiquarian interest, and thus deprives it of the right claimed for it by some near-sighted scholars to be regarded as genuine literature. A glance at those old writings will reveal, beside, the difficulties that beset any attempt at a philosophical history of them ; for their arrangement fluctuates with the tides of criticism, an important piece being assigned by different authorities to different generations or centuries even; nothing is known about the authors of some of the most important works, and little that is certain about those whose names are known. These facts, lack of original thought, and uncertainty about dates of composition, — to which we may add the gaps in the literary record, — render a philosophical interpretation of the phases of the literature almost impracticable. A survey of its main divisions gives evidence, however, in a general and unsatisfactory way, of a certain movement.

Before and above all its relics stands the epic of Beowulf, — the solitary finger of the sun that rises from the Saxon plain to take rank among the mighty monuments of world literature.

The tale possesses a deep and ever vital interest, in that it is a record of the conflict between heathen and Christian ideas in the Teutonic mind; and as it reflects the passage of Saxons and Angles over the wild North Sea from their old to their new home, so too it marks the great transition from faith to faith, — in it we may see the revolution in belief in very process.

The most significant antithesis of ideas in this old poem, this Christian graft upon a heathen stock, is that of the two explanations of world history offered by Fate and by Providence that divided the author's and redactor's minds. That man's life is bound by fate is the thought that lies deepest in the mind of the hero Beowulf as he prepares for the deadly conflict with the monster Grendel, — but at last he decides to lay aside his weapon and to wrestle with the foe, leaving the outcome of the fight to the disposition of the all-wise God, the holy Lord. Over and over again the poet expresses his faith in a righteous and all-powerful God of battles, the true governor of human affairs, — and yet at the end, when Beowulf is about to die by the fire-dragon's bite, it is said that his Weird, that is, his Fate, was approaching. In one place the poet tries to overcome the antithesis by identifying the blind Fate, the gloomy Destiny of heathendom, with the holy will of the personal sovereign of the world: Fate, he says, is the Providence of God.

The thought about nature revealed in the poem is of deep interest, and shows that in the convert's mind his former gods did not cease to be, but were simply metamorphosed into demons, and believed to haunt the fens, moors, crags, and waste places of the earth. He seems to have thought that powers of nature malignant to man were directed by evil spirits. The dreadful Grendel is a sort of personification of the deadly miasma of the marshes, and of any other natural influence hostile to human life. He towers at last to the dimensions of a Satan; he is an outcast, dwelling in darkness and the shadow of death, tormented by sight and sound of human happiness; he stalks over marsh and moor with a company of monsters, giants, and ogres, — the brood of Cain; he is the abomination that makes desolate, the foe of man, at once the thrall and the thane of hell, the adversary of God. Yet he retains something of human form, — he is a Caliban, only more ghastly; he destroys thirty warriors in one night. Night is the time when the fire-dragon flies abroad, when fiends have power,— they flee at the approach of dawn. By night the splendid hall of Hrothgar is deserted; the king and his train come trooping back by day. This horror of darkness and joy in the daylight illustrate the dualism that underlies the whole work; its theme is the ancient conflict between good and evil.

One striking touch is the gladness of nature when Grendel's horrid dam, the hag of the mere, whose home is a cavern under a torrent, is slain by Beowulf with a magic sword; instantly the sunlight grows brighter, the turbid water clears.

The lingering influence of heathenism is shown by those warriors who seek to save themselves from Grendel by propitiating the goblins, by sacrificing to idols; 'They knew not God,' is the stern comment of the poet. At last Beowulf is sent to destroy the pest, by the high grace of the holy God.

Beautiful is the picture of the friendly relations of Beowulf and his band and the sage old King Hrothgar; beautiful the stately courtesy of the queen to the hero. Throughout the poem loyalty is lauded as the crown of human virtue, the very bond of social life; disloyalty receives the severest condemnation. Charming, too, are the scenes of mirth in the royal hall; the warriors and their guests seated at long tables decked with barbaric gold, passing around ornamented ale-cups and flagons, while gold-embroidered hangings wave along the walls.

The next most important relic of Anglo-Saxon poetry is Cædmon's paraphrase of portions of the books of Genesis and Exodus, the story of Daniel and the Three Children, and fragments of a life of Christ. The fall of the rebel angels and the rage of Satan are described with spirit and power; the fall of man is boldly told, with interesting variations from the Biblical account; but after that the paraphrast becomes tame and dull, goes lumbering through the genealogies, sticks closely to his text,—not attempting, for instance, to harmonize the conflicting details in the story of the flood. The escape of the children of Israel from Egypt is more freshly treated. Though of far less value than Beowulf, this paraphrase, with its variations, is significant by reason of its deep earnestness of tone; in those two works we seem to see the Teutonic mind coming to itself.

It ought to be said that Cædmon's poem is regarded by scholars as a composite work, traces of many hands being found in it; also that neither it nor the tale of Beowulf are extant in manuscripts older than the tenth century, — later by many ages than the originals, and, moreover, written in a different dialect from theirs.

About the time when those poems were being composed, that is, at the end of the seventh century and throughout the first generation of the eighth, the erudite and saintly Bede — the glory of the Northumbrian monasteries — was preparing in Latin a veritable encyclopaedia of the knowledge of his age. The most remarkable passage in his works is, perhaps, the account in the "Ecclesiastical History" of Brother Drithelm and his vision of hell. Bede finished while on his death-bed a translation into the vernacular (long since lost) of the Gospel of St. John.

To the same period, probably, belong the poems of Cynewulf; but which and how many they are, and who Cynewulf was, are still vexed questions among scholars. That ancient bard is indeed a problematical character ; he has roamed like a restless ghost through centuries far apart, appearing now in the latest, now in the earliest period of the literature. He has been identified as an abbot of the eleventh century, as a bishop of the eighth, and, finally, all ecclesiastical rank has been denied him. To increase our uncertainty, there has been a tendency to attribute to him almost all the floating, anonymous minor poems in the language ; beside his Riddles, the Phoenix, and Elene — the Finding of the Cross, — Andreas, Crist, Juliana, Guthlac, and the Wanderer have been fathered upon him. His case is a notable example of the difficulty that attends any attempt at a reliable interpretation of the development of the literature. The genuine specimens of Cynewulf's work that have come down to us possess considerable beauty of thought and style ; they show that their author derived real pleasure from the gentler aspects of nature : his ideal landscape was a smooth plain, green and flowery and dotted with sunny groves, under a bright sky traversed by little clouds.

With the lamentable decay in Northumbrian power and prosperity that was going on through the eighth century, a shadow fell upon Anglo-Saxon literature that rested upon it for more than a hundred years. And yet that was the period of the rise of the power of Wessex, under Egbert, who had spent many years at the court of Charles the Great, in company with his countryman Alcuin — the leading scholar of his age in the west, — and had returned in the year 800 to assume the crown, and to put in practice as far as he could what he had learned from the example of Charles. By the year 827, the authority of King Egbert was recognized over all England ; and his able administration, his military and political success, must have been accompanied, it would seem, by some intellectual awakening. We should expect at this epoch some manifestation of interest in the operations of the mind, some study of logic and the laws of thought, and therewith a development, however slight, of the critical faculty, and of argumentative composition. The age of great poetry being past, we should look, with the study of grammar and rhetoric, for the formation of a good prose style. Some evidence of observation, if not investigation, of external nature might be expected : the motions of sun, moon, and stars, of winds and rivers and the sea, the properties of plants and minerals, the habits of animals. Already the Arabians were beginning their chemical studies, and were fascinated by watching the effect of herbs and minerals upon the human system. With his training and executive ability and capacity for organizing, it might be supposed that Egbert would introduce in his realm of Wessex a more thorough and comprehensive system of education ; that he would teach his people the benefits of an improved economy, and would encourage agriculture and handiwork of all sorts and the erection of better buildings ; and that in every way he would promote social stability and domestic comfort. But if there was movement in any or all of these directions, we have no literary or architectural proofs of it. This, to be sure, does not prove that there was no such movement — for fire destroys both books and buildings, and Egbert's reign went out in the darkness of Danish invasion. The probability is, however, that there was no great intellectual activity in that age ; perhaps King Egbert found that he could not communicate to a backward people the ideas that he had gathered at the court of Charles the Great, and so left much to be done by his grandson Alfred, fifty years later.

That noble prince, steadfast, wise, and good, the very personification of moral energy, was nourished as a boy upon the songs of his native land and language; and was of himself sufficient to create a literary age. In tranquil intervals amid his Danish wars, while engaged in recovering his realm from barbarism, in rebuilding cities and restoring arts and commerce, he made time to do an astonishing amount of literary work. He translated for the instruction of his people the History of the World by Paulus Orosius, a Spanish churchman, contemporary and friend of St. Augustine ; the Pastoral Care of Pope Gregory I ; Bede's Ecclesiastical History ; and (most significant of all) Boethius' Consolation of Philosophy. The aim of this latter work is to inculcate self-knowledge and self-mastery: it discusses the supreme good, the problem of evil, vice and virtue, misery and happiness, and seeks to reconcile the freedom of the human will with God's foreknowledge. Various comments of his own which the king incorporated in his translation show what a strong interest he felt in those great themes. It will be seen that Alfred's work partakes of the imitative nature of Anglo-Saxon writing in general; none of it is original, except the annotations just mentioned, and an account of the voyages of Ohthere and Wulfstan which he added to his translation of Orosius. Yet by his labors he became the father of Anglo-Saxon prose-style. In his time, too, the meagre entries of the ancient Chronicle become more copious, and swell it into a record worthier of the national history.

The next literary epoch was shaped by the influence of great ecclesiastics like Odo and Dunstan, who elevated the altar above the throne, controlled the course of political events, and brought their church into closer conformity to the Roman model. The central point in their policy may be divined to have been the introduction of the doctrine of transubstantiation, in support of which miracles even were alleged: it was currently reported that once, while Odo was breaking the consecrated bread, great drops of blood fell from it—to the confusion of the incredulous. In this respect those English churchmen shared in the general heightening of dogma that was in progress upon the continent of Europe. Odo was translated from the see of Sherborne to the archbishopric of Canterbury in the year 942; the year following, Dunstan was appointed abbot of Glastonbury. The cathedral of Canterbury was rebuilt at this time.

Upon the death of Odo, Dunstan was raised to the primacy in 961, and was the ruling spirit throughout the reign of Edgar. With the king's help he restored many monasteries all over the land, naturalized the Benedictine order, and ejected secular canons from cathedral chapters, putting monks in their place. This last measure was carried out at Winchester by Bishop Ethelwold, in the teeth of furious opposition; it was approved, however, by a voice that seemed to come from the great crucifix. In this reign the practice of receiving the sacrament fasting was canonically enforced.

The long and remarkable career of Dunstan, as monk, artist, and musician, scholar, and ecclesiastical statesman, came to a close in the year 988.

Such were some of the conditions under which the new literature arose; and its most celebrated names were those of ecclesiastics, Ælfric and Wulfstan. It was almost exclusively religious in its character, consisting of sermons, translations of the Scriptures, a paraphrase of the Psalms, and lives of saints; and it was chiefly in prose, — the most conspicuous exception to the character thus given of it being the spirited song of the fight at Maldon, in the year 991.

Ælfric was a pupil of Bishop Ethelwold, and taught grammar in the school at Winchester. Eighty homilies of his have come down to us, fine specimens of pure and mellow Saxon prose; in composing them he depended largely upon the writings of the Fathers of the church, freely translating and compiling from their stores. He translated beside the first seven books of the Old Testament. Ælfric was made an abbot; he has even been identified (erroneously, as it seems to many) with the archbishop of Canterbury of that name, who died in 1006. One homily of his, though not original, is important as giving evidence of a reaction in the mind of the English church against the recent development of eucharistic doctrine and toward the ancient, spiritual view.

Wulfstan, archbishop of York from 1002 to 1023, composed homilies in a rugged, picturesque style quite different from Ælfric's; in one fervent address, of great interest and value, he describes the forlorn condition of the country under the oppression of its Danish marauders. The political and social outlook was so dark, indeed, that it seemed to both those preachers as if the coming of Antichrist, the day of doom, and the end of the world were near.

The sun of the Saxon state, after suffering a long eclipse during the supremacy of the Danes, shone out again with a pathetic, evening light in the time of Edward the Confessor, and set forever upon the field of Hastings. By the year 1071, the Norman conquest of England was complete; and Saxon nationality, as a freely developing, self-conscious entity, as an end in itself, existed no more. Its extinction is fitly typed in the failure of the male line of the Saxon kings. The church, too, was involved in the ruin of the state : native bishops were ejected from their sees to make room for foreigners, — a process significantly illustrated by the deposition of Stigand, native archbishop of Canterbury, and the installation of Lanfranc, an Italian, in the year 1070. Canterbury cathedral was destroyed by fire in the first year of the Norman conquest, — a loss that seriously impairs our knowledge of Saxon architecture. The national literature participated, inevitably, in the general decline; yet it lingered on, a thin stream, ever ready to die in the sand, until the middle of the following century. Some homilies were written and the Chronicle was brought down to the year 1154 — when, with the Norman dynasty, it too came to an end. And then ensued a period of half a century which is practically a total blank in the history of composition in the language of the conquered people. A few more homilies belong to that period, composed in a dialect already so far removed from the form of the Saxon classics that those who spoke it could no longer understand the earlier writings : Ælfric's homilies had to be modernized for their benefit. Anglo-Saxon language and literature had shrunk into a possession for monastic antiquaries.

Even from a survey as swift as this of ours has just been it is apparent that these compositions form a distinct literary department which cannot legitimately be merged in any other but must be isolated for special study. To understand and enjoy this literature a special discipline is necessary: the language must first be learned — a language which those who know most about it admit to be totally new and strange to the Englishman of to-day, only to be acquired by long study. By reason of its peculiar form Anglo-Saxon verse especially is hard to understand, — as much so indeed as difficult German. The literature, moreover, is circumscribed in its scope; Beowulf alone soars into the empyrean of universal poetry; for the rest it consists almost entirely of paraphrases, translations, and homilies largely compiled from foreign sources, for the sake of a special audience in a period long since gone by. Its work has long been done; it is now of interest only to the philologist, the antiquarian, the student of Saxon civilization. It is a literature at second-hand, for the Saxon mind, assimilative, imitative, cared chiefly about the reproduction of the thought of stronger minds. And finally, the gaps in the record, and our ignorance or uncertainty about the authorship or approximate date even of much that remains, are such that the result of the most patient attempt at a philosophical interpretation of it must still be somewhat unsubstantial. Fresh discoveries and closer agreement among critics must precede any complete and comprehensive theory of its development.

I.

In the twelfth century the intellect of England found expression in Latin and Norman-French, and though works composed in those languages cannot, of course, be included in English literature merely because they sprang on English soil, and though at first sight they seem further removed from it than the Saxon classics even, yet in reality, from a literary point of view, some of them are much nearer, being allied to it in subject: in them appeared those images of chivalry and devotion that have swum in enchanting vision before the eyes of great English poets; have stirred the emotions of myriads of hearers and readers, and still have power to charm; that run like a golden chain through all these seven centuries of English literature, binding them in one, — the tales of Arthur and his knights of the Round Table, of Lancelot and Galahad and the search for the mystic Grail.

The charm of those old stories, the surpassing beauty and mystery of the conception of the Grail, invite us to consider the genius of the age from which they sprang.

For several generations there had been in progress a remarkable religious revival, which, beginning silently in centres far apart, had gradually widened in influence and gathered such strength that at the close of the eleventh century it gave a distinctive character to the age. As far back as the close of the tenth century a young nobleman of Ravenna named Romuald was suddenly converted from a worldly to an ascetic life; he exerted an extraordinary influence upon all who came in contact with him, and converted many, so that he became at last the founder of a new brotherhood: he left his cell in the Ravennese marshes, in the year 1009, to found a monastery at

Camaldoli, in the region of Arezzo. Even before his time the monks of Clugny, in Burgundy, had developed an intense religious zeal which told at last upon the papacy itself, and raised it from the turpitude into which it had fallen : in 1049, a brother of Clugny mounted the papal throne as Leo IX, and carried out stringent reforms, with the aid of his friend and counsellor, also a brother of the order, the mighty Hildebrand. In 1038, a Florentine named Gualbert, inspired by a visit to Camaldoli, started in Vallombrosa — a vale of willows — a fraternity pledged to observe in all its strictness the primitive rule of Benedict. Several affiliated houses were soon formed ; at the time of the founder's death, in 1073, there were twelve in the order. Still the deepening of the religious life went on ; the enthusiasm for starting new orders continued unabated; in 1084, Bruno of Cologne founded in a desolate site near Grenoble the first Carthusian monastery, to which, following an example set by Gualbert, he admitted lay brethren ; in 1098, an aged Benedictine monk named Robert started in a wood at Citeaux, in the neighborhood of Dijon, a brotherhood which, after it was joined by the fervent young Bernard, in 1113, out-rivalled all others in popularity. Soon after, Bernard became abbot of an affiliated house which he had founded in the wild valley of Clairvaux. His genius dominated the age; for a generation he exercised throughout Europe a primacy of piety. Norbert of Cleves, cousin and almoner of the Emperor Henry IV, was converted from a life of luxury to one of rigorous asceticism in consequence of an accident which had nearly proved fatal to him : while out riding one day he was over-taken by a fearful thunderstorm, and was thrown by his horse, terrified at lightning which struck near at hand. Donning beggar's clothes, Norbert travelled about in Germany and Brabant, preaching repentance. On Christmas day of the year 1121 he established forty monks in a spot which had been shown him in a vision, — the lonely wooded valley of Prémontré.   This was the germ of the Premonstratensian order, which soon ramified over Europe, and exerted great influence. At the same time, Gilbert of Sempringham, in Lincolnshire, — the only English founder of an order, — instituted one, chiefly for women, which was known by his name.   At meals, Gilbert always had beside him what he called "the dish of the Lord Jesus," in which he put aside, for the poor, the best of whatever was on the table.

The spiritual fervor of these ascetics ; their phantasmal view of nature ; their abnormal mode of living, — their prolonged silence, fasts, and vigils ; their periods of rapt contemplation ; the beautiful services in which they took part, — the chanting of the hours at evening and in the night-time, — all tended to produce occasional conditions of ecstasy, especially when, after long fasting, in a state of physical and mental tension, they assisted at what was the supreme event of their life and worship, the celebration of the mass.   About that their visions clustered thickest, and serve to render intelligible to us the apparition of the Grail.   Thus, for example, a young Norman nobleman named Walthen, who joined the Cistercians at Rievaulx Abbey, and died as abbot of Melrose in the year 1160, once, while celebrating mass, saw the host in his hands vanish into the figure of the infant Jesus, who smiled upon him, and was changed into the host again.

Beside this religious strain, the next most important characteristic of the age was the spirit of warlike adventure which the Normans infused into Europe.   Their bounding blood, their fresh activity found relief in voyages of discovery, in freebooting expeditions and feats of arms, which easily took on a religious cast, and the freebooter became a pilgrim, combining the congenial search for further adventure with the search for relief from the consciousness of past crime.   Robert the Magnificent (also called the Devil), father of William the Conqueror, who lies under grave suspicion of having poisoned his brother in order to attain the ducal crown, died in Asia Minor upon his return from a pilgrimage to the Holy Land. The Normans were indefatigable pilgrims, — many doubtless from compunction of conscience; many drawn by mere religious glamour blended with the longing to see strange lands; many from a desire to dignify or make decent with a pious motive their aimless search for adventure, their plundering expeditions even.

Now just at the time when Norman power was in the ascendant, and when the new birth of devotional enthusiasm was urging increasing numbers of pilgrims and penitents toward the Holy Land, the fierce Seljuk Turks got possession of the holy places, and made access to them difficult and dangerous. This was all that was wanting to fire the zeal of the enthusiast, to make the blood of the Norman boil: the tide of pilgrimage, checked by the barbarities of the Turks, steadily mounted against the barrier until at last it poured over it in the First Crusade. The main motive-power of the Crusades was the instinctive conviction, rooted ineradicably in the human breast, that there are places where man can draw nearer to God than he can elsewhere; and to the mind of that age Palestine was preëminently the place where heaven touched the earth. The crusading armies, spite of all alloy of baser motives, were in reality pilgrim hosts, going armed that they might repel force by force, and obtain for themselves and others unimpeded access to the scenes of the Saviour's life. That chivalrous devotion to the person of Christ and loyalty to his memory that were the very flower of the feudal age, that blind feeling after his humanity and longing to make it real to mind and heart that inspired the Crusades, certainly make those mighty movements deeply affecting as well as impressive. It was the thought of Incarnation, indeed, which gave to that and succeeding ages their strange spiritual glow, midway between the gloom of the dusk ages and the glare of modern times. On the eve of the First Crusade the saintly Anselm began in England and finished in a Calabrian monastery his epoch-making treatise — a conspicuous sign of the stir of a new intellectual life in Western Europe — in which he grounded the necessity of the Incarnation upon the fact of sin.

In the armed devotion of the Holy Wars, in which bishop and baron, monk and knight took part, we see revealed the very form and pressure of the time. Emotional self-abandonment was the note of the era; men were extreme in whatever they did. The swing of the soul from tumults of military ferocity to a tumult of devotion is vividly exemplified in the case of Godfrey and his crusaders, when, after the carnage at Antioch and after having marked with blood their course through Syria, they arrived at last, on that day in June of the year 1099, within sight of Jerusalem, and in a moment their souls were melted to contrition, and they fell on their knees, weeping and groaning, and kissed the earth, and laid aside their armor, and in the raiment of pilgrims walked barefooted toward the holy city; then armed again, and after a fearful siege took the city, heaped the streets with slain, waded in blood, — and then donned white garments, went to the church of the Holy Sepulchre, and bowed down in a passion of humiliation.

In the excitement of battle as well as in the silence of monastic cells men saw visions, or transmuted what they saw into wondrous apparitions. The Crusaders were nerved in their assault upon the walls of Jerusalem by the figure of a knight that appeared over upon Mount Olivet, whom they took to be St. George the Martyr.

The incident of the discovery at Antioch of the tip of the lance said to have pierced the Saviour's side, and its immediate effect in reviving the spirit of the host, is a striking example of the belief of those days in a miraculous virtue, a mysterious power of communicating influence, inhering in the bones of saints and martyrs, or in objects that had touched their bodies. But most significant of all was the discovery at Caesarea, in 1101, of a bowl of greenish glass, said to be emerald, which was fully believed to be the dish out of which Christ ate the broth of bitter herbs at his last passover, and in which Joseph of Arimathea afterward caught the blood issuing from his crucified body.

An important development of the Crusade and of the age was the order of the Knights Templars. In those military monks we see the perfect blend of the two passions of the age, worship and warfare. Within twenty years after the founding of the Latin Kingdom of Jerusalem, a few knights banded themselves together to protect pilgrims on their way to the holy places ; they obtained from Baldwin II the right to lodge in the precincts of his palace, on the site of Solomon's temple, —thence their title was derived. They chose as their habit a white mantle marked with the red cross of the Crusaders. As members of a religious order they were bound to attend the daily services of the church ; and at their meals no voice was heard save that of the reader of the Bible-lesson for the day. Upon entering the order, in sign of utter self-renunciation, the knight gave up all his private property, pledged himself to chastity, and to kiss no woman, not even his nearest relative, and vowed unquestioning obedience to the master, whose bidding should be to him as God's. Two forms of disobedience, which were yet one, were punishable by expulsion from the society : one was desertion to the infidels, the other, disloyalty to the faith, that is, heresy, — and both were treason. A few years after the institution of the order Bernard was chosen as its patron, and after that it gained great and speedy prestige ; before the Second Crusade, of which their patron and they were the chief promoters, the knights had established themselves in Italy, France, Spain, Germany, and England.

In England the twofold interest of the age was illustrated by massive monuments that still endure — the castles and

cathedrals that the Normans raised.   Gundulph, military
architect and engineer of William the Conqueror, was also
bishop of Rochester; 'he re-built his cathedral, and reared near
by it the castle whose mighty keep still frowns upon the
Medway.   Bishops were famous castle-builders' in those days :
King Stephen got into trouble by attempting to destroy some
of their fortresses.   All over the land, on commanding sites,
rose the threatening walls, the massive keeps with machicolated
battlements of the castles of the Norman lords, temporal and
spiritual.   Meanwhile, the splendid fanes of Winchester, Dur-
ham, Norwich, Peterborough, Ely, and Gloucester were also
rising, and in its lovely vale the stately nave of Fountains
Abbey, over whose ponderous pillars the pointed arches — the
first to be seen in England — gave evidence, possibly, of the
influence of Saracenic art.

Such was the world into which Geoffrey of Monmouth was
born, and before which he held up the figure of the legendary
Arthur as the mirror of chivalry.   Geoffrey came, like his hero,
from the west of Britain; he was the son of a priest named
Arthur, of the household of Robert, Earl of Gloucester, natural
son of King Henry I.   He studied at Oxford, and became a
man of learning according to the pattern of the age.   There
he gathered material for his history; there, at a churchman's
bidding, he rendered into Latin the " Prophecies of Merlin."
About the year 1140 he was appointed archdeacon of Llandaff,
through the influence of his father's brother, who was bishop
there.   Meantime he was slowly shaping his Latin " History
of the Kings of Britain," making use, probably, of some old
collection of legends long since lost.   The work assumed its
final form, it is believed, in 1147 — the year of the Second
Crusade.   In 1151, Geoffrey was promoted to the bishopric of
St. Asaph; he died at Llandaff in 1154.

During his lifetime and for half a century after there was
extraordinary literary activity among the Welsh.   Beside his

friend, the chronicler Carodoc, there appeared a veritable galaxy of bards. Through Geoffrey part of this energy was projected into the general literature of the world.

In his work appeared a troop of figures that were destined to a literary immortality. Herein is manifest the difference between a vein of Anglo-Norman writing and the whole body of Anglo-Saxon literature: the latter contributed not one great theme to English literature, while the stories of British kings that Geoffrey told, the error of Lear, the conquests and magnificence of Arthur, and his mysterious end, have exercised over it a sovereign charm. It is interesting to notice that, just at the time when the Norman Conquest had drawn England into the current of European history, Geoffrey coördinated the legendary history of the island with that of ancient Rome: both were made to spring from the same Trojan stock. His book played an important part in the literary awakening of mediaeval Europe; its influence upon the continent was as great as it was in England. It was soon translated into French verse by Robert Wace, a Norman trouvère, under the title of " Brut," or Brutus — the grandson of Æneas, fabled to have become the first of the British kings.

During the life-time of Geoffrey another literary tradition, deeply religious in its nature, was taking shape, which was destined shortly to be grafted upon his and to transform it.

Among the chroniclers of the twelfth and thirteenth centuries who compiled in Latin their Histories of England, — men who were scandalized by Geoffrey's presumption in calling his fictions a history, — William of Malmesbury only is connected with our subject through his Latin treatise "On the Antiquity of the Church of Glastonbury." He is believed to have been the son of a Norman father and a Saxon mother; he certainly exemplified in his person that union of conquerors and conquered which was in process earlier than is commonly supposed, — an historic illustration of it is the marriage' of

Henry I to Matilda, daughter of Queen Margaret of Scotland — a princess of the Saxon line. William entered the Benedictine monastery at Malmesbury, and after a time was made custodian of its manuscripts. He was befriended by Geoffrey's patron, the earl Robert of Gloucester. His history of England ends with the year 1142, and probably indicates the time of his death. His treatise above referred to tells of the wandering of Joseph of Arimathea and his companions to Glastonbury, where they preached to the natives, and gathered the first Christian church in Britain. It is worth noting that in the legend Joseph and his fellow-missionaries make up the mystic number twelve.

Now the romantic interest of the story of Joseph centred in the dish that he had brought with him, which had been used at the Last Supper, and which held the blood that issued from the five wounds of the Lord. Moreover, his body and King Arthur's both lay enshrined, according to fable, in the sacred precincts at Glastonbury. When we consider this and bear in mind the general character of the age, we see clearly how just one touch of poetic imagination might fuse the two lines of romance in one, illumining the secular with the sacred, changing tales of bloodshed, passion, and demonic arts into descriptions of the search for ideal purity and holiness, as suddenly and wonderfully as the mood of the Crusaders was changed when they came within sight of the walls of Jerusalem. It was apparently by a churchman named Walter Map, or Mapes, that that final touch was given.

He was born, probably, in the west of England. He attended lectures at the University of Paris, and after his return to England was made a canon of Salisbury — in the Arthurian region. His talents gained him the favorable notice of King Henry II; he was employed at court, and accompanied the king upon his progresses through the realm. In 1173, he visited Gloucester as itinerant justice of the district. The same year, Thomas à Becket, archbishop of Canterbury, who had been slain three years before, was canonized by Pope Alexander III.

It must have been about this time that Walter wrote, in Norman-French, his prose romance of the Quest of the Holy Grail. We cannot but feel some connection between that work and the great events of those years, — the barbarous murder of the archbishop, who murmured with his last breath, that in defence of the church he was willing to die, — the disasters that soon after ensued, and almost overwhelmed the king, — the canonization, — the painful humiliation of Henry before the shrine of the martyr at Canterbury, — these events produced that excitation of imagination that precedes a great conception, that atmosphere of horror and fearful expectancy, of wonder and religious awe, upon which flashed in blinding light the apparition of the Holy Grail.

Walter also wrote, in part at least, the romance of Lancelot du Lac. He was present, as an English delegate, at a council held by Pope Alexander III, — probably that of the Lateran in the year 1179. In 1196, he was appointed archdeacon of Oxford. He was still living in the reign of King John. With his Latin works we are not concerned here.

A significant fact in connection with the Quest of the Grail is that in the twelfth century the sacramental wine began to be generally withheld from the laity. Parallel with this change came a change in the thought of the Grail : from the dish it became the cup used by Jesus at the institution of his supper, — that is, the chalice, — a symbol of the central mystery of the Christian faith. The thrill that accompanied its appearance is like the touch of a ghostly presence. And so the vision of the Grail became the ideal of the Middle Ages ; it was a glimpse of heaven, God's presence with men ; it was purity and holiness and perfect faith and peace. And only like could comprehend like. Indescribably beautiful and pathetic is Arthur's grief when his knights, with one accord, vow to undertake the quest: he knows that the charm of the Round Table is overcome by a more potent spell; that its glory is departing forever; that his company of gallant knights will gather round him no more. It is the sundering of human ties by the constraining power of a great ideal.

Like Geoffrey's romance of Arthur, the legend of the Grail soon won wide popularity upon the continent; it stimulated the imagination of the age, deeply impressed its finest poets, and was the motive of its most spiritual poetry. At the French court Robert de Boron produced his prose version of the story of Joseph of Arimathea, and Chrestien de Troyes, a prolific versifier, who flourished in the years 1180–1190, made the Grail the motive of his romance of " Percevale." A profoundly imaginative version of this work was the " Parzival " of the German knight, Wolfram von Eschenbach.

In lighter vein, with frequent touches of satire, Wolfram's contemporary and rival, Godfrey of Strassburg, recounted the history of the fateful passion of Tristram and Isolde — a theme that hardly yielded to the legend of Arthur in popular interest.

At this period the great popular epic of Germany, the Nibelungenlied, took its final form — a form interesting to compare and contrast with that of Beowulf, — a savage, heathen core with a faint burnish of Christian or rather ecclesiastical terms. And as Denmark was drawn in the twelfth century into the political system of the Empire, so do her ancient ballads seem to circle, like satellites, in orbits more or less remote, round the great luminary, the Lay of the Nibelungen. In France, the " Chansons de Gestes," a mass of verse dealing with Charlemagne and his paladins, deeply imbued with the feudal spirit, had already been produced. This, too, was the era of the troubadours, chief among whom were Geoffrey Rudel, Bertrand de Born, and Pierre Vidal; it was indeed the golden prime of that Provençal poetry of love and war, so soon to be extinguished by the ferocious crusade that desolated Languedoc, and by the Inquisition thereupon established. In Spain, the first and greatest monument of the young Spanish language, the grand poem of the Cid, champion of the faith and of the nation, emerged at this time amid the tumult of the Holy Wars that were going on in that peninsula. The history of Spain, partly by reason of its very aloofness from the common interests of the rest of Europe, presents the more striking analogies to them, chief among these being the religious orders of knighthood that emulated the glory of the Templars and the Knights of St. John. The order of Calatrava originated in an heroic defence of that place against the Moors in the year 1158 ; and the Knights of Santiago, who for many years had protected pilgrims to the famous shrine of Compostella, were formally instituted in 1175 by a bull of Alexander III.

It is believed that the epic of the Cid as we have it was shaped from an earlier collection of ballads that sprang from the fierce border warfare of Moors and Spaniards by an ecclesiastic who refined, idealized, and Christianized the whole. This gentle graft upon a savage stock would then present an interesting parallel to the introduction of the Grail-motive into Arthurian romance. And now, at the close of the chapter, we return to England, to take note of the poet Layamon, in whose work the course of English literature, properly speaking, begins.

It may seem that we have travelled far and wide before making a beginning, — but it will prove to have been well worth our while to do so. We have gained a general impression of the character of the age ; have traced the working out of a great conception; and have seen how widespread and productive was the fresh literary enthusiasm of the twelfth century. Now our footing is firm; we have secured a point of departure for the literary developments that are to come.

The latter half of the twelfth century, though remarkably barren of English writings, was, for that very reason largely, the seed-time of English speech. Freed from the restraining influence that works of genius exert upon the tendency to linguistic change, unused in the services of the church, in the homes of the learned and the great, the language of the people passed through a period of confusion from which it emerged as archaic English. The changes it underwent were chiefly of two kinds, inflexional and lexical: first, a general reduction of the various Anglo-Saxon endings for case, gender, number, person, mood, to *e* or *en* on its way to *e*; and second, the introduction of new words from Norman-French. Both modes of development are exemplified in Layamon's poem, although, long as it is — it contains over thirty-two thousand lines — there are hardly one hundred and seventy words of French derivation to be found in it.

Layamon was a priest who lived on the banks of the Severn, in Worcestershire. His alliterative poem — in which now and then a stammer of rhyme is heard — belongs to the threshold of the thirteenth century, and stands at the head of English literature: its author has been called the English Ennius. A qualification is necessary, however; Layamon wrote in a dialect, in the speech of the south of England — one of the three dialects among which English writings are to be divided for the next hundred and fifty years. His language is difficult, no doubt; special preparation is required to understand it, and a glossary must be constantly consulted; but it is not like learning a foreign tongue, — two or three hours of study a day for three or four days would make one master of the grammatical difficulties that stand in the way of one's enjoyment of the poem.

It is called the "Brut," and is a translation, with many additions, of the Brut of Robert Wace. It is the first account in English of those mythical British kings that were to play so great a part in English literature. Here we have the story of Lear (who, as romance says, gave his name to Leicester), as

Geoffrey of Monmouth told it: the injured king visits his daughter "Cordoille" in France, and obtains from the king her husband a force sufficient to re-conquer England, over which he reigns gloriously until his peaceful death, three years after. Following this comes the story of "Fereus and Poreus," and shortly after of "Kinbelin," in whose time Christ was born, — who, in the theology of our poet, is "Father in heaven, Son on earth of the good maiden, and holds with himself the Holy Ghost." Soon there ensues the voluminous account of the deeds of Arthur, who became king at the age of fifteen years; he was prosperous, rich in gold, liberal, strong, stern to wrong-doers, dear to those who did well, — the noblest of kings, the Britons' darling. The most interesting portion of the vast work, and that which best repays reading, is the description of Arthur's coronation, which extends for about five hundred lines onward from line twenty-four-thousand two-hundred and forty-one. Here are reflected the brilliant display of regal power, the stately ceremonial, and all the external magnificence of the poet's own age — the age of Richard I and the Third Crusade. The coronation takes place on Whit-sunday at the British capital, Kaerlion-on-Usk, — a wealthy and splendid city, second only to Rome in the whole world. Thither have gathered from every quarter Arthur's vassal kings, earls, and thanes, and ladies in gay array. Dubricius, archbishop of Kaerlion, and the archbishops of London and York, take part in the solemn ceremony ; Dubricius, the chosen of Christ, the Pope's legate, leads the procession, and places the crown upon Arthur's head. Then follow the coronation feast, and the games, all through the long summer afternoon, upon the meadows about Kaerlion.

Thus sweetly, with the glamour of poetry, did the Britons and their king take captive the descendants of their Saxon conquerors, as they had already, through Geoffrey's Latin romance, enthralled their conquerors' conquerors. Thus, too, by the memory of Saint Dubricius, was the fame of the ancient British church restored.   The harmonizing effect of these old legends upon the mixed population of England must have been great indeed.

II.

REMARKABLE differences appear between the work of Layamon and the writings of the age that succeeded his, — differences that were rooted, of course, in the altered character of
the time. Certain notable events help us to determine the
bounds of the new period: it extended from the year 1204,
when Normandy was lost to the English crown, to 1265, — the
year of the first typical English parliament, the battle of Evesham, and, let us add, of the birth of Dante Alighieri. It is
hardly necessary to say that the formative influences of the
period were at work years before the former date (they are dis-
tinguishable upon the continent at least as early as 1170), and
though waning were yet operative years after the latter.

A conspicuous sign of the time was the decay of crusading
zeal. Early in the thirteenth century the name crusade was
prostituted by being applied to shameless attacks upon Christians. A great expedition designed for the recovery of the
Holy Sepulchre was diverted, by the pride and greed of the
Venetians, into a siege and capture of the city of Zara, and
soon after of Constantinople, and resulted in the temporary
subversion of the hollow Empire of the East. The ruthless
"crusade" against the Albigenses, which for twenty years
desolated the fairest provinces of France, was another instance
of abuse of the name for purposes of mischief. The crusade
of Andrew of Hungary in Palestine, in 1217, ended in failure
and speedy retreat. Europe and Asia alike were growing
weary of the long and costly struggle; the only considerable
successes of the time were the bloodless victories of the
Emperor Frederick II, in 1229, and Richard, Earl of Cornwall, in 1240, who, by negotiation with the infidels, obtained

possession of Jerusalem and neighboring towns. The zeal of the former age burned brightly in the breast of Louis IX alone, and never with a purer flame; but his first expedition was disastrous in the extreme, and he died, in the year 1270, upon the torrid sands of Tunis ere the second had fairly begun. That was the last of the crusades. The forces of the Saracens drew round the doomed town of Acre, the last stronghold of the Christians in Palestine; but the crash of its walls awoke not an echo in Europe, and the reddened waves washed the corpses of its defenders along the coast.

At the other extremity of the Mediterranean, Ferdinand III, the sainted King of Spain, was achieving great success in his struggle with the Moslem power; he took town after town in Andalusia, and in 1236 had the pleasure of converting the many-pillared mosque of Cordova into a cathedral. In 1249 he took Seville, the largest city in the peninsula, after a protracted siege; and at last all that remained to the Moors was their province of Granada, enclosed, like a promontory, by the Christian power. But the absorbing interest of the age was the deadly strife between the papacy and the house of Hohenstaufen, which ended in the extermination of the latter in the year 1268, when the boy Conradin, grandson of Frederick II, and last of his line, went to a cruel death upon the scaffold in a public square at Naples. Grievous as the conflict was, it yet shows that the mind of Europe had become more deeply engaged in its own concerns than in the support of a shadowy kingdom far off upon the Asiatic shore. It is this introversion of the mind that gives tone to the whole period.

The most remarkable religious phenomenon of the thirteenth century, — and in religious movements the philosophy of all these ages practically consists, — was the foundation of the great mendicant orders. Their originating principle was that longing for complete disengagement from the world that was manifested with fresh force by Francis of Assisi, who proposed a self-renunciation so absolute that it seemed fanatical and impracticable even to the churchmen of those days. We cannot but honor the motive that underlay the practice of such excessive poverty; it was designed to disencumber the brothers of all burdens so that they might move around freely among the growing towns, preaching the word of God. A similar zeal for preaching joined with a similar poverty had already been manifested by the Waldenses, whose apostolical missionaries had penetrated, in the time of St. Francis, into all the great countries of Western Europe, having even crossed over into England. We must recognize this movement as the evangelical phase of mediaeval piety.

Francis' attitude respecting this world's goods was determined by a thorough-going change in his character. Between the lines of his life we may read something of the pain that attends every transition from one age of the spirit to another, the misunderstanding of the new by the old, the condemnation of the old by the new, the mental distress, the domestic agony, that should teach us a deep reverence and sympathy for the heroes of every spiritual renascence. Francis practised strange austerities to bring and keep his body in subjection; with that quaint humor that helped to win him others' hearts he called his body "Brother Ass," because it was made only to slave and be beaten and to be supported by the coarsest food. His order was recognized by Pope Innocent III in 1210, and from that time to his death Francis held the primacy of piety in Christendom. In 1219, it was estimated that five thousand friars attended the general chapter of the order. The virgin Clara, also of Assisi, founded an order for women under Francis' rule, which soon numbered twelve houses in Italy, with others in Germany. A little later, the princess Isabel, sister of St. Louis, became the patroness of the Clares in France. Clara was as deeply enamoured of poverty and ascetic practices as was her model: she went barefoot; wore a shift woven with sharp bristles; lived on bread and water, and slept upon the bare floor.   We are not surprised to hear that she suffered much from sickness, — yet even her ill turns she improved by spinning fine linen thread to be woven into altar-cloths and corporals for the churches of Assisi.

After the death of Francis, in 1226, his work was carried on in the same spirit by Anthony of Padua (born in Lisbon, in 1195).   He was the most noted preacher of his age, and undertook long missionary tours in France, Spain, and Italy. Within a few years the Franciscan order produced its brightest light, the saint and doctor Bonaventura, who was five years of age at the time of the founder's death, took the habit at the age of twenty-two and became erelong general of the order. Among his voluminous works is one that he wrote at Francis' retreat upon Mt. Alverno: the little golden treatise of mediaeval mysticism, — the " Itinerarium Mentis in Deum."

At the same time the rival mendicant order, the Dominican, brought forth its great saint and doctor, Thomas Aquinas, whose " Summa," or system of theology, is a monument of industry and exhaustive analysis.   Aquinas drew a strict line of demarcation between the provinces of faith and reason in matters of religion, — a psychological distinction fertile of future controversy and speculation.

The three other mendicant fraternities, Carmelite, Augustinian, and Servite, never attained the popularity and power of the former two.   The Servites originated in Florence, about the year 1233.   The devout Filippo Benizi was one of the founders, and in time became general of the order.   He was an earnest preacher, and once undertook an extensive missionary journey through France and Flanders.   The glory of the Augustinians in this age was Nicholas of Tolentino, in the march of Ancona.   He too was a fervent and persuasive preacher, but his usefulness was impaired by his ascetic rigors, which brought upon him many painful infirmities, which he

mistook as punishments for his laxity. He chastised his re-
bellious flesh by binding it about with heavy iron girdles; he
ate only the simplest and coarsest food ; his bed was a board,
his pillow a stone.

The little that we have said of the monks and friars is the
very least that was due to men who contributed a large part of
the literature of mediaeval Europe, and copied and preserved
the rest in their libraries.

An interesting episode of the time was the military mission-
work of the Teutonic Knights. As the crusading fever abated,
they devoted their attention more and more to their boreal
provinces about the Baltic Sea. Having converted the natives
to Christianity at the point of the sword, and having established
some scattered bishoprics in Esthonia, Livonia, and Courland,
they caused the whole region to be erected into an ecclesiastical province, with its archiepiscopal see at Riga, in the
year 1255.

As it was throughout Europe in general, so was it in England
in particular: interest in home affairs and a spirit of religious
reflection superseded the interest of the preceding age in things
without and far away. The conquest of Normandy by Philip
of France served greatly to stimulate, even if it did not create,
this new self-consciousness of the English people. That event
was followed by two generations of internecine strife, the most
confused period of English history, yet fruitful of future good
beyond almost any other. It was a protracted struggle between a monarchy that aimed to be absolute, that carried
beyond endurance its abuse of power, that rested upon external sanction and support, and a nobility that however turbulent was yet determined to be free ; between sovereigns like
John and his son Henry III on the one hand, the first tyran-
nical, cowardly, and evil, the other capricious and weak, who,
to gain the support of the Roman curia against their own
vassals, and to wring from them the sums of money of which

they stood in perpetual need, were willing to sell the liberties of the English church, and on the other hand, a series of able and independent ecclesiastics, like Langton, Edmund of Canterbury, and Robert Grosseteste, who resented the intrusion of Italian prelates into English livings and the exactions of the popes, together with the great barons, led by the Marshalls and Simon de Montfort, who resented the insolence of royal favorites, the heaping of favors upon foreigners, and all the injuries of irresponsible, personal government by the king. It is evident, moreover, that this opposition to royal incapacity and oppression which was in truth the national party, in spite of the selfish motives that may have swayed many of its adherents, was buoyed up by the sympathy of the people, and the rising influence of the towns. It was a dark and troublous age, yet in it were planted upon imperishable foundations the rights of persons, the liberties of Englishmen. The charter drawn up by barons and churchmen at Runnymede, and signed by King John in June, 1215, was confirmed over and over again in the following reign; and Henry's bad faith and neglect of its provisions led at last to the events of the year 1258, when a wearied nation decided that he was unfit to rule.

Matthew Paris, the best of England's mediaeval chroniclers, through whose monkish Latin can be clearly discerned a kindling national consciousness, is our authority for a great part of the reign of Henry III, and exhibits in the plainest way the dependence of English upon papal politics; the supreme importance of the contest between empire and papacy, and the distress it caused all thoughtful minds; the plunder of the English and their church to which the pope's necessities drove him, and the king's connivance at it for his own selfish ends. The chronicler shows, too, with startling distinctness, how that awful contest palsied all crusading effort, partly by withholding aid from Europe, partly by stirring up strife between Hospitallers and Templars in Palestine. And further, by an occasional naïve remark he discloses the ill-feeling that existed among members of the long-established monastic orders toward their young, active, and popular rivals, the friars.

In the midst of these manifold antagonisms, and offering, as it were, a refuge from them, there rose those chaste examples of early Gothic architecture in which the deepening religious consciousness of the time found expression. In France, the cathedrals of Chartres, Rheims, and Amiens, in Germany, those of Freiburg and Strassburg were more or less advanced toward completion, and the reconstruction of the choir of Cologne was begun. A significant change in the ground-plan of churches accompanied in England the substitution of the pointed arch for the round: a square eastern end replaced the Norman apse. The cathedral of Lincoln was covered with a substantial vault, the first probably that was constructed in the kingdom. At Salisbury was rising, between the years 1220 and 1258, the most symmetrical of English cathedrals, the only one that was completed according to the original design in the same generation in which it was begun. Westminster Abbey was rebuilt by King Henry III in the latter half of his reign.

It is necessary to bear these noble monuments in mind in order to do justice to an age that is inadequately represented by its literary remains. The truth is that the spirit of poetry expressed itself mutely then in cathedral columns, walls, windows, pinnacles, and spires, — it had not yet found a tongue.

How inadequate as a literary medium the English language yet seemed to educated men is shown by the fact that the patriotic Grosseteste, bishop of Lincoln, used French in writing his doctrinal and allegorical poem, the " Château d'Amour " (the " Castle " being the body of Mary the Virgin), in which he told of Creation, Redemption, the Judgment, the pains of Hell and the joys of Heaven.

Now to gather in a focus all that has been said of the period, to tell its secret in a word, we must recur to the thought of the

Grail. That was the supreme ideal of the preceding age, at once its culmination and the beginning of its dissolution; it was the pivot on which thought revolved into a new stage. The vision of the Grail, that is, a foretaste of heaven, could only be attained by those whose lives were spotlessly pure; and in the thirteenth century, chastity meant the extirpation of physical desire. For the body was regarded as impure, and as the seat and source of impure appetites and imaginations. To quell them, therefore, its strength must be reduced; to live out of the body, as if one had no body even, was the ideal of Francis of Assisi and his companions. Hence the ascetic rigors already noted, hence the snapping of all ties held to be earthly, hence the straining to be free from worldly pursuits and possessions. Thus only, it was thought, could one live a heavenly life. Erelong the inevitable consequences of such a mode of striving toward the ideal made themselves felt; the flesh, which men abused and attempted to ignore, rebelled, thrusting itself upon their notice; then ensued a more desperate struggle to overcome it, followed by more violent revenges; the ideal seemed ever more remote, and the spirit, groaning under the bond it hated yet had to endure, conscious of its own weakness, vexed by prurient suggestions, torn by doubt, became a prey to melancholy. It is in such mortal strife between body and soul that self-consciousness grows clear; in such a time psychology begins.

The course of English literature in this period may be thus summarized: devotional works appear, aiming to excite enthusiastic love for the Redeemer by pictures of his suffering; lives of saints hold up examples for imitation; sermons instruct, exhort, and endeavor to make religion a more inward thing, a matter of the heart; soon an undertone of sadness begins to be heard, a consciousness of failure, and marks of what the mystics well term "interior desolation"; and this ends in a realization of the antithesis between soul and body as a fierce antagonism, which induces final despair.

The first and lengthiest specimen of this group of writings is a series of sermons in metre called the "Ormulum" by its author, who was an Augustinian canon named Orm. He wrote in the dialect of the English midland. His plan was simple; patience only was needed for its execution, and of that quality Orm had good store. It was to turn into English the gospel-lesson for the day, and then append an exposition of it, — and in compiling the latter the author often laid under contribution the writings of the great patron of his order. How laborious he was may be gauged by this, that the fragment of his work we possess, though amounting to more than twenty thousand lines, only reaches, with many gaps, to the thirty-second sermon, — and beyond that stretched, in endless perspective, scores, perhaps hundreds of gospel paraphrases with their homiletic commentaries. That such a work should be composed or read was owing, probably, to the fact that some knowledge of the Scriptures — which were now being withheld from the laity — could thus be imparted in a form not subject to censure by the ecclesiastical authority. A council at Toulouse, in the year 1229, inhibited the use of translations of the Scriptures, but left a way open for paraphrases of portions of them like the work of Orm.

The Ormulum flows on in unrhymed lines of eight and seven syllables alternately. Its iambic metre is exceedingly regular, and does certainly course onward with a lilt that bears the reader easily along.

In the Southern dialect and in prose were composed the Lives of Saints Juliana, Margaret, and Katharine ; the "Ancren Riwle," or Rule of Anchoresses, — giving in detail the pattern according to which nuns should frame their lives ; a long homily called "Soul's Ward" (or "Guardian") which urges, in allegorical fashion, rejection of Self-Will and submission to heavenly Wisdom as the guide of life; and a devotional treatise, "The Wooing of Our Lord," which in the swoon of divine love that it labors to induce by holding before the gaze the picture of Jesus' poverty, humiliation, passion, flagellation, and crucifixion, reminds one of the ecstasies of St. Francis, and of the morbid desire of many in that age to produce in their own flesh a semblance of the five wounds of the Lord.   Similar to this in spirit is a short poem called "A Good Orison of Our Lady," — in halting lines on the basis of the iambic pentameter, rhyming in couplets, — in which the beauty and glory and power of Mary are chanted, and she is entreated to bring her worshippers at last to the blessed heaven where she is.

To a later date than any of these — about the middle of King Henry's reign — belong a quaint metrical Bestiary that breaks into occasional rhyme, and a freely flowing version in octosyllabic couplets of portions of the books of Genesis and Exodus.   Both are couched in the Midland dialect.

The Bestiary is a version of a Latin work ; it is a curious example of that mixture of legend and allegory that passed as natural history in the middle ages.   After the description of an animal and its supposed habits, often apocryphal, but accepted without suspicion on the authority of the author, there follows an application to human conduct — for every habit, imaginary or otherwise, was believed to be symbolical, and capable of conveying a moral lesson.   As the Ant, for instance, gathers food in season, so should we gather spiritual sustenance ; as winter is to her death is to us ; and as she drops the barley she is carrying when she finds a grain of fine wheat, so should we discard the old law, — the new is better.

The representative piece of the period, and best worth conning, is a rhyming homily of not quite four hundred lines which has been poorly entitled "A Moral Ode."   "An Earnest Call to a Godly Life" would be a better description of its character; its burden is, "Do Good while yet there is Time."   The author's soul was heavily weighted with a sense of the extent

and power and fearful end of sin ; he felt a pressing responsibility for the souls of others, — he must "warny" all his friends
to shun the path that leads to endless pain.   His voice comes
sounding to us out of the very heart of that sad age; this is
proved by the demand that there was for the poem through
many years : several copies of it are still extant, some dating
from the beginning, some from the end of the period.   Its long
lines, with their monotonous rise and fall, chime well with the
solemn thought they convey.   It begins with a lament for
wasted time : the poet's youth is past, and now he cannot do
the good he then neglected to do ; his example and his regret
should incite his readers to do well while they can, else like
him they will sorely repent.   Every man must stand by himself,
trust no kinsfolk, not even wife or child, — and the wife must
not trust her husband : none but Christ can save another's
soul.   Let each avail of every opportunity of doing good, for a
time of reckoning is to come, when every man will be judged
by his works.   God is gracious; to him a little gift that comes
of good will is dear : ah, do good before it is too late.   At the
day of doom devils will be our accusers; they will bring to
light all our evil deeds, — and we shall be our own judges, for
there is no witness like a man's own heart; every man knows
himself best, his works and his will, and shall judge himself as
the testimony of his works may compel him, either to death or
to life.   The pains of hell are terrible and without end ; a
week's pleasure here must be paid for with seven years of
sorrow there ; if one could experience that pain for only one
hour now he would abandon wife and child, father, sister and
brother, and all the pleasures and possessions of the world, and
be ever in prayer that he might escape hell-fire and arrive at
last in heaven.   Oh listen ! — in hell are hunger and thirst,
heat and cold; no rest, but ever-burning fire for the false, lustful, and covetous ; adders and snakes to tear and fret the
proud ; darkness and smoke and dreadful fiends, — no tongue

can tell the horrors of that place ; compared to them the greatest pain we suffer on earth is glee.   And many bad Christians
are there, without hope, — oh, warn your friends as I do mine.
We are weak and sinful ; we suffer for our forefather's fault ;
but God is merciful.   Two words, love to God and man, sum
up the whole of God's law : if we have those two loves we
shall taste the joys of heaven.   Reflect before it is too late ;
keep yourself from the world and its love ; nine men in every
ten are pressing down the broad way ; few take the narrow
way of God's commandment, surrendering their own wills.
Let us take that path, for it leads to heaven ; there God is all
in all, those who are near him lack nothing.   There shall those
see more of him who loved him more here, and find in him all
that man can desire : they have enough that have him who
possesses all things.   May God bring us to that bliss.   Pray,
dear friends, for the soul of him who wrote this, that he may
attain it.

The earnest dualism of this pathetic exhortation gives place
to despair in a remarkable poem called " The Debate of the
Body and the Soul," which was widely popular in many lands
in the thirteenth century.   Its grotesqueness and savage dualism were highly characteristic of the age.   The author dreams
that he sees a knight's body lying on a bier, and the soul that
has just parted from it standing by.   The soul gibes at the
body, and curses it for its disobedience : it would go its own
gait, and now its gluttony and lust have brought them both to
hell.   The corpse slowly rears its head and replies : " Thou
dost wrong to lay all the blame upon me.   I was entrusted to
thy guidance, and did nothing but what thou didst whisper in
my ear.   Thou art lost by thine own fault, and but for thee I
should be as a sheep or an ox, and not be bound to hell."   The
soul retorts : " I could do nothing without thee.   We were both
born of one woman; I loved thee, but thou wast unruly; I was
thy slave, and now must suffer for thy deadly sins."   " Nay,

the thought of every sin came first from thee, Soul ! I knew
not what was right or wrong except as thou didst teach me. I
was inclined to sin, as is the race, and thou didst allow me my
pleasure, though it was for thee to beat and bind." "I gave
thee good advice," says the soul, "but the fiend and the world
deceived thee. O ye traitors ! combining against my bliss : ye
led me as an ox is led by the horn, and have brought me to
hell-pain. Now no prayer avails !" "Oh that I had died at
birth !" cries the corpse, "then I had not known sin." " 'Tis
too late, Body! We must go our way, — but oh, that thou
hadst amended only a little while ago! Here come the fiends,
— farewell ! We shall meet at doomsday." Then the devils
swoop upon the wretched soul, strike their claws into it, tousle
it hither and thither, drag it to the pit of hell, hurl it over the
brink — and the dungeon door closes upon it. With the horror
the sleeper rouses up, aghast; and thanks God that he is still
in the land of the living, and by repentance may hope to
escape that fearful fate.

If we turn to contemporary literature upon the continent of
Europe we shall find there also interesting evidence that a
serious spirit was abroad that was quite out of touch with the
spirit of those light romances, full of love and war and adventure, in which the former age delighted. Among the songs of
Walther von der Vogelweide — the prince of the Minnesingers
(the German troubadours) — there are many verses that show
how acutely he felt the discord of his time. Although he is
remembered now for his love-songs, and especially for his lively
touches of natural description, a serious, moralizing strain was
yet the chief characteristic of his genius. The shadow of the
end seemed to him to be falling upon the world; he saw corruption spreading in the church, and anarchy impending in the
state. The correctness of this latter forecast appeared before
the next generation had passed away; the fall of the house of
Hohenstaufen was followed by the disorders of the Interreg-

num, during which the flower of German song faded, and the line of Minnesingers, like their imperial masters' line, became extinct.

Sometime about the year 1250 appeared a book of moral instruction called "Der Winsbecke," purporting to be a father's advice to his son. At this time all Germany was ringing with the eloquence of Berthold Lech, a friar of the order of St. Francis, a preacher of repentance, and of interior piety as contrasted with reliance upon indulgences, the merit of pilgrimages, and the intercessions of saints. So vast were the crowds that thronged to hear him that no building would hold them, and he had to preach in the fields. His sermons are models of clear German prose.

In France, too, the religious revival stimulated by the mendicant orders gave rise to much sermon-writing in the mother-tongue. How generally prevalent was the didactic spirit exemplified by "Der Winsbecke" is shown by the appearance of a similar work in French, "Le Castoiement d'un Père" — "A Father's Counsel" — in which rules of conduct are impressed upon the memory by apposite stories. The contrast between the two great periods that we have been studying is well illustrated by the works of the famous chroniclers, Villehardouin and Joinville : the former wrote a history of the conquest of Constantinople (in which he took part) in the year 1204, which is full of the stir and color of the times; the latter wrote, in a sober tone that was suited to a graver period, a history of his royal patron, St. Louis. Of writings in verse we can do no more than mention the lays and fables of Marie de France ; the lyrics of Thibault de Champagne ; and the "Roman de la Rose," begun by Guillaume de Lorris, who died about the year 1260. This voluminous work, popular for ages in many lands, has been suggestively termed a "psychological epic"; it is an allegory, and through it all a moral purpose runs ; the Rose, to obtain which is the object of the lover's endeavor, is the recompense of faithful love, and personified sins — such as Sloth and Hatred — stand in the way of its attainment.

After the blighting Albigensian crusade the sceptre of poetry passed from Provence to Northern Italy, where it was wielded by the severe Sordello of Mantua, — whose shade in after years guided Dante through the valley to the gate of Purgatory. A few troubadours, leaving the desolate halls of their patrons, who had fallen in the wars, wandered over the Pyrenees and sought a livelihood in Catalonia and Aragon. Chief among these was Pierre Cardinal, who found a patron in Jayme I, king of Aragon ; but his spirit was embittered by misfortune, and in satirical songs he poured contempt upon his age. The last of the troubadours was Giraud Riquier of Narbonne, who was befriended by Alfonso the Wise, king of Castile. His verses suffer from that didacticism which is the death of poetry.

The representative poet of Spain in this age was the priest Gonzalo of Berceo, in the neighborhood of Calahorra. He composed rhyming lives of saints, "The Martyrdom of St. Lawrence," and the "Merits" and "Miracles of the Blessed Virgin Mary." He died sometime after the year 1260. At the end of the century appeared a Spanish version of "The Debate of the Body and the Soul."

III.

THERE stands a church upon the embattled acropolis of Carcassonne — the old church of St. Nazaire — the body of which, dating from the eleventh century, is gloomy indeed. Its western end was walled up long ago, in time of war, and lets in no light ; half a dozen heavy pillars on either side divide the aisles from the nave; overhead lowers a cavernous vault, pierced by no openings. The chancel end is bright, and going toward it one finds himself surrounded by tinted light that almost dazzles after the darkness left behind. Right and left extend spacious transepts, — above are springy vaults, — and round about are graceful columns, carvings, and large windows filled with the elegant tracery of the fourteenth century, and the gleam of painted glass. Something like that is the change we experience on passing from the shadows of the last age into the light of the one before us.

We are greeted by an English carol that begins in this way: "Spring is come with love in its turn, with blossoms and with birds' songs, that brings all this bliss ; day's-eyes in the dales, sweet notes of nightingales, — every bird sings its song. The thrustlecock chides them ever ; away is their winter woe when woodruff springs. These birds sing wondrous many, and whistle in their winter joy so that all the wood rings."

This is one of a number of refreshing little songs of love and budding branches, spring flowers and returning birds.

A clever poem of considerable length, showing the same genial appreciation of nature and a new-born sense of humor, is "The Owl and the Nightingale," in which, in sprightly couplets well suited to the theme, those birds flout each other, peck each other's character to pieces, and celebrate their

own good qualities. "Each said of the other's habits the
very worst that they knew"; it was a "stiff debate." The
nightingale sat on a fair bough, among blossoms, in a thick
hedge mingled with spire (tall grass) and green sedge; near
by, on an old ivy-covered tree-trunk, stood the owl. The nightingale taunts her enemy with her evil look and "guggling"
note; she is a tyrant, hated by small birds; moreover, she
feeds on nasty creatures like snails and mice and such "foul
wights." The owl swells with rage: "Why won't you fly out
into the open," she says, "and let us see which of us two is
fairer?" "I don't care to have you claw me with your sharp
cleavers," retorts the nightingale; "shame on you for your
treachery! Tell me, monster, why do you sing your doleful
song by night, never by day? 'Tis a grisly shriek to hear.
You fly by night too, — you love darkness." "I sing better
than you, chatterer! My loud note is not like your feeble
piping. You sing all day and all night long; your piping tires
everybody." "Not so, owl! Everything is glad when I come.
The blossoms begin to spring and spread on tree and in
meadow; the lily with her fair beauty welcomes me, prays me to
fly to her; the red rose too, on the thorny bush, begs me to sing
for her love." "I have a fine dwelling too," rejoins the owl:
"big trees with thick boughs, all overgrown with green ivy that
never fades in frost or snow; in winter it keeps me warm, in
summer cool; my house is bright and green when nothing is
left of yours. You jeer at me for my food, — but what do you
eat, pray? Is it not spiders and flies and worms? But I keep
men's houses and barns free from mice, — churches, too, I
cleanse of them; no foul wight that I can catch ever comes to
Christ's house." At this the nightingale is out of all patience:
"One song of my mouth is better than all that ever you could
do. My notes are sweet, like the songs of Holy Church; in
heaven there is such singing. I help the priests at matins, and
they rejoice in my song." After further wrangling, the night-

ingale bursts out, as if victorious, into loud warbling, in which a choir of other birds join, thrush and throstle and wood-wale; the wren calls for a decision ; Nicholas of Guilford (the author's name, no doubt) shall be the umpire. Away they fly to find him — " but how they sped in their judgment I can't tell you; here is no more of this tale."

In verse similar to that of this playful piece but far more fluent, brighter yet in color, sprightlier in fancy, is a short poem called " The Land of Cokaygne " — " Kitchen-land." It is a satire upon the luxury that was already beginning to invade and corrupt conventual life, but its tone is by no means bitter, — it is rather that of amusement ; it was written in the spirit of a wag, not of a reformer. Better than Paradise — where there is fruit but no meat, and nothing but water to drink — is the land of Cokaygne, that flows with oil, milk, honey, and wine. " Well is him that there may be." In that land there is an abbey of white and grey monks where there is store of flesh and fish ; the very walls are built of pasties ; in the cloister is a tree of spices ; a well of treacle is hard by. To that abbey roast geese fly, bringing garlic. After dinner, the young monks go out to play, — and here the humor of the piece becomes outrageous. In conclusion it is said that to reach that delectable land one must wade for seven years up to his chin in swines' filth.

" The Land of Cokaygne " is one of the best specimens of light satire in the language. The appearance of such a piece signifies much : it means that a critical spirit is abroad ; that fresh powers of observation are coming into play ; that thought is growing independent.

Collections of proverbs — those digests of popular experience — were made at this time, and were in great demand. One of such goes by the name of Hendyng — some legendary sage, some rustic Solomon, whose name became a generic term for all makers of proverbs. After a ballad-like stanza, in which some bit of popular observation is unfolded, the whole is compactly summed up in one of Hendyng's sayings, and often made yet more portable by being clinched with a rhyme or an assonance. In this old collection occur many proverbs that are still current: "A good beginning makes a good ending," — "a burnt child dreads the fire." Other examples are: "Hope of long life beguiles many a good wife," — "when need is highest, help is nighest," — "seldom comes loan laughing home," — "well he fights that well flies." In the last two the assonance is still preserved, — it is obscured by our modern pronunciation in the following: "A fool's bolt is soon shot."

The poetical pieces thus far noticed were simply the prelude to masses of rhyme. Long rhyming chronicles appeared, in which Arthur and the other ancient British worthies figured again upon the scene. Romances full of love and fighting and adventure gathered bulk proportionate to the popularity of their heroes. It is plain that there was a resurgence in some measure of the spirit of the age of Layamon.

Portions of Scripture history, beginning with the birth, death, and resurrection of Christ, were dramatised and acted in connection with the Corpus Christi festival, — first instituted by Pope Urban IV in 1264, and appointed to be kept on the Thursday following Trinity Sunday. These representations were called miracle-plays, and at last mysteries (in order to distinguish them from other miracle-plays founded on the lives of saints): it is believed that a series of them was acted at the town of Chester within a few years from the date given above.

This promising, fresh beginning of English literature is to be explained by the spirit of the age of Edward I. As unlike his father's as was the character of that great sovereign, so unlike the former age was that which had supervened. The pendulum of thought and feeling had swung over a wide arc; a new set of ideas had replaced the old. Whereas the world, in its double sense of external nature and human society, had seemed to be hopelessly evil, opposed in its very essence to heaven and to God, and whereas the human body had been despised and hated as the loathly prison of the soul, now, on the contrary, instructed doubtless by the unhappy consequences of that view of things, men began to discover goodness and beauty in the world and the body; regarded nature with the genial interest we have already noted; and received gratefully the pleasures of the senses. The human spirit began to feel at home in the body, looked about it, and exerted itself to improve its condition. Thus was a higher unity secured after the painful discord of the previous period.

At such a time natural science is born; and the striking witness to this fact is the renowned Franciscan friar, Roger Bacon. The story of his troubled life marks him out conspicuously as the intellectual pioneer and martyr of his age. His investigations having aroused the suspicion of his superiors in the order, he was kept under guard in Paris for a whole decade, and was deprived of instruments and books. Happily for him, a friend of former years was raised to the papal throne in 1265 as Clement IV; for him Bacon managed to compose a work — the "Opus Majus," a synopsis of science as he understood it, — which brought about his liberation, and in 1268 he was in his native land of England once more. He was too eager to be discreet; his impatience with ignorance and mental immobility in high places made him enemies; the general of the Franciscans in special disliked and suspected him; and in 1278 he was confined at Paris again. Ten years later, the general was chosen pope, with the title Nicholas IV; and it was not until his death, in 1292, that Bacon was set free. He returned to England to die.

By making mathematics the ground of all science Bacon gave unity to his speculations. He excelled in alchemy and optics, — studies in which the Saracens had been without peers for fully five centuries. As an explanation of the backwardness of science throughout Christendom, Bacon alleged four causes : unquestioning submission to authority, the force of habit, prejudice, and self-sufficient ignorance. The only remedy, he said, was to go directly to nature, and question her without fear and without prepossession. The scholastic method of argument had failed to increase or advance knowledge : that could only be done by experience, by experience in its twofold sense, external observation and experiment and internal comprehension, conception, understanding. The causes of sensation, the two principles of physical existence, he made to be matter and " virtue " (in the sense in which we speak of the virtues, properties, or powers of herbs): these were the elements of natural science. Creation, motion, any effect he explained by the action of a " virtue," or quality, or power, upon matter.

Out of mere justice to the age one is obliged to say thus much about Bacon, although his writings, being all in Latin, do not belong to English literature.

It is interesting to compare with him his almost equally misunderstood and ill-used contemporary, the star-gazing king of Castile, Alfonso X. To him we owe the simplification of our arithmetic by the introduction of Arabic numerals.

Bacon had experimented much with lenses, but it was left for an Italian, Alessandro Spina, first to put them to practical use in the manufacture of eye-glasses.

Another Italian meanwhile, the Neapolitan Flavio Gioja, was experimenting with the loadstone, and about the year 1302 devised a compass and magnetic needle.

The epoch was further signalized by the dissection of two human bodies at Bologna, in 1315, by the professor of anatomy, Mondini di Luzzi, in the presence of the medical students of the university. Up to that time, the interior structure of the human body had been inferred from that of lower animals: the great Galen even derived what he knew of it from the

bodies of apes. Mondini's work — the result of his investigations — was not superseded as a text-book in anatomy for two
hundred years.

The head of the medical profession in England at this time
was John Gatesden, or Gaddesden, a graduate of the newly
founded Merton College, Oxford, who about the year 1299
began to study medicine, and soon became a successful practi-
tioner in London. He gained celebrity by his fanciful treatment of a son of Edward I for small-pox, — and the boy
recovered. Toward the close of that king's reign Gatesden
compiled his " Rosa Medicinae," drawing heavily upon the
writings of Arabian doctors. He lived to a great age, dying in
1361; and not many years after he was ranked by Chaucer
among the greatest physicians of all time.

A feature of the age quite as remarkable as this progress of
science and medicine was the development of another profession, that of the law. Out of the tumult of the previous period
sprang a longing for order, for security of life and limb and
property, that favored the growth of law, and goes far to
explain the rise of strong governments in Europe toward the
close of the thirteenth century. In England, that longing was
responded to by Edward I, one of the greatest of her kings,
whose name is a synonym for order, able government, and
legal and political reform. The battle of Evesham, in 1265,
had established anew the royal authority, and Edward took
advantage of the tranquil period that ensued to go to Palestine
as a continuator of St. Louis' last crusade. There his valor
and military prowess gained him high renown, stirred the
patriotic pride of his people, and won him their admiration and
affection ; upon the death of his father he returned to England,
in 1274, to take up the reins of government in an auspicious
season. The kingdom was at peace, and commerce was flourishing. The year after his return, parliament made a beginning of customs legislation by according him a duty on

exported wool, which was all that was needed to replenish his treasury. From the first Edward directed his attention to the strict execution of justice throughout the realm, and to the development of law and of a better judicial system. Interest in the subject had been greatly increased by a valuable compend, "Of the Laws and Customs of England," by a late learned jurist, Henry Bracton. Edward broke up the old king's court into its constituent parts, and established these as distinct courts, — those of King's Bench, the Exchequer, and Common Pleas; he also parted the martial from the civil function of the justices (the union of which was characteristic of the feudal age), — it is said that Ralph Hengham, first chief justice of the reconstructed court of King's Bench, was the first who did not wear under his ermine a coat of mail.

Great as Edward was as a law-giver and administrator, he was equally great and successful in his military undertakings; indeed, it is the brilliant extension of his authority over all Britain, whereby he made of it an island-empire, that mention of his name in general first suggests. Those conquests of his, moreover, accelerated the growth of sound constitutional government, for the king's necessities forced him to have continual recourse to parliaments, and to gain the confidence and support of shires and towns by giving them representation, — and grants of money were secured by concessions on his part. In 1282 came the conquest of Wales (one cause, without doubt, of the revival of interest in Welsh legends which we have already observed); the year following, Edward called four knights from every shire and four burgesses from every corporate town to devise some means of meeting the cost of the war. In 1294, in consequence of a serious quarrel with Philip the Fair of France, he had to make a similar appeal; and in 1295 there met a parliament that became the model of all such assemblies in the future. Then followed the war with Scotland — for Edward had allowed himself to be persuaded by his lawyers that he had a just claim to the overlordship of that kingdom, — and this time his necessities led to the confirmation of the charters, in the year 1297.   In the winter of 1301, he had again to make large concessions in order to obtain from the barons unanimous rejection of the arrogant and unprecedented claim lately put forth by Pope Boniface VIII to the suzerainty of Scotland.   In 1303, Edward made a triumphant military progress through that kingdom, his fleet meanwhile skirting its shores.

Among contemporary sovereigns Edward had no equal as a great national king.   Philip IV (the Fair) was a successful despot, but he was not great; he was selfish and cruel; his influence and example, and the result of his strongly centralized government, were disastrous to France.   Yet in many respects the careers of the two monarchs were remarkably like, and show in an instructive way with what different motives the same line of policy may be pursued.   Like Edward, Philip bent all his energies to the depression of feudalism, and to that end favored the jurists, extended the jurisdiction of the Parliament of Paris to the virtual suppression of lesser courts, and called the people to his aid.   In 1302, during the height of his contest with Boniface VIII, he convened, beside the clergy and nobles, representatives of the Third Estate.   It was the first meeting of the States-General, and was analogous to Edward's parliament of 1295.   That contest between pope and king was the chief concern of the era; it was a mortal combat between a declining and a rising power; the legal, critical, slightly skeptical temper of the time was all on the king's side. After the collapse of the papal power, Philip's influence in the conclave secured the election of a Frenchman as pope, who took the name of Clement V, was invested at Lyons, and fixed his residence at Avignon.   Having humbled the mightiest institution of the middle ages and made it subservient to his ends, Philip continued his war with feudalism by attacking its wealthiest, proudest, and most powerful representatives, the Knights Templars. He forced the pope to his will, and Clement abolished the order in the year 1312.

The tone of French literature was prevailingly satirical in this period, as is shown by the poems of Rutebœuf, and yet more conspicuously by the continuation of the "Romance of the Rose" by Jean de Meung — he introduced into it a new and significant allegorical personage, "False-Semblance," and grafted upon a dreamy exposition of the metaphysic of love a prolix satire upon the society of his day. A consummate example of long-drawn and remorseless satire was also taking shape, — the great beast-fable of the middle ages, the "Roman du Renart." There is something terrible in the cynical contempt of honor displayed in this poem, this apotheosis of baseness, this triumphant career of coarse and cruel trickery, hypocrisy, and lust. It is indicative of the emergence of an ignoble element in the social life of the time, destitute of any high ideal, yet quick to discern any discrepancy between profession and practice on the part of its superiors, and stirred to admiration only by successful cunning.

Late in the thirteenth century the sarcastic Adam de la Halle produced the first comedy of modern times — "Li Jus Adam."

Interesting evidence of the reaction against the gloomy ideas of the former age is afforded in German literature by some of the songs of Friedrich von Sonnenburg. The world, he declares, is fair and good ; and he proves it in true mediaeval fashion by reference to the bodies of Christ and his saints, which were formed of its substance and by it were nourished; the resurrection bodies of the redeemed, moreover, will be framed of it. We should not despise the world, he concludes, but be glad that we are in it.

While Friedrich was preaching this wholesome doctrine, the energetic Rudolf of Hapsburg, king of the Romans, was making his part of the world pleasanter to live in, by restoring order and maintaining the peace of the Empire as far as he was able. He repressed the violence of the barons, razed the castles of the refractory, and cleared the highways of the robber bands that infested them. He was wise in his generation, and made friends of the people.

With the rise of the people in political importance, a vein of satire cropped out in German literature also, appearing most conspicuously in the homely verse of Hugo von Trimberg.

Even the hastiest survey of the age would be incomplete were we not to mention again that remarkable man, Alfonso X (the Wise), brother-in-law of Edward I, — his sister, the noble Eleanor, become Edward's queen. Alfonso had the Bible translated into Spanish, and had a chronicle of Spanish history and a great code of laws and customs compiled, also in the native language. The Code took its title — "Las Siete Partidas" — from its seven main divisions. These were the first great monuments of Spanish prose. A little later the fluent Italian language was moulded by the mighty genius of Dante, who stands, Janus-like, between two worlds, his backward gaze piercing depths of gloom until it is lost in the silvery light of classic literature, while his forward face, flushed with the sunrise of the Renascence, seems to command all coming time.

To Aquinas and Bonaventura Dante was profoundly indebted, and he more than paid what he owed them: the theology of the one and the mysticism of the other, transmuted by him into poetry, were freed from the shackles of the technical and professional, and attained a universal validity. It is, of course, unnecessary to look beyond the sixth book of the Æneid for the suggestion of the general design of the Divine Comedy, but in the middle ages more than one monkish visionary had made the same awful journey as Virgil's hero, and had not been deterred, as he was, from exploring the terrific city of Dis, — and in their steps Dante trod. Bede's account of Drithelm's vision was mentioned long since; yet more striking and detailed is the account given by Roger of Wendover (a precursor of Matthew Paris), among his annals of the year 1196, of a certain monk of Evesham who, while his body lay in trance, was conducted by St. Nicholas through the doleful regions where souls received fitting punishment for their sins.

The Divine Comedy may be read as the history of a soul that has struggled from darkness into light. It is a record of the travail of its author's own century, as it passes out of the horror of great darkness, the lurid gleams and deadly fear of the Inferno, through the milder shades of Purgatory, to the peace and faith and radiance of the Paradise. The lofty invocation to the Virgin at the very close of the vast poem merits special attention; it was in Dante's time that the cultus of Mary reached its consummation; it was firmly established henceforth as an essential element in the popular faith, was defended and expounded by doctors, enriched the services of the church, and became the inspiration of poets and artists. To the Franciscan order this access of devotion was primarily due; St. Bonaventura composed a Litany of the Blessed Virgin, and about the year 1300 Duns Scotus, the subtle schoolman, defended with many refined arguments the lately developed doctrine of her immaculate conception. In this he antagonised the conservative Aquinas, as he did his theological system in general, enlarging the domain of faith in doctrinal matters at the expense of that of reason. The Carmelites strove to outdo the Franciscans in devotion to Mary; they called themselves her friars, and boasted that she had shown their order peculiar favor. The Servites took their title from the special service they professed to her. The first great Christian painter, Giovanni Cimabue, thrilled the heart of Florence with joy by his colossal picture of the Madonna, and a little later the new cathedral of that city, built by the eminent architect Arnolfo, was dedicated to St. Mary of the Lily.

A clue to the secret source of this outburst of devotional fervor is afforded by the two wonderful hymns of the thirteenth century, the "Dies Irae" and the "Stabat Mater," the former uttering in awe-struck accents the burden of the first half of the century, the latter opening out in the last half a way of relief. Both are believed to have been composed by Franciscan friars. The Dies Irae exhibits a soul conscious only of two awful facts — itself and God: its poverty, helplessness, sinfulness, and abysmal alienation from a terribly majestic and offended Deity. The Stabat Mater interposes a screen between the trembling soul and its Maker; the Virgin Mother is the intermediary who dispenses grace and pardon from above, stirs up holy affections in the human heart, and will plead for the sinner at the judgment so shudderingly expected. Thus the awful gulf was bridged, and the guilt-burdened spirit poured itself forth in the very abandonment of adoration toward that gracious figure, all mercy and mildness, who had herself sounded the depths of human sorrow, and forgot its own anguish in contemplating hers.

This motion of sympathy broke up the stony ground of the heart, and a spring-tide of art ensued. To the year 1288 — the first of the pontificate of Nicholas IV, for whom it was done — belongs the great mosaic representing the Coronation of the Virgin in the apse of Sta Maria Maggiore at Rome. In the church of Sta Maria sopra Minerva a mosaic over the tomb of Durandus, who died in 1296, presents the great symbolist and ritualist on his knees before a Madonna that might have been designed by Cimabue. At Florence and Siena flourishing schools of fresco-painting arose under Giotto and Duccio. Those great masters loosed the swathing bands of art; their work is characterized by a mobility, lifelikeness, and varied expression of feeling before unknown. In his department Giotto was as eminent a man as his friend Dante (whose portrait he painted) was in his; it is pleasant to think of the intercourse between them at Padua, Dante looking on and conversing while Giotto covered the walls of the Arena Chapel with scenes from the lives of the Virgin Mother and her son.

The epoch was further rendered illustrious by a revival of sculpture, under a fresh and direct study of nature and of remains of ancient art. Now it was that the Pisani carved and cast their pulpits, statues, tombs, and doors.

The reign of Edward I was the flowering time of mediaeval English art. Gothic architecture then attained its relative perfection in the introduction of geometrical tracery, which, coming midway between the severity of the lancet style and the weakness of flowing tracery, was capable of endless variety without extravagance and of perfect adaptation to openings of any form. This beautiful style is exhibited in the Angel Choir at Lincoln, which belongs to the early years of Edward I, and in the nave of York and the Chapter-house at Wells, begun about the middle of his reign. The sculptures of the Angel Choir, too, give evidence of the taste and skill of the period. The leafy capitals of columns show the effect of the new study of nature, as do the carvings of the exquisite crosses reared by Edward wherever the body of Queen Eleanor rested on its way to interment in Westminster Abbey. The fine recumbent figures in bronze upon the tombs of Henry III and Eleanor were the work of William Torel, — but who he was it is impossible now to ascertain; some insist that he was an Englishman, others, that he was an Italian of the school of the Pisani. The latter claim at least testifies to the excellence of his work. The beautiful grille by Eleanor's tomb is a specimen of the delicate iron-work of his time.

After this sweeping glance at the manifold activity of the age we turn again to the literature, which we are now better prepared to appreciate. One of the first points to arrest our attention is the great influence of French literature and language upon English: the statutes of Edward's reign were couched in French (instead of Latin as before); chronicles, romances, mysteries, were done into English; and French words were naturalized in the language in such numbers as to make this an epoch in its history. The first who thus enlarged the vocabulary was the monk Robert of Gloucester, who, about the year 1300, wrote in the southern dialect a rhyming history of England that begins with the mythical Brutus and ends with the reign of Henry III. Thus the first part of his chronicle covers the same ground as Layamon's, but Robert greatly abridges the history of the British kings in order to make room for later dynasties. Like Layamon, he dwells upon the story of Arthur in a tone of admiration and regret. This new invasion of English literature by the Britons made amends for the recent conquest of Wales. One cannot fail to see in the good monk's record of British, Saxon, Danish, Norman, and Angevin dynasties an evidence of patriotic pride, of the rising national spirit, and of the union of races now happily achieved. His chronicle contains twelve thousand lines — equivalent to twice as many of the short lines of Layamon. To Robert has been ascribed a set of Lives of Saints — Katharine, Lucy, Christopher, Ursula and the Eleven Thousand Virgins, Swithin, Dunstan, Edmund the Confessor and others — that are written in the same dialect and verse as his history. In the life of St. Swithin occurs an interesting touch of criticism of the bishops for their pageantry in the consecration of churches, — the good Swithin did not make such display.

In the year 1303, Robert Mannyng, of Brunne, in Lincolnshire, a member of the order of St. Gilbert of Sempringham, translated into English verse a French treatise called " The Hand-book of Sins." He called his version " Handlyng Synne" — using the term " handling" in the sense of " touching" or " concerning." It deals with the seven deadly sins — pride, envy, anger, covetousness, sloth, gluttony, lechery, — illustrating them with stories that enforce the duty and advantage of practising their contrary virtues. Many years later, at the bidding of his prior, Mannyng translated, also out of the French, a rhyming history of England. This work, which was designed for the instruction and entertainment of the common people, goes over the ground that Robert of Gloucester had lately occupied, with the addition of the reign of Edward I — whom Mannyng greatly admired. An English version of St. Bonaventura's "Meditations on the Lord's Supper, and Hours of the Passion," which is marked by much sweetness of phrase and feeling, has been attributed to him.

These writings are of importance in the history of the language. They are in the Midland dialect, and show it in its final phrase, just before it rose to recognition as the English language proper. The changes that we noticed in connection with the speech of Layamon have been progressing; the various terminations of Anglo-Saxon have become (with few exceptions) indistinguishable, having been melted down to a universal *e*, — and even that is beginning to drop off, especially from adjectives; *es* is now established as the regular plural of substantives; and the vocabulary has been swelled by new words of French derivation that greatly outnumber those even that were introduced by Mannyng's elder contemporary, the monk of Gloucester. Already the language has a decidedly modern look : it is hardly if at all more difficult to understand than Chaucer's.

A certain melancholy interest attaches to Adam Davy's " Dreams about King Edward II," because their glowing vaticinations of his miraculous escape from assassination, his election as emperor, coronation by the pope, and subsequent crusade under Christ's guidance, are in such woful contrast with his unhappy career and horrible end.

As the Corpus Christi festival had not yet attained great popularity or come into general observance, Pope Clement V promulgated it anew at the Council of Vienne in the year

1311. Five years later, Pope John XXII ordered that it should be celebrated everywhere with solemn processions. As the festival rose thus rapidly in importance, so, we may presume, did the dramatic representations that were connected with it increase in number and popularity. Those five years may be referred to as the time when a fresh impulse was given to the performance of mysteries ; then the famous collections known as the Chester, Wakefield, Coventry, and York plays were taking shape. These sets contained from two- to four-dozen plays apiece ; it took days, sometimes even a week to present them ; they were acted by members of the town guilds upon movable scaffolds in the market-places or open spaces before churches. In some instances they became an accompaniment of the annual fairs that drew a great concourse of country people to town. They were in truth the chief means of popular religious instruction, for sermons were few : Archbishop Peckham of Canterbury had lately had to require his priests to preach at least once every three months. The mysteries unfolded in long panorama the great events in the history of man's redemption ; a series of them would embrace these and similar subjects : the Fall of the Angels — the Creation — the Fall of Man — Cain and Abel — Noah — the Sacrifice of Isaac — the story of Balaam — the birth of Christ, Visit of the Shepherds, and of the Three Kings — the Flight into Egypt — Massacre of the Innocents — Miracles of Christ, especially the Raising of Lazarus — the Conspiracy of Pilate and Caiaphas — the Crucifixion — Harrowing of Hell — Resurrection — walk to Emmaus — Ascension — appearance of Antichrist, and Day of Judgment.

This list reminds one of the frescoes of the same scenes and subjects that were at this very time beginning to bloom upon the walls of Italian churches. The passion of the age for such graphic synopses of Bible history is revealed again in the high popularity of the "Cursor Mundi," or Course of the

World, a voluminous poem in the Northern dialect, ascribed to the latter part of the reign of Edward II. Its prologue, which consists of only two hundred and seventy lines, is really interesting for the glimpse of contemporary romance with which it begins ; in it, too, the author has kindly told us just what he is going to write about, and has spared us the necessity of reading further. Men love (he says) to hear rhymes and romances of Alexander, Julius Caesar, and the strong strife of Greece and Troy ; of Brut, Arthur, Gawain, and Kay, their adventures and the wonders that befell them ; of Charles and Roland, and their wars against the Saracens ; of Tristram, Isambras, and Amadas, — vain shadows all. Earthly love is a phantom ; those who can should rhyme of the blessed Mother of God, and her love. In her honor he will write and tell of the old and new law, — of the fall of the Angels, of Adam, Noah, Abraham and Isaac, Jacob and Esau, Joseph, Moses, David, and Solomon ; then of Christ's coming, of Joachim and St. Ann, the birth of Mary and of her Son, the Three Kings, Herod's slaughter, the flight into Egypt, the baptism and temptation of Christ, his miracles, crucifixion, harrowing of hell, resurrection, and ascension ; and finally of the lives of the Twelve Apostles, the assumption of Mary, the revelation of Antichrist, and the Day of Doom. All this he will write in English tongue, for the love of Englishmen, that the common folk of England may understand it. Everywhere one finds French rhymes, — but let there be to each his own language.

In this list, as in that of the mysteries, one is struck by the width of the leap from Old to New Testament times : the great prophetic period seems to be entirely ignored. But the author of the "Cursor Mundi" is better than his word, and in the body of his work partly fills the gap by some account of Elijah, and of the prophecies of Isaiah and Jeremiah. He devotes about ten thousand lines to Old Testament history and prophecy, and about fourteen thousand to the (partly apocryphal) Gospel story, and the Last Things. All through the work much legendary matter is inwoven. The popularity of a production like this is to be explained (as in the case of the "Ormulum") by the ecclesiastical prohibition of translations of the Bible. The Psalter only was permitted to be translated ; and a version of it was made in English prose by William of Shoreham, in Kent, about the year 1327.

To the same date belongs a series of rhyming homilies in the Northern dialect. The preacher begins with a slight paraphrase of the Sunday's lesson, proceeds to an exposition of it that inclines strongly to allegory, and points the whole with an appropriate tale. It was an age of story-telling ; one misses its full flavor unless he perceives the naïve and childlike delight with which men and women listened then to tales of marvel and adventure.

The prologue to "Cursor Mundi" classifies excellently the rhymed romances that were steadily increasing in popularity through the reign of the first two Edwards. To the groups there indicated should be added certain suggestions of an old Danish and Saxon group, the "Lay of Havelok the Dane" and "King Horn." These are both translations from the French — as, indeed, all the romances are. Horn was a banished prince, courteously received by King Aylmar, whose daughter Rimenhild falls desperately in love with him. Before he can marry her he must be knighted, and prove himself worthy of her by valiant deeds. So he goes in search of adventure, beheads hundreds of Saracens, enters the service of the King of Ireland, kills the giant champion of a heathen host, — and is suddenly called home by a messenger from Rimenhild, who has been betrothed against her will to a neighboring prince. Horn braves the king ; tells him he will conquer his own land and return for Rimenhild ; he does so, bears her away in triumph and makes her his queen. This is in brief the simple theme upon which a host of romances merely ring the changes.

In the cycle of stories about Charlemagne and Roland echoes of the old " Chansons de Gestes " sounded in England. One cannot but feel more interest, however, in stories that were native to the soil, such as the Arthurian legends, chief among which were those of Joseph of Arimathea, Merlin, Lancelot of the Lake, the Quest of the Grail, and the Death of Arthur. The Tale of Troy derived its popularity partly from its imagined connection with the history of Britain.

A set of tales and apologues of Oriental origin that goes by the name of the " Seven Sages" is significant because it taught western writers to string together a number of stories upon a slender thread of narrative. The tales referred to are fourteen in number; seven of them are told by a wicked queen with intent to prejudice her husband's mind against his innocent son, who must be speechless for a week; their effect is counteracted by the other seven, told by the sages; and the king is thus amused until the fatal week is past, after which the prince's tongue is loosed, he clears himself completely, and the bad queen is put to death.

The adventures of two English heroes, Bevis of Hampton and Guy of Warwick, were unsurpassed in popularity — if we may judge by their great length, and the way in which they have been patched and added to by later hands. Bevis was the son of an English earl. Even as a child he performs wonderful feats of strength and valor, but his wicked mother sells him into slavery to the Saracens. The Sultan's daughter Josyan falls in love with him; after manifold adventures in paynim and Christian lands, he marries her; and their son Guy is crowned king by the dying Sultan. Much better is the romance of Guy of Warwick, with whom, as a type of chivalry, we may close this account of the literature of the age. Guy was a son of the steward of the Earl of Warwick; he was shapely, brave, and strong. He dares to love the Earl's daughter, Felice, — but she disdains him. In a vision she is warned to be kind to him ; she bids him be knighted, and when that is done, bids him seek adventure that he may prove himself worthy of her. For a year he fights and jousts, and returns famous : still she is not satisfied. He sets off again, meets with unimaginable adventures, kills the Sultan, is betrothed to the daughter of the Emperor of the East, — but is reminded of Felice by the sight of the wedding ring. He escapes the match by getting into a broil with a courtier ; leaves Constantinople, and after more adventures arrives in England. He slays an invulnerable dragon that was wasting Northumberland ; is joyfully received at Warwick, and is wedded to Felice, whose scruples are now entirely overcome. Erelong, compunction of conscience sets him roving upon a pilgrimage : he visits Jerusalem, and after a few final adventures, returns home to fight a giant, the champion of an invading Danish host ; and then retires to a forest hermitage to die.

These romances were the delight of the feudal aristocracy, and continually bring before the mind's eye the gay business of their lives, their hunting, hawking, jousting, fighting, and feasting ; and present beside pictures of the castles — barbican, drawbridge, portcullis, gloomy gate, and open bailey surrounded by parapeted walls and towers — in whose sombre halls they were chanted by the minstrels. Edward I built castles on a new plan, of which those he reared at Carnarvon and Conway are splendid examples : the keep now left its lordly central position and was engaged with half-a-dozen other towers in the castle wall, which enclosed a bailey of a rudely oval outline. The apartments in the towers, lighted by loopholes for windows, so dim that lamps had to be lit while it was yet day, badly ventilated too, filled with smoke from the gusty fireplace when the wind blew the wrong way, must have been uncomfortable enough, in spite of the sparse rushes strewn upon the floor, the arras that covered the damp walls, and the soft divans — memorials of intercourse with the East.

The rest of the literature, — rhyming chronicles, paraphrases of Bible history, and religious poems — sprang from another source, the monasteries. The antithesis between these two classes of writings — the romantic and the religious — is well expressed in the prologue to "Cursor Mundi." Of the grand churches, rivalling cathedrals, that bounded the cloisters on their northern side, the most beautiful was Tintern Abbey, re-built in the perfect style of the time of Edward I. About the cloisters and the little sunny gardens they enclosed were the chapter-house, scriptorium, or library, where the work of copy-ing and illuminating manuscripts went on, hospice, where trav-ellers were entertained, dormitories for the brothers, almonry where food, clothing, and medicines were doled to the poor, refectory, kitchen, cellars, and offices. The mere enumeration of these buildings indicates how important an agency such an institution must have been in the social life of the time. The life of the monks was regulated by the canonical hours ; after service at prime (6 o'clock in the morning) they worked, in summer, for four hours ; then read until sext (midday), when they had a meal ; rested through the heat of the day, and after nones (3 o'clock) worked until evensong. They were allowed each a pound of bread a day, and two meals of two cooked dishes and a dish of fruit. At bed-time compline was sung, and then they went to rest upon their mattresses of straw. But the severity of this rule was beginning in many places to be relaxed, and the simple life of former years to be corrupted by worldliness and self-indulgence.

Castle and convent were now declining institutions, types of a system passing away, its work nearly done. The centre of interest shifts to the growing towns, and homes of the people. Everywhere there were rising, at first under the protection of baron, bishop, or abbot, but now, in securer times, farther away, villages of perhaps one hundred souls, farmers', weavers', and tanners' families, their cottages arranged in line along a road, near a stream. The cottage floor was simply trodden earth; around the walls were chests; a brass pot, wooden trenchers, and pottery were the household utensils; chimneys were perhaps just beginning to be built, but as a rule the smoke of the fire was allowed to escape through a hole in the roof. A ladder led to the snug sleeping loft overhead, under the thatch. The house was scented by the heap of refuse that fermented for months at a time just outside the door. The farmer's clumsy cart rolled to field on stout iron-bound discs of wood that did duty as wheels. The only breaks in the dull round of hard labor were the services on Sundays and saints' days, and for the favored few a visit to the annual fair at a distant town. The church was the centre and light of village life in those days. It was often fortified, especially if it were by the sea and in danger from freebooters; to its massive square tower the people ran for refuge, carrying their little property of value, when threatened with danger. The consecration of a church was the event of a lifetime; then the bishop came with his clergy, marched in procession round the building, bade the doors be opened, entered, sprinkled holy water about, blessed the corners of the church, and then the altar, on which twelve candles shone, chanted the litany, — and then the people, who had been waiting without, were admitted to see the rest of the ceremony. In like manner grave-yards were consecrated, the four corners blessed, and crosses set up. The bell that was to call the village to service was washed, named, and blessed against lightning and evil spirits.

The church's watchful care encompassed every individual from the cradle to the grave, supporting him at the great crises of his life, and hallowing them; receiving him, an infant, at baptism, confirming him at the age of puberty, applying for every spiritual ailment the antidote of penance, nourishing him with the Eucharist, solemnizing his marriage, smoothing his passage to another world with extreme unction and the viaticum.

Unless one apprehends such facts as these genially, without prejudice or contempt, it is not for him to understand or enjoy the culture of that age.

It is estimated that in the fourteenth century the population of England amounted to as many as two million, five hundred thousand souls, of whom at least two hundred thousand were gathered in the towns. London numbered about forty thousand; Norwich, the second city in the kingdom, perhaps a third as many; then came York and Bristol, with about ten thousand each. The streets of the cities were narrow, the houses low. In London, an ancient ordinance required that the buildings should be of stone; there, at the time of which we treat, gabled upper stories were beginning to appear, projecting so boldly that they almost met above the narrow streets. The rooms on the ground floor were then commonly converted into shops. Chimneys and glazed windows were becoming general in the houses of the well-to-do, behind which often pleasant gardens stretched. More than half the land of London was in the hands of ecclesiastics; fine monasteries like those of the Black and Gray Friars gave character to the city. Over all the world-famous spire of St. Paul's shot into the air to a height of nearly five hundred feet: its dedication, in the year 1315, signalized the completion of the old cathedral, after a century of reconstruction and addition. The vast building, with its cloisters, chapter-house, and episcopal palace adjoining, enclosed a wide square, in the middle of which rose a large cross of sculptured stone. In a neighboring row, manuscripts, pictures, and rosaries were sold. A single bridge — old London bridge — spanned the river Thames; it was lined, like a street, with houses on either side. From Southwark the tide of pilgrimage, travel and traffic set toward Kent, and all the counties that bordered on the English channel.

Living was plain and poor in those days, and throughout the winter absolutely unwholesome, for owing to lack of provender for that season vast droves of cattle had to be killed in November, and on their salted meat people lived for more than half the year. The salt used was made by evaporation, and was dark in color and poor in quality. In Lent, of course, salt fish was the only fare. As the supply of vegetables was quite insufficient to correct the ill effects of so unwholesome a diet, it is no wonder that the people of England were plagued with scurvy in those long winters. An immediate result of so much salt fare was intolerable thirst; vast quantities of ale and small beer were required to quench it. The tables of the rich were supplied with Gascon wine.

Such, in brief, was the world into which Chaucer and Gower, Langland and Wyclif were born.

IV.

THE office of Edward III's reign was to fill with feeling, and thereby modify the intellectual forms of the time of Edward I. It was an era of sentiment, of a fresh stir of the affections, of freer fancy and humor, of a new pathos. This it is that makes it so attractive to the student of history; the soul feels more at home in it than in any preceding age.

The settled participation of the people in the government of the country begot an interest in the common welfare and a sense of national unity and glory that were more genial and general than before. In theology, a further departure was made from the scholastic method which heralded the dissolution of the system: the logical proofs of church doctrines that were employed in preceding ages were abandoned as inadequate; the reason was declared to be ineffectual in the sphere of the supernatural; and faith was proclaimed as the only organ for apprehending spiritual truths. From such an attitude diverse consequences sprang: among pious souls a more ardent devotion was stimulated, a warmer coloring was cast over religion, and it became a matter of feeling; while the stirring intellect of the time, gladly relinquishing all spiritual concerns to the direction of an external authority, exercised itself in the sphere that was left to it of the secular and the human, and revelled in the glory of nature and the treasures of classic literature. In architecture, the chaste forms of the last age were moulded into mild curves of excessive elegance and grace that bear the impress of the refinement, sentiment, and fancy of the new epoch. The choirs of the cathedrals of Lichfield, Ely, and Wells are examples of this Decorated style; but the acme of flowing tracery (seeming in this case to copy the deli-

cate curves of leaves and flower-buds) was attained in the east
window of the cathedral of Carlisle. And now at last the
spirit of the age found a tongue, and in the young Chaucer's
liquid lines, his " ditties and glad songs " (which sparkled, we
may be sure, with dew and sunshine), his " Court of Love,"
" Complaint to Pity," and " Complaint of Mars," warbled forth
the exultant joy in existence, the delight in springtime, in the
fragrance and beauty of flowers, and the song of birds, the bliss
of happy love, the woe of unrequited love, that were the product of this new birth of the soul. Chaucer's first literary work
(significant of the French influence that dominated all his early
poems) was a translation of the " Romance of the Rose." He
also translated from the French a prayer to Mary, in which the
thought of the tender compassion of the Virgin Mother rouses
in the poet's heart the very abandonment of love and passionate entreaty. He flees to her, he has no comfort except in her,
the queen of misericord, the cause of grace. In her is abounding pity ; she has ruth on our adversity. This word *ruth* is
most characteristic of Chaucer of any in his vocabulary ; it is
his own abounding sympathy, his broad humanity, that has so
endeared him to every later age. This quality gave him access
to the hearts of his characters, and his mastery of language
enabled him to tell their secrets to others. The woes of mythological personages even were real to him ; his beautiful lament
for the Duchess Blanche of Lancaster opens, appropriately,
with the sad story of Alcyone, and

> " Truly I which made this book
> Had such pity and such ruth
> To read her sorrow, that, by my troth,
> I fared the worse all the morrow
> And after, to thinken on her sorrow."

In the same poem, the inconsolable grief of the man in black
(the widowed Duke) — an impersonation of sorrow, — and the
poet's sympathy with him, are affectingly portrayed.

The central figure in this epoch of feeling, of a national enthusiasm which he himself did much to create, is that of the spirited young king, Edward III. He stands in the heart of all the stir and glitter of that day. Enthroned when he was only fourteen years old, he wedded, at fifteen, Philippa of Hainault, and in 1330, when he was but seventeen years of age, became the father of a son who is known to history as the Black Prince. A few months later he assumed in full the sovereign authority; sent to the gibbet the worthless Mortimer; and fairly began his brilliant reign. In 1333, his victory over the Scots at Halidon Hill wiped out the lingering disgrace of Bannockburn, and his overlordship of Scotland was admitted by the king whom he placed upon the throne of that country. In 1337, in his resentment at the assistance afforded by Philip VI of France to the refractory Scots, Edward revived his claim to the French crown as grandson of Philip the Fair; entered into an alliance with the Flemings, — a connection that had an important bearing upon the industrial development of England; and began the long drama of the Hundred Years' War. The splendid victory of the English fleet off Sluys, in the year 1340, was the first great naval battle of modern times. In 1346, on the field of Crécy, King Edward defeated a French army three times as numerous as his. The following year he reduced Calais. At Poitiers, in 1356, the Black Prince overcame and put to flight a host that outnumbered his as five or six to one ; took the French king captive, carried him to England, and exhibited him in courteous triumph in the streets of London. These dazzling victories swelled to the utmost the pride of Englishmen in their king and country, and greatly diminished the influence over them, before so potent, of the French language and literature.

Parallel with these events were the Statutes of Provisors and Praemunire, — declarations of the independence of the English church. The papal curia, still situated at Avignon, was quite

under French control. Those statutes forbade papal fore-
stalling of the rights of chapters and patrons by appointing
successors to living incumbents, and declared the king's court
the court of final appeal, threatening with outlawry any ecclesiastic who carried his case to the curia for settlement.

King Edward enhanced the lustre of his monarchy by intro-
ducing, for princes of the blood royal, an order of nobility elevated above the ancient orders, — that is, the dukedom.   He
created the Prince of Wales, while yet a young child, Duke of
Cornwall, and soon after made his cousin Henry Duke of Lancaster.   But it was the institution of the Order of the Garter
that sums up for us picturesquely and completely the magnificent qualities of his reign.   With it was connected the rebuilding of Windsor castle, — a truly national work, in which
laborers from every shire in England coöperated, — and both
confess the magic power of Arthurian romance.   A Round
Table was set up in the Round Tower at Windsor; knights
and noblemen from far and near contended in splendid tournaments; twenty-five of the bravest were decorated with the
insignia of the order; and song and feasting concluded
the day.

Edward was interested in the intellectual culture of his young
subjects: at Cambridge, where Clare Hall had lately been
founded, he founded, in 1332, King's Hall, or College.   About
the same time, Oriel and Queen's Colleges were instituted at
Oxford, the latter in honor of Queen Philippa.   These foundations are to be compared with the universities that were rising
at the same period in the large towns of southern Europe.

There was no noted man of science in this reign, if we except John Ardern, the first celebrated English surgeon, — and
he was not as eminent as his French contemporary, Guy de
Chauliac, physician to several of the Avignonese popes.   Ardern began his study of the human frame at the time when the
Black Death was devastating Europe; after the year 1370 he

had a flourishing practice in London, where he attended the Black Prince and the chief of the nobility.

When we turn to the literature of the reign we catch at first, to our surprise, echoes of the lugubrious strains of the time of Henry III. It is as if a fountain of bitter water had flowed underground for a hundred years to well up darkly amid the sunshine of a happier age. This sense of incongruity is lessened when we consider that the writers of the beginning of Edward III's reign were reared in the midst of the fierce antagonisms of his father's time, and voice its tragic spirit. It is apparent, moreover, that a deeper religious sentiment was abroad than in the period immediately preceding.

An excellent illustration of this is afforded by the following sentence, out of a work translated from the French by Michel of Northgate, Kent, in the year 1340: "If thou wilt know what is good and what is evil, go out of thyself, go out of the world, learn to die, part thy soul from the body by thought, send thine heart into the other world (that is, into heaven, hell, and purgatory) — there thou shalt see what is good and what is evil." The work of which this dualistic effort is the key-note goes by the name of "The Ayenbite of Inwyt" (Again-biting of the Inner-wit, or Remorse of Conscience). It is written in the uncouth Kentish dialect. It is an exhaustive classification and description, with divisions and sub-divisions quite in the manner of a philosophic treatise, of the seven deadly sins and the virtues that correct them.

Michel's injunction above quoted was followed to the letter by his contemporary, Richard Rolle, hermit of Hampole, near Doncaster, Yorkshire, who died in the year 1349. He wrote, in the Northern dialect, a dreary yet interesting poem, "The Prick of Conscience," in which he expatiates, with infinite detail, upon the misery of man's life. Every period of it, he says, contains mickle wretchedness; as soon as a child is born it begins to cry; it is pitifully feeble, and until it is baptized is the fiend's son; even if it lives to grow up a stalwart and comely young man, evils of all sorts, fever, dropsy, jaundice, phthisic, gout, and other maladies will cause his strength to abate, his beauty to fade; then comes doting old age, heavy of heart and head, dim of sight, hard of hearing, short of memory, — and then death, whose tokens are remorselessly described; nor is the poet content to leave the grewsome theme until he has harrowed our feelings to the uttermost by unveiling the horrors of the charnel-house. He enlarges next upon the uncertainty of life; the world is unstable, as variable as the sea, as full of danger as a wilderness haunted by wild beasts or a forest full of thieves and outlaws; man's life is a series of chances and changes; Dame Fortune turns her wheel, and while she lifts some from woe to weal, plunges others from weal to woe. Fascinated, like an Egyptian of old, by the thought of death, the hermit-poet turns to it again to dilate upon its physical and spiritual terrors; he enumerates four reasons why death is to be dreaded: the pain of the parting of soul and body; the vision of devils about the death-bed; the account of his life that the sufferer must shortly give; and his uncertainty whether he is passing to joy or pain. As to the first point, a figure employed by a "philosopher" is quoted with approval; suppose a tree planted in a man's heart, its roots twisted about every joint and vein in his body, its top shooting out of his mouth, and then suppose that that tree, with all its roots, were suddenly pulled out, — the pain would be like, yet not so fearful as that of the parting of soul and body. The next portion of the work treats of Purgatory (its least pain being greater than the greatest pain of earth; a spark only of its fires being hotter than all the fires of earth), — the next of Doomsday, — and the last of the Pains of Hell and the Joys of Heaven. Some of the pains of hell are Dantesque and terrific; there men suffer such hunger that they tear their own flesh; they thirst, and have only fire to drink; they are tortured by conscience, and by devils whose aspect would drive men mad for fear.

Violent as the contrast seems to be between this dismal poem with its lurid touches and the brilliant reign in which it appeared, there was yet a fundamental agreement between them, — they represented the two poles of feeling. The hermit of Hampole's aim was emotional coercion ; he would save men by exciting to an agony the sentiment of fear.

The other extreme of feeling, that of desire of glory, joy in victory, and patriotic pride, was voiced by Laurence Minot, Edward III's rustic laureate, who composed, in the Northern dialect, eleven poems that celebrate the great deeds of Englishmen and their "comely King" in the war with France and Scotland. The ground of this sentiment, in large measure the cause of those triumphs, was a conviction that God was on the side of the English in the struggle, and that he regarded their king with peculiar favor. Proof of this is quaintly recorded by Minot : one dull morning, when the spirit of the English army was depresssed by a thick fog, King Edward made his prayer to God, "and God sent him good comfort soon, — the weather grew full clear."

All through this period, we should bear in mind, miracle-plays and mysteries were enacted in due season before eager crowds, and metrical romances were as popular as ever. About the middle of the reign a French romance, "William of Palermo," was translated into the midland dialect, in alliterative verse. It is a tale of a Sicilian prince who was kidnapped by a were-wolf, found by a shepherd, and finally adopted by the emperor of Rome ; the were-wolf, who was in reality a Spanish prince, suffering under the baleful enchantment of his wicked step-mother, is in the sequel restored to his right shape, and returns to his native land to reign. It is a pretty story; and the best descriptive passages it contains were added by the English translator. More interesting yet, because smacking of the soil, is the "Tale of Gamelyn" — a youth who is abused and betrayed by his eldest brother, and escapes to the greenwood, where he is made "king" of a company of outlaws. His story is evidently connected with that of Robin Hood. The gathering hatred of the people toward the regular clergy is strikingly exhibited in this poem. The best of all these romances, either of this or the previous period, is that of "Sir Gawayne and the Grene Knight." It is of considerable length. Each section, of about twenty alliterative lines, is pointed with a jaunty quatrain. Sir Gawayne is King Arthur's nephew; he is a paragon of knighthood, an exemplar of the five chivalric virtues, frankness, fellowship, chastity, courtesy, and pity — or sympathy. The scene opens with the Christmas festivities at Camelot; Guenore the queen is there in gay apparel; after the bounteous feast Arthur calls for tales of marvel and adventure. On a sudden a giant, as green as grass, appears before the court; his beard is like a bush, his bristly brows are green, and "all his vesture verily is verdure." He is seated upon a green foal; his saddle is embroidered with birds and flies, his stirrups set with green stones. He holds no weapon but a holly-bough and axe of sharp green steel. The company is daunted by this singular apparition, who dares any knight there present to smite him on the neck three times with the axe, on condition that that knight shall seek him out a year from that day and stand as many strokes in his turn. Amid the forebodings of the ladies, Sir Gawayne undertakes the adventure : his first two blows are ineffectual; the third severs the Green Knight's head from his body; the monster catches up his head and gallops away. The seasons come and go, but no thought of escape from the conditions he has accepted ever enters Gawayne's mind — to a knight it is an unspeakable disgrace not to keep his faith. The warm showers fall, the trees grow green, the birds build and sing, "for solace of the soft summer," the "donkand dew" drops from the worts, the sun is bright and hot, the wind blows, the dust drives, the leaves fall, the grass grows gray, — and winter winds round. It is time for

Gawayne to start on his quest for the Green Knight. First he wanders through North Wales, and in the winter woodland meets many wonders, — but none can tell him of the Green Knight. At Christmastide he arrives at a fine castle, and is courteously entertained there three days. His host goes hunting, after making Gawayne promise that he will return him anything that may be given him in his absence. The descriptions of the arming of a knight, and of deer, boar, and fox-hunting, are given with spirit, and are entertaining episodes in the story. Meanwhile the lady of the castle tempts Gawayne; it is a difficult predicament, — he must be courteous to the lady, yet not a traitor to his host; he withstands her enticements gracefully and honorably. She gives him a magic girdle to protect him in his encounter with the Green Knight, whose haunt (he discovers) is not far away. In the evening, when his host returns, Gawayne gives him his lady's kisses — but says nothing about the girdle. The next morning, he sets out to fulfil his compact with the giant. It is a wild winter's day; the north wind blows, the "snittering" snow drifts in the dales, every hill has a hat and cloak of mist. At last he comes to a cave, overgrown with herbs; it is the green chapel of the giant, — an "ugly oratory, where devil-wise devotions might well be paid; a cursed kirk!" Out of a hole in the ground comes the Green Knight, — his host of the castle, though he knows it not. Gawayne bares his neck for the blows; the first two are only feigned; the third time the axe just cuts his skin. Then the Green Knight tells him he has borne himself well save in the matter of the girdle: the third stroke was his punishment for that little blemish upon his honor. Gawayne is deeply humiliated, and curses his cowardice and untruth.

As we read, we feel instinctively that the figures of this story have a hidden meaning, and we are justified in seeking it by the known passion of the Middle Ages for allegory. What is the Green Knight but a type of nature, — not the inanimate world, but the deathless life that is in nature? Then the teaching of the tale is that that Protean life can only be conquered and made harmless, even friendly, by perfect self-control and the strength and fearlessness that spring from purity and good faith.

The most popular book of the age, and an important monument of early English prose, was Sir John Mandeville's story of travel in the Orient. Sir John left England in the year 1322, and was gone for more than thirty years. Upon his return from the East, he submitted a Latin version of his narrative to the pope at Avignon; having gained his approval of it he translated it into English, in 1356. His motive in composing the book was to afford pilgrims a guide to Jerusalem and the Holy Land. So he points out, in the first part, four ways to the holy city: one by Cyprus and Jaffa, another by Tyre, another northward from Egypt, another, almost entirely by land, through Constantinople and Antioch. In the second part he takes a wider range; traverses Armenia, the land of Job, India, Java, and Cathay; describes the gardens, palace and throne of the Grand Khan, and the customs of the Tartars; and then tells of Media, Georgia, and the Land of Darkness; of twenty-two kings pent up between the mountains and the Caspian Sea, who will break forth in Anti-Christ's time; of the dominion of Prester John and his palace at Susa; of the Vale Perilous, the Devil's Head, and the isles of Bragman and Taprobane. Though some of Mandeville's geography seems to be of fairyland, and though he records marvels prodigious enough to satisfy even the eager craving of that childlike day, yet that very interest in geography and the doings of strange folk in far-off lands was at once a sign and a means of a remarkable intellectual and imaginative awakening, and the many manuscripts of the work show how general that awakening was. One notable trait of Mandeville's is the interest and subtle sympathy born thereof with which he describes the religious beliefs of various peoples, the strange ways of the Greek and Syrian Christians, the belief of the Saracens and of the Fire-worshippers. He actually speaks in that day of the Inquisition, of the "Holy book Alkoran, which God sent by his messenger Mohammed,"— a dangerously liberal sentiment!

Such was the literature produced in England while Chaucer was a boy. Meantime, in Germany, William of Occam, an Englishman, who had already drawn the last conclusion from that theological nescience on which Duns Scotus had lately insisted, was defending, under the protection of the Emperor Louis IV, and in his behalf, the rights of the civil power as against papal autocracy. It was not by any means by chance that the flourishing period of German mysticism in the Rhine valley, at Constance, Basel, Strassburg and Cologne, coincided with Occam's career, — that Eckhart, Tauler, Suso, and the author of the "German Theology" were his contemporaries. Scholasticism was dissolved into mysticism through the medium of feeling, — by the doctrine of intuitive apprehension of the being of God and of all spiritual truths. In matters of faith, moreover, both yielded unqualified submission to the authority of the church.

In the year 1362, a priest of Strassburg named Closener finished his German prose chronicle of his own time. The most remarkable passages in it are those descriptive of the Black Death, and the emotional extravagances (connected with it) of the Flagellants. The whole of the fourteenth century was prolific in the homely, mechanic verse of the Master-singers.

The rise of sentiment in that century was signalized by a revival of poetry in the South of France. A court of love was instituted at Toulouse, and on the first of May, 1324, a golden violet was awarded to the author of the best poem in the Provençal dialect. This was the occasion of the Floral Games, and of a renewed flourish of the "Gay Science." In 1355, second and third prizes were awarded, — a silver eglantine, or flower of jasmine, and an acacia-blossom to the author of the best ballad. And now, in the north, the young Froissart was meditating the first part of his chronicle of the gorgeous spectacles, the splendid feasts, and all the pride, pomp, and circumstances of the glorious wars of his day. By this time, too, the wave of enthusiasm for classic culture, propagated by Petrarch, had reached northern France, and Nicholas d'Oresme, a canon of Rouen, said to be the most learned Frenchman of his day, headed a revival of letters, in the course of which translations into the vernacular were made of works of Cæsar, Sallust and Cicero, Livy, Ovid, Valerius Maximus, and Lucan, and of the Latin version of works by Xenophon and Aristotle.

A delightful collection of tales that deserve to be better known than they are was composed in Spanish prose by Don Juan Manuel under the title " El Conde Lucanor." The tales purport to be a wise counsellor's answers to the Conde's questions concerning the conduct of life. Witty and wanton stories, parodies of hymns, and a satire on the papal court for its luxury and greed of gold, were written in Spanish verse by a daring priest, Juan Ruiz de Hita. It is no wonder that he languished, for the last thirteen years of his life, in the prisons of the archbishop of Toledo. The history of Don Juan's young relative, King Alfonso XI of Castile, bears comparison in brilliancy, movement, and romantic coloring with that of Edward III. Alfonso founded in the year 1332 the short-lived Order of the Belt, which very probably suggested the institution of the Order of the Garter. Edward admired his young Castilian contemporary exceedingly, sought an alliance of their houses, sent him aid during the siege of Algeciras. Alfonso's love for the beautiful Leonora de Guzman, and the ill-fated passion of Pedro, prince of Portugal, for the yet lovelier Inez de Castro, make this the most romantic era in the history of the peninsula: and its enthusiastic and often irregular loves, its melting sentiment, martial daring and adventurous spirit are all enshrined in a work of pure imagination, the vast romance of Amadis of Gaul.

To Italy, alive with the inspiration of Dante's genius, the literary supremacy of the fourteenth century unquestionably belonged; and the name of Andrea Orcagna, goldsmith, painter, sculptor, and architect, a contemporary of Petrarch and Boccaccio, reminds us that her preëminence in the arts was yet more absolute. Taddeo Gaddi, a pupil of Giotto, emulated his master in some frescoes in the church of Sta Croce, Florence, illustrative of scenes in the life of the Virgin; and to her Petrarch addressed a fervent hymn. That exquisite poet refined the Italian language, and gave it flexibility, elegance, and grace. His sonnets to Laura are, many of them, antithetical, ingenious, studied, — but some, especially of those written after her death, are instinct with a tender and exquisite sentiment that bathes even hills, woods, and waters in its pensive light. Thus Petrarch became the clearest spokesman of that age of feeling. Sentiment like his, moreover, is one of the mightiest agents in self-knowledge : in him the ideal of culture, of self-development as contrasted with the monastic ideal of self-repression, came once for all into full relief. His very name seems to shed visible radiance over the whole age. After his coronation with the poet's laurel wreath at Rome, in the year 1341, he was the literary dictator of Europe.

At the same time Boccaccio began his contributions to Italian literature. He had already composed in Latin an erudite work on the genealogy of the ancient gods which bears witness to the passion for antiquity that characterizes every return to nature. In 1341 he visited Naples, and became the chief ornament of the gay court of its cultivated but dissolute queen. There he wrote, in the octave stanza that he made his own, a diffuse romantic poem intended as an epic, " La Teseide." This he followed with the " Filostrato "; and then

taught the Italian language to wind and flow in light and graceful prose in his " Decameron."   In this work the tales of the
fourth and fifth days — the first set treating of unhappy, the
other of happy love and successful intrigue — strikingly illustrate the range of sentiment (albeit in this case somewhat
artificial) which we have learned to associate with that time.
Tears, smiles, and mocking laughter chased each other in
quick succession over the countenance of the age.

Among Boccaccio's most admired works were two, written in
Latin, on the sad fortunes of illustrious men and on famous
women.   Soon after his return from Naples, where he spent
the seven best years of his life, he met Petrarch, and the two
became fast friends.   One of Boccaccio's chief claims to distinction is that he stimulated a great yearning among scholars
to learn Greek.

A contemporary of his, Giovanni Villani, the historian of
Florence, proved by his work that Italian was a fit instrument
for historical composition.

Such, in brief, was Chaucer's immediate literary background;
and with him English literature began a new course.   Up to
this time, as has been constantly forced upon our attention, it
was at best but a dialect literature, provincial and narrow in
scope and interest ; but in the last forty years of the fourteenth
century the Midland dialect became the English language, and
writings in it enjoyed no longer a merely local but a national
popularity.   Henceforth we shall have occasion to mention
the Northern and Southern forms no more, save as the former
may re-appear under a new name as the Scottish dialect, — the
first monument of which, a product of the sturdy struggle for
Scottish independence, was honest John Barbour's poem, "the
Bruce."   Various reasons have been brought forward to account for the interesting linguistic development just mentioned:
it has been said that the Midland counties exceeded the others
in extent, wealth and populousness; that in them were situ-

ated the great institutions of learning at Oxford and Cambridge; that within their bounds the king held his court; that the language of the midland could be understood by men from north and south who could not understand each other; and finally, that Chaucer's poems and Wyclif's translation of the Bible were sufficient of themselves to raise the dialect in which they appeared into a commanding position. These reasons serve to account for the supremacy of the Midland dialect, but a deeper cause underlay them all which alone satisfactorily explains the rise in importance of English speech, — and that was the elevation of English sentiment in consequence of the splendid successes of the war with France. An interesting expression of it was an act of parliament of the year 1362, — two years after the treaty of Bretigny, which put a term to the first period of the Hundred Years' War, — which required that henceforth in the courts of law all cases should be pleaded, defended and judged in the English tongue, "the tongue of the realm," instead of in French as before. And now, at this favorable juncture, a great master arose to make the forming language flow in verses of captivating melody.

Something has already been said, by way of anticipation, of Chaucer's character: that sympathy which was then emphasized as its dominant note remained with him through life. Over and over again he proclaims his poetic creed, that a truly noble heart is quick to feel and show compassion:

" For pity runneth soon in gentle heart."

That line sums up his observation of life, and that we may not miss its import he repeats it, weaving it into works that belong to different periods of his career. It appears first in the prologue to the " Legend of Good Women," and is repeated in the tales of knight, merchant, and squire. In the man of law's tale the thought is otherwise expressed: "a gentle heart is fulfilled of pity." In the same, the pathos of Constance's story is too poignant for the narrator:

> " I may not tell her woe until to-morrow,
> I am so weary for to speak of sorrow."

He uses the felicitous expression "pitous joye" to suggest the indescribably affecting blend of various and deep emotions when relatives, long parted, meet again. That gentle and beautiful relation of sympathy between human beings, that noble and refining sentiment of which true courtesy was the expression, was admirably suggested by the word *mansuetude* —much used in Chaucer's time; it is a pity that we have lost it.

Chaucer's love of nature—God's "vicar general"—is proved by innumerable passages: by the well-known description of his romantic homage to the daisy—"the emperice and floure of floures alle"—in the prologue to the "Legend of Good Women"; by the pretty lines in the knight's tale :

> "The busy larke, messager of daye,
> Salueth in hire song the morwe graye;
> And fyry Phebus ryseth up so brighte
> That al the orient laugheth of the lighte,
> And with his stremes dryeth in the greves
> The silver dropes hongyng on the leeves ";

even more by such examples of delicate observation as these (from the " Parliament of Fowls" and the squire's tale) :

> "Therwith a wynd—onethe it myght be lesse
> Made in the levys grene a noyse softe
> Acordaunt to the bryddis song alofte."
> "The vapour, which that fro the erthe glood,
> Made the sonne to seme rody and brood."
> "Herkneth these blisful briddes how they synge,
> And seth the fressche floures how they springe;
> Ful is myn hert of revel and solaas "—

cries Chanticleer, in the nun's priest's tale.

Chaucer had a keen eye for artistic beauty: in the second nun's tale occurs this stanza of pictorial quality as distinct as any fresco of the school of Giotto:

> Valerian gooth hoom, and fynt Cecilie
> With-inne his chambre with an angel stonde ;
> This angel hadde of roses and of lilie
> Corones two, the which he bar in honde ;
> And first to Cecile, as I understonde,
> He yaf that oon, and after gan he take
> That other to Valerian, hir make."

There are traces in other works of his of an art more advanced than that of any contemporary Italian artist, — for Chaucer died before the boy-painter was born who first dared to depict the unclad human form. In the "Parliament of Fowls" there is a picture of Venus recumbent on a golden bed : her golden hair is loose, she is nude to the waist, her limbs are covered with thin valence. In the "House of Fame" the poet dreams that he is in a temple of glass, and among statues and portraitures sees a figure of Venus "naked floating in a see," a garland of red and white roses on her head, and doves fluttering around. Not till a hundred years later did any work of Italian art appear that at all resembled that description.

A mythologic touch that would be startling were it not naïve, and that was subtly characteristic of the Renascence, occurs in the story of Dido, who was so fair that God the Creator might take her for his love, if he would wed a mortal woman. It cannot be denied that this is paralleled by the relation conceived by mediaeval devotion to exist between the Holy Ghost and the Virgin Mary : there is a bold expression of it in the prioress's prologue to her tale.

Chaucer's journey into Italy at the end of the year 1372 was a turning point in his literary career. He went in King Edward's service, and was away until the end of the following year. It is supposed that upon that visit he made the acquaintance of Petrarch : it is certain that his Clerk's tale was a free version of Petrarch's Latin translation of the last tale in Boccaccio's Decameron. That Italian journey put a term to the literary influence of France upon his spirit, and opened its gates to the more potent influence of the great authors of Italy. There is not one of Boccaccio's works before mentioned to which Chaucer was not deeply indebted. His stanza is but a slight modification of Boccaccio's octave. In 1378, he went on another embassy to Northern Italy, and some time after his return composed "The House of Fame," in which Dante's influence is plainly apparent. An eagle bears the poet to the echoing palace of fame, midway between heaven, earth and sea. It is built of beryl, and stands on a high rock of ice which is written all over with famous names, the least known of which have partly melted away. In the splendid hall sits the goddess of Fame on a ruby throne; on pedestals beside her 'stand Statius, Homer, Virgil, Ovid, "the great poet Dan Lucan," and others. This idea of individual glory, this hope of living in the memory of the race, was a salient feature of Renascent life and thought: men longed to stand well in others' estimation, to gain their approbation by brilliant achievements. That desire arose naturally out of the character of the age: it was simply a longing for sympathy raised to fever heat. It was a highly important agent in the cultivation of individuality, in which the broadest and deepest distinction between mediaeval and modern literature consists. Literature proper was henceforth no longer to be provided by cowled monks whose personality was lost in their profession, or by wandering and nameless minstrels. Chaucer's personality is surprisingly distinct when seen against the background of all previous English literature; he was in truth a modern man. We should not forget to mention as a significant factor in his intellectual development, his translation of Boethius' treatise "On the Consolation of Philosophy."

By the year 1388, Chaucer had worked free of Italian influence, and entered upon his third, last, and thoroughly English period, — that of the shaping of the Canterbury Tales. To that period belong the inimitable Prologue, and in all probability, the tales of miller, reeve, friar, summoner, etc. —

stories of broad humor and coarse satire for which Chaucer himself apologizes: he must not "falsen his mateere." His own "Rhyme of Sir Thopas"—in the midst of which he is impatiently interrupted by the host—is a delicious satire on the metrical romances still in vogue, on their fantastic characters, motives, and incidents, and prosy detail. A playful piece like that is worthy of attentive reading; it is an evidence of independent thinking such as generally marks the boundary between epochs; it is the criticism of a new age on that which has gone before.

The Canterbury Tales comprise a veritable world of thought and feeling. Scattered through them, especially the later ones, are many allusions that help us to reconstruct with tolerable completeness the domestic life of Chaucer's time. The franklin's tale—one of the most pleasing of all,—its subject borrowed from Boccaccio,—opens with a beautiful description of wedded love: "Love is a thing as any spirit free." The wife of Bath's tale (for a wonder) concludes in the same strain: yet it may be doubted whether Chaucer had such a lofty idea of marriage as some of his critics, deceived by the seeming seriousness of certain playful passages, have declared that he had. How could he have when for ages after his day the traditional view of marriage as a declension from the better state of celibacy still cumbered the ground?—when he could write that in the consummation of wedlock a woman lays half her holiness aside?—a notion that poisoned the stream of domestic life at its source. It is true that he says, correctly enough, that "marriage is a full great sacrament"—but then that line, with its accompanying (ironical) praise of a wife occurs in the one and only thoroughly and hopelessly corrupt tale that he ever wrote. In the parson's sermon is a rebuke that throws a sad light upon a grave and only too common wrong: "above all things men ought to avoid cursing their own children, and giving their offspring to the devil: surely it is great peril and great sin." The doctor of physic cautions parents against negligence in chastising their children. The franklin has a son whom he brings up on the vicious though common principle of " snubbing," because the youth is not as virtuous as he should be.

It seems impossible to doubt that the plan of the Canterbury Tales was suggested by the Decameron, but its working out was entirely independent and national in movement and color. Boccaccio's story-tellers, ten in number, are all young and of the same station in life; they meet in the church of Santa Maria Novella, and leave the plague-stricken city to shut themselves from their suffering kind in the safe seclusion of a stately palace amid delicious gardens and rèfreshing fountains; there they divert their minds from all thought of the misery left behind by telling tales which, as we have seen, tend toward classification, — one set dealing with happy, another with unhappy love-affairs. The English poet gathers thirty people together, of all ranks and ages, and of the most varied experience of life; they meet in an inn, and their motive is a genial one : they are pilgrims to the shrine of St. Thomas of Canterbury. In the morning they set forth, all on horseback, and pass before us in a gay and shifting cavalcade; though of varying degrees of reverence or no reverence, their common motive, and the free intercourse of travelling acquaintanceship, give them all a pleasing equality. The tales they tell are of infinite variety, and are adjusted with nice art to their several characters.

So Chaucer has preserved for us a world of life that moves and has its being forever. How potent the spell of his gently lapsing verse!

> " In Surrye whylom dwelte a companye
> Of chapmen riche, and thereto sadde and trewe,
> That wyde-wher senten her spicerye,"

yielding to the current the reader is quickly borne over the tide of years to that far-off, almost ideal time when Constantinople

was the centre of the world's commerce, and the precious
stuffs and jewels of the Orient, brought thence in Genoese and
Venetian argosies, were distributed over Europe, and exchanged in the ports of Bruges and London for the produce of
northern shores scoured by the fleets of the Hanseatic League ;
when along the line of those fertilizing streams of trade stately
monuments of art were rising ; when the Dukedom of Athens
still existed, a last fragment and fading memorial of the Latin
Empire of the East; when Genghis Khan and his sons were yet
mighty and marvellous figures in a not distant past ; when bow,
sword and buckler had not yet vanished before powder and
shot ; when English knights served in Lithuania with their
Teutonic brethren, or under Castilian banners against the Moors
of Granada or sought adventure even further away, in Anatolia
and Armenia ; when dreamy legends of saints were still
devoutly believed ; when pilgrimages to Compostella and the
Virgin's house at Loreto were popular ; when Rome was the
religious centre of Christendom, and her emissaries were
omnipresent and numerous as the motes that people the sun-
beams.

V.

IN relation to his times, Chaucer would have been happier
had his whole career been set back ten years or so: he lived on
into an era of discord, folly and crime in which his spirit must
have felt belated and something of an alien, — nor can he have
fully understood and sympathized with the moral struggle of
those troubled years. Even his early manhood had been dis-
turbed by jarring cries, — the cry of poor against rich, of
laborers against idlers, of earnest men against worldly churchmen, and worthless monks and friars. The spokesman of this
popular discontent was William Langland; his allegorical,
severely didactic, preaching poem, in dialect and in alliterative
verse, was in great demand: many manuscripts of it are still extant. Langland found the social condition of the England of
his day to be lamentably unsound ; in the prologue to his work
he passes in review various classes intended to represent the
sum of English society, and finds that in the mass evil vastly
preponderates: plowmen labor hard to produce what the waste-
ful scatter in gluttony ; the proud array themselves in outward
splendor ; jesters — " Judas' children " — make fools of themselves instead of working as they might ; beggars rove about,
getting food by feints, fighting over their ale — greedy, lazy
ribalds!; pilgrims and palmers seek the shrine of St. James, and
saints at Rome, — and have leave to lie all their lives after ;
some great lubbers that are loth to work call themselves her-
mits and take their ease ; friars of all the four orders preach for
their own profit and glose the gospel as seems good to them ;
pardoners and parish-priests divide the people's silver ; ser-
geants at law plead for pence and pounds, — but will not part
their lips for love of our Lord ; bishops bold and bachelors of

divinity become clerks of account, to serve the king ; deacons and archdeacons, instead of preaching to the people, "lope" to London to plunder the country as clerks of King's Bench ; bakers, butchers, weavers, tailors, tanners, masons, ditchers and delvers do their work badly ; there are some truly pious people, some honest merchants, some minstrels who get guiltless gold, — but most men now on earth have their honor in this world, and reck not of any other heaven than here. The body of the poem is a rambling allegory of things seen in dreams ; a lovely lady, Holy-church, explains their meaning, and preaches about truth and right ; Flattery, Falsehood, and Meed (this world's goods) appear on the scene : Meed is to be married to Falsehood, but he leaves her in the lurch ; the king offers her to Conscience, but he rejects her with horror, and gives a catalogue of her enormities. In the next dream the deadly sins are moved to confession, and go in search of St. Truth ; they are directed on their allegorical way by the ideal personage who gives his name to the work— Piers the Plowman. In following visions occur interesting and affecting descriptions of the hard life, improvidence, and sorrows of the poor.

Langland's conviction was that the times were out of joint, but could be set right if only the rich would have *ruth* on the poor, and if every man would work diligently at his calling, and be guided by right reason, common sense, and conscience. This appeal to conscience, to the sense of duty, is of deep significance ; it means that the mind of England was struggling to reach a higher moral level than feeling could afford. Another and more satisfactory guide of life was being sought for in the midst of that moral confusion into which mere sentiment must ever degenerate. Into such confusion, toward the close of the fourteenth century, England and the world at large were plunging; a light shade falls over the face of history at this point, and dims the brightness of the First Renascence.

The treaty of Bretigny was soon infringed by the French king, Charles V; his forces made serious encroachments upon Poitou and Guienne, and the boundary-line of the English possessions in France began steadily and rapidly to contract. The Black Prince had sadly embarrassed his cause by his ill-advised interference in Spanish affairs, — he found to his cost that he was upon the wrong side in the struggle for the Castilian crown. He achieved his last famous success in the recapture of the city of Limoges, in 1370, and sullied it by an act of ungovernable passion which has left an ineffaceable stain upon his memory: the town had revolted from him, and in the fury of revenge he ordered a general massacre of its inhabitants: three thousand persons, all defenceless, many of them innocent, fell victims to this sanguinary mandate.

In England, King Edward III, though yet in middle life, was fast declining in vigor and honor. After the death of his faithful queen Philippa, in 1369, he resigned himself completely to the influence of a courtesan, the notorious Alice Pierce: the scandal was such that parliament had finally to bring about her removal from court. In 1376 the Black Prince died; the year after the king followed him to the tomb; and the Prince's only surviving son, then but eleven years of age, acceded to the throne as Richard II. The story of his reign is a depressing account of incapacity and misgovernment, of a long struggle for power between the dukes his uncles and the king, of a series of crafty and vindictive strokes and counterstrokes of selfish policy. In 1381, the smouldering discontent of the people was fanned into flame by the imposition of a hated tax to pay the costs of the futile war with France; but the insurrection was soon suppressed and its leaders were put to death. In 1386, the French collected a great army and a multitude of ships for the invasion and subjugation of England, — but a storm at sea and divided counsels among the commanders brought the vast enterprise to naught. The next year, King

Richard, restive under the control of his uncle the duke of Gloucester, and swayed entirely by the influence of his favorite, the handsome but profligate De Vere, obtained from the submissive Chief Justice, Robert Tresilian, and his colleagues a declaration against the Duke's attempt to minimize the royal authority. This scheme failed of success : the duke and his party rose in arms, De Vere fled to the continent, and Tresilian, caught hiding, was hung. In 1389, however, Richard managed to secure sovereign power; but an unpopular step which he took, in 1396, led to his fall : he made peace with Charles VI of France for a term of twenty-eight years, and took to wife his daughter Isabella. Trading upon the general dislike of this connection in England, Gloucester began fresh intrigues, which were foiled by a stroke of kingcraft : he was arrested and made way with, and his chief adherents were executed or banished. Richard now plainly revealed the temper of a tyrant, and, satisfied that he had crushed all opposition, he shortly crossed over into Ireland to maintain his authority there. But while he was away his cousin Henry, duke of Lancaster, whom he had banished from the realm and whose possessions he had seized, landed in England and speedily attracted to himself a numerous following. At the news, Richard returned precipitately, and found himself alone in his kingdom : he was taken captive, deposed, removed to some secret spot, and was never heard of more.

It was in the midst of this period of disintegration, of dissolution of family and social ties, while the political pendulum oscillated between anarchy and tyranny, that a great and much needed appeal to Conscience and the Bible was strenuously and resolutely made by John Wyclif and his band of "poor priests." This reformatory movement originated at Oxford: Wyclif first appears upon the scene as Warden of Balliol College. About the year 1366 he was drawn into the current of political life, and powerfully defended the refusal of the English government to pay the tribute demanded by Pope Urban V. At this time he sketched out his cardinal doctrine of Dominion, that all authority depends upon God's favor. This weapon he turned against the papal claims : like a sword with double edge it cut right and left. While the English people obey God, he said, they hold directly of him and not mediately, through the pope. Thus at a stroke he lopped off both the temporal and the spiritual authority of the pope in England. For on the one hand he gave the national idea a deeper ground than had been recognized since Israelitish times : the state, he said, as well as the church derives its power from God and does him service ; and, on the other hand, by insisting upon the immediate, personal relation of man to God, that as man sins against his Maker and may sin secretly so by secret repentance and confession to him he may obtain forgiveness, he banished all intermediaries between the creature and the creator, levelled the celestial and terrestrial hierarchies, and revealed the emptiness of the heavenly treasury and the deceitfulness of indulgences. Wyclif would have earnestly exhorted or sternly rebuked the Canterbury pilgrims had he met them at the Tabard inn : he would have shown them that pilgrimage was no sure sign of genuine contrition or means of grace. His was a ringing appeal to the conscience of the people. "Some good judgment," he wrote, "is of men's out-wits [senses] ; some, of men's wit within, as men judge how they shall do by law of conscience." "Men of conscience " say that only Christ can hear shrifts. When Wyclif thought of man he took it for granted that he was free in choice and act : "each man hath a free will and choosing of good and evil." To convert that will to righteousness was the motive of his and his followers' fervent preaching, and of their translation of the Bible. "It is Antichrist," he said, "who forbids the study of God's word, and who says that preaching is useless because God ordains to weal or woe."

This evangelical activity was a necessary consequence of the doctrine of dominion : the condition by which the English people received from God the right to govern themselves, without interference from pope or emperor, was that they should serve and obey him, should do him homage (an application of the feudal principle) : they lost that right by failure to fulfil the condition, by disobedience and sin.   Hence it was imperatively necessary that the English should be a godly people ; to that end it was necessary that they should know the will of God which it was their duty to obey; that will was embodied in the Bible : that therefore they must thoroughly know by reading and exposition.   Wyclif grasped in a manner granted to few in the world's history the thought of God as absolute will : when he fixed his gaze on him he was a predestinarian.   He held together the doctrine of God's unconditioned sway and of human freedom, and felt, perhaps perceived that there was, no conflict between them.

One aspect of his position which needs further illustration is the conflict between religious authorities that it occasioned. The theory of theological nescience that was in the ascendant before and during Wyclif's day left it to faith alone to apprehend spiritual truths, — but faith was capable of mistaking temporal errors for eternal truths ; faith bowed unquestioningly to the authority of the church, — the mystics gave it an all but unqualified submission ; and opinions and institutions purely human, from which divine efficacy had evaporated, and which were becoming noxious, might be and were generally accepted on ecclesiastical authority as divinely revealed dogmas and polities.   Any one who would alter anything in the established order of things must seek another court of appeal, — and that Wyclif found in the Bible.   There, he proclaimed, was a clear expression of the will of God, with which the confused and changing authority of the church might and often did come into conflict.   For many years that antagonism found

daily expression in the controversies between the friars and the
"poor priests," or preachers whom Wyclif sent out, who erelong came to be known by the unexplained but evidently
opprobrious term "Lollards." They regularly closed their
argument by an appeal to "God's law," which their opponents
as regularly attempted to offset by instancing the practice of the
church. The inefficacy of this latter appeal, and the farthest
reach of intellectual independence in that day, are exemplified
by Wyclif's naïve assertion that the pope's approval of a thing
indicates that it is probably wrong !

From this view of the Bible as the supreme authority in
religious matters its translation into the vernacular followed as
a matter of course. That translation was in its best sense a
popular act ; it was an act of trust, — of trust in the intelligence of the people, their capacity to understand the book, and
in their moral sense, their will to use it rightly. Distrust of
these was then and for ages after the ground of all objections
to such translation : the people would misconstrue and abuse
the teaching of the book, it was said. To this suspicion Wyclif
opposed a firm faith in the good sense of the majority, and an
argument capable of infinite application : he could not deny
that some might abuse their liberty, — "but should food be
forbidden to all because some are gluttons?" Against his
opponents the friars he adduced the example of Christ, who
taught the people deepest truths in their mother-tongue ; the
spirit, moreover, spoke in divers tongues on the day of Pentecost ; St. Jerome translated the Scriptures out of the original,
sacred languages into Latin ; they have been translated into
French ; and the friars themselves teach the Lord's Prayer in
English, — why not then the whole Gospel? "Englishmen
know Christ's lore and life best in their mother-tongue."

Wyclif and his coadjutors addressed themselves, therefore, to
the great task of turning the Vulgate into the speech of the
English Midland. He toiled especially at the New Testament,

beginning with the Gospels, proceeding to the Epistles ; a faithful friend of his named Nicholas Hereford, chief pillar of his party at Oxford, devoted his attention to the books of the Old Testament. Hereford's translation was painfully literal, and had to be revised ; so John Purvey, one of Wyclif's wandering preachers, and later his curate at Lutterworth, went over the whole work, clearing up obscurities and polishing the style ; by the year 1388 his labor was done, and the English Bible stood forth, a splendid monument of energy and zeal.

Next in importance to the translation of the Word of God was its exposition ; Wyclif imputed to preaching an extraordinary efficacy : it is better, he said, and more esteemed by Christ than the consecration of the elements. Hence his institution of itinerant preachers, his "poor priests," who in their evangelical poverty resembled the primitive Franciscans. It is interesting to know that he bade them everywhere do all they could to strengthen those ties of social and domestic life that were being so rudely strained in his day. One of his later English treatises, "Of Servants and Lords," was occasioned by the insurrection of the year 1381. It discusses the relations of classes to each other, and dwells upon the important fact (generally ignored then and for ages after) that masters have some duties toward those whom they employ : that all the rights are not on their side, and all the duties on the other. At the same time, the author is careful to disavow, on the part of the "poor priests," the doctrine attributed to them that tenants may refuse to pay rent to wicked landlords. The impression was general that the new religious teaching was at the bottom of the social disturbances of the time ; and some incautious followers of Wyclif's may very likely have drawn extreme but not illogical conclusions from his doctrine of dominion. The insurrection was certainly an embarrassing circumstance ; it forced Wyclif to define his doctrine anew, and expressly to restrict its applicability : tenants may not keep back rent due to wicked lords, he said, though they may withhold tithes from sinful priests. This limitation to the ecclesiastical sphere of the great principle that dominion is lost by sin, though inconsistent, was natural; Wyclif shrank with horror from revolutionary inferences from it which he had not foreseen when he first enunciated it, during the contest with Urban V, years before. Finally, he guarded himself and his doctrine in a way that emptied it of all practical significance: in this world, he concluded, one can never know that a man is void of God's grace and may justly be deprived of the power conferred by it.

As regards his attitude toward the fine arts, Wyclif was no iconoclast: in his " Trialogus " an approved speaker points out that Christ did not condemn signs in themselves, but only abuse of them; the brazen serpent, the crucified Lord himself, were both signs. Nevertheless, in Wyclif's nature the moral element was developed to the sacrifice of the ideal: his intense seriousness, his fear lest symbols should become to the simple occasions of idolatry, made him suspicious of the use of the arts in the service of the sanctuary, while his deep sympathy with the poor made him intolerant of the diversion of wealth that would relieve their necessities to the production of works of art. He seems to have felt that though statues, "gay windows, and paintings " were not wrong, they were at least inexpedient, and might have evil effects. " They worship false gods who seek blind stocks or images and offer to them more than to poor, bedrid men. Rich men clothe dead stocks and stones with precious clothes, with gold and silver and pearls and gayness to the world, and suffer poor men go sore a-cold and at much mischief." His dislike of the elaborate ritual of the Middle Ages — a gorgeous form closely allied in its nature to the fine arts — was determined by his belief in the potency of preaching, which seemed to him to be interfered with by the time spent in ceremonies; while the pains that had to be taken to avoid mistakes in these intricate "rites and rules of sinful men" made them as intolerable as the requirements of the Jewish law, — the freedom of the gospel was quite done away by such "novelry." As for church music, "descant and counter note, organ and small breaking — vain japes — stir vain men to dancing more than to mourning. Where there are forty or fifty in a choir, three or four proud lorels sing so that none can hear the sentence, and all others shall be dumb and look on them like fools."

It is well known that up to the time of the papal schism, in 1378, Wyclif's heresies concerned no doctrinal point, but only such questions as the relation of church and state, the government and worship of the church, and the morals and manners of the clergy. He had become so formidable, however, by his earnestness and ability, the indisputable strength of his moral position, and the ever increasing number of his followers, that the great prelates, monks, and friars whose worldliness he assailed began to feel that something must be done to suppress him, and he was summoned by the bishop of London to answer for his errors before a synod at St. Paul's in the winter of 1377. But the influence of the University of Oxford, where he had troops of friends; the favor of the government, which he served so well during the controversy with the papacy; the enthusiasm of the people, who regarded him as their champion; and the powerful protection of John, duke of Lancaster, eldest surviving son of Edward III, neutralized the utmost efforts of his enemies; it was impossible to secure his conviction, and the synod broke up in confusion. Foiled at home, his embittered foes appealed to Pope Gregory XI, who, in May of the same year, fulminated five bulls against the reformer. It is to be noted that the propositions condemned in these were practical consequences of the doctrine of dominion: they concerned the power of prelates, and points of government and discipline, — the constitution of the church, and not her doctrinal decisions. Thus fortified, Wyclif's opponents attempted again to bring

him to judgment : he was cited to appear before the bishop of
London and the archbishop of Canterbury at Lambeth, in 1378,
— but nothing of significance was done by them. In the summer
of that year occurred an event of rare magnitude in European
history, an immediate effect of which was Wyclif's complete
spiritual enfranchisement. Upon the death of Gregory XI
the cardinals elected as his successor Prignano, a Neapolitan,
who assumed the title of Urban VI. More than seventy years
had elapsed since an Italian had worn the tiara. Urban fixed
his residence at Rome, and began at once, and with some
acerbity of temper, considerable disciplinary reforms. Dissat-
isfied with his proceedings, the proud and luxurious French
cardinals, who were in a large majority in the conclave, pre-
tending that their choice had been made under compulsion,
and was therefore invalid, proceeded to elect one of their own
number in Urban's stead. He took the title of Clement VII,
and established his court at Avignon. Thus originated the
memorable Schism of the West, which shook the very foundations of papal power. Rival lines of pontiffs divided the
suffrages of Europe ; they made desperate efforts to crush
each other, — it was a shameful but instructive spectacle.
" God hath cloven the head of Antichrist," exclaimed Wyclif,
exultantly ; it seemed to him a God-given opportunity for the
English to throw off the papal dominion altogether. Now
began the last and busiest period of his life, in which he translated the New Testament, questioned and ere long boldly
controverted the received opinion concerning the eucharist,
and appealed to the intelligence of the people in tract after
tract, couched in vigorous English. It was inevitable that a
strenuous thinker who, as we have seen, regarded with cold
dislike the details of the worship of his day, should sooner or
later penetrate to the central point of that worship — the doctrine of the eucharist — and bring it into question ; that a clear
thinker should revolt from that confusion of thought which

supposed a conversion of one substance into another, the phenomena meanwhile remaining unchanged; that a zealous reformer should at last fall foul of a doctrine that seemed to be the innermost intrenchment of the worst evils that afflicted the church. Wyclif utterly rejected the dogma of transubstantiation as unscriptural and idolatrous: Christ, the apostles, and the saints of the primitive church all taught, he maintained, that "the sacred host, white and round," is at the same time true bread and the Lord's body.

This daring definition brought on another crisis; many of his followers, fearful of the innovation and its possible consequences, fell away from him; and a council was held in the spring of the year 1382 at which this and other statements in his works were condemned. Personally, however, Wyclif suffered no harm; he withdrew to his quiet rectory in the pleasant village of Lutterworth, and after two years of faithful work there, died in peace at the close of the year 1384. And now, as his grand figure fades into that distant past from which we have summoned it, it were best, perhaps, that some recollection of his firm hold upon spiritual realities should henceforth be associated with his name; that we should pay his memory the honor due to it for his undaunted claim for man to an immediate, personal relation with the eternal Origin of things. Few have pierced with as keen a vision through the outward shows of things to the realities that underlie them, — few have been as thoroughly convinced of the vanity of all forms that are not vitalized by spirit. "Baptism by water is nothing without baptism by fire — that is, the Holy Ghost," — he said. "Crown [tonsure] and cloth make no priest, nor the emperor's bishop with his words, but power that Christ giveth." "Not babbling of the lips but a holy life is prayer." And this noble sentence lingers like music in the memory: "God the Trinity is with each creature by might, wisdom, and goodness to keep it, for else it should turn to nought; but God is with good men of virtuous life by grace, and dwelleth in their souls as his own temple."

To the series of moralists and reformers belongs the poet John Gower; he is to be classed with Langland and Wyclif rather than, as he customarily is, with Chaucer. It must not, however, be inferred that he was affiliated to the "new sect of lollardy": he is emphatic in his denunciations of it; he adjures his reader:

> "Beware that thou be not oppressed
> With Antichristes lollardie: . . .
> — this newe tapinage
> Of lollardie goeth about
> To sette Christes faith in doubt —
> Such newe lore I rede eschewe."

He thus affords interesting and valuable evidence that the reformatory impulse of the hour was deep and general, — too wide to be confined within sectarian lines.

Gower was several years older than Chaucer, and he outlived him by some years. His "Vox Clamantis," in Latin verse, was occasioned by the insurrection of 1381: it is a searching analysis of the social and moral evils to which he referred the discontent of the peasantry, and the outbreak of revolution. The condition of England seemed to him deplorable, — "the end of the world is fallen upon us." At the head of the government was an ignorant and careless boy. A shocking schism in the papacy was bringing manifold woe upon the church: "we fall between two stools." The governors of the church were corrupt; they committed every deadly sin; the parish priests and roving friars followed their example, — they were greedy and drunken, lustful, hypocritical. Soldiers were extortionate and licentious, merchants dishonest, lawyers crafty and unjust, laborers discontented, and voracious as a pack of wild beasts. In the midst of such corruption what was to be done? Gower's reply is like Langland's, —

let every man take care of himself, have faith in God, who is over all, do his duty to his fellows, and use the world well, remembering that its pleasures and possessions pass away.

This anxious interest in the social problem contrasts strikingly with the unconcern of Chaucer, who ignores it so airily that from his works one would never guess that one of the most serious convulsions in English history had happened in his time.

Gower wrote, in French, another moral essay in verse, the "Speculum Meditantis." This does not appear to have been a successful effort; no copy of it is known to exist; but his last and greatest work, the "Confessio Amantis," was extremely popular in his own day and for ages after. It is written in English, in smooth, octosyllabic couplets. It consists of a really interesting prologue, and eight books, one for each of the deadly sins, and one a summary of the philosophic and moral, scientific and liberal learning of the poet's own age. The different books consist of groups of tales that illustrate the deadly sins; they are borrowed from the Bible, from Ovid, Cassiodorus, and Isidore, from the "Tale of Troy," of Alexander the Great, and of Lancelot du Lac, and from the popular collection known as the "Gesta Romanorum," and the "Speculum Regum" of Godfrey of Viterbo. Gower was a learned, not to say a bookish man, according to the fashion of his time. "I read as the cronique saith," — "In a cronique this I read" — "This find I written in poesy" — are formulas of frequent occurrence in his work. He strings his stories together upon the tenuous thread of a supposed confession made by a young lover, whose father confessor examines him in the seven sins, and points his precepts with appropriate tales. Some of these are tedious enough, and one cannot but echo the unhappy young penitent's unguarded admission :

> "The tales sounen in min ere,
> But yet min herte is elleswhere."

But what makes Gower truly great, and worthy of lasting remembrance, is his moral view of the universe. To him in truth preëminently belongs the title "moral" — bestowed upon him, half mischievously perhaps, by Chaucer. Two great ideas were the fountains of his inspiration : the thought of a mysterious correspondence between the physical and moral spheres, between nature and spirit, and that of human freedom, of a power in man to rise above the force of circumstance, and to put the stars under his feet. Gower believed that the Black Death was incurred by man as a punishment for his sin.

> "The sun and moon eclipsen both
> And ben with mannes sinne wroth ;
> The purest air for sin aloft
> Hath ben and is corrupt full oft."

The ground of this belief lay in a supposed interdependence between the world and man the microcosm. The four elements of the external world had their counterparts in the four humors of man's body, and between his soul and these there was mysterious union. But between soul and body strife has arisen, — and the result is sin :

> "For sin of his condition
> Is mother of division."

Disturbances in the realm of nature are the portentous signs and punishment of this moral discord.

> "The man, as telleth the clergie,
> Is as a world in his partie,
> And when this little world misturneth
> The grete world all overturneth ;
> The land, the sea, the firmament,
> They axen alle jugement
> Against the man."

The other thought, which he wearies not in reiterating, is that man, if he is true to himself, is not the sport of chance. Duty, not Fortune, determines his success and happiness. The

world is out of joint, and why? Some say, Because of Fortune, or, Because of the aspect of the stars. Then the poet
delivers his message :

> — " The man is overall
> His owne cause of weal and woe :
> That we fortune clepe so
> Out of the man himself it groweth."

An invigorating truth, banishing a host of grisly superstitions
whose presence benumbs the soul ! "All earthly things which
God began," he says, in reassuring tones, " were only made to
serve man." The planets do indeed control mundane affairs,
diseases, tempests, wars, — but good and wise men need not
fear the stars — (and then come the immortal lines) :

> " For one man, if him well befalle,
> Is more worth than ben they alle
> Towardes Him that weldeth all."

A flash of insight like that penetrates the profoundest
depths of the mysteries of creation and redemption and makes
them luminous ; a cheery call like that out of the ages gives
fresh meaning to life, inspires with new courage, and lightens
the oppressive weight that natural science with its mechanical
processes would lay upon the soul. With one sweep of her
pinion the heavenly muse of poetry exalts little man to the
sublime station that is rightfully his ; from that altitude the
world, weary, heavy, and unintelligible before, becomes trans-
parent and intelligible. Thus, in the evening of the fourteenth
century, did John Gower transcend the superstitions of his
time ; and thus may we in this latter day shake off with him
the nightmare of fatalism, and transcend the no less enfeebling
superstitions of a school of scientific thought that would arro-
gate to sensuous experience all reality, and that despises and
denies the ideal. As long as science lasts, as long as the world
endures, poetry will endure to give the spirit its due, to correct

the one-sided and therefore faulty and dangerous estimates of a science blind to the moral and ideal, and to resist the materializing tendency of our every-day life.

It is worth noting upon how much higher a moral level than Chaucer's Gower stood. Chaucer never worked free of the eery influence of the constellations; how numerous his references to judicial astrology are every one familiar with his works knows well. "In the stars," he says, "clearer than is glass, is written the death of every man, without a doubt. Certainly our appetites here, be it of war or peace or hate or love, are all ruled by Destiny. Fortune can turn her wheel and out of joy bring men to sorrow." With him a favorite maxim is, "Make virtue of necessity."

A memorable characteristic of Gower's (reminding us how far we have travelled from the era of the Crusades) is his recognition of the rights even of infidels. He believes that Christian men run counter to their Lord's commands when they shed the blood of heathen folk, for these too have souls to save. His missionary zeal recalls the evangelical labors of his Spanish contemporary, Vincent Ferrer, among the Mohammedans of Granada.

> " And for to sleen the hethen alle,
> I not what good there mighte falle
> So mochel blood though there be shad.
> This finde I writen, how Crist bad
> That no man other shoulde slee . . .
> To sleen and fighten they us bidde
> Hem whom they shuld, as the boke saith,
> Converten unto Cristes feith . . .
> A Sarazin if I slee shall
> I slee the soule forth withall, —
> And that was never Cristes lore."

Passages of natural description, sometimes quite pleasing, generally conventional, are scattered through the "Confessio

Amantis." The woful lover seeks the solitude of the woods and there gives way to his feelings :

> " — In the moneth of May,
> Whan every brid hath chose his make
> And thenketh his merthes for to make
> Of love that he hath acheved, . .
> Unto the wood I gan to fare,
> Nought for to singe with the briddes,
> For whan I was the wood amiddes
> I fonde a swete grene pleine,
> And there I gan my wo compleigne."

In another place there are a few pretty lines about the sun

> — " which is the worldes eye,
> Through whom the lusty compaignie
> Of foules by the morwe singe, —
> The freshe floures sprede and springe, —
> The highe tre the ground beshadeth,
> And every mannes herte gladdeth."

Hopelessly conventional, pedantic, and arid are Gower's references to the arts. Amid the glories of mediaeval architecture and sculpture, for which he seems to have had no eye, he nods over names gathered from his books :

> " Zeuzis found first the portreture,
> And Prometheus the sculpture ;
> After what forme that hem thought
> The resemblaunce anon they wrought."

and then (O discriminative Gower !), —

> " Berconius of cokerie
> First made the delicacie."

And yet to this poor, prosy old poet was granted the supreme vision of that age : "One man, if he behave well, is worth more than planets and stars to Him who wields them all."

When Gower wrote the " Confessio Amantis," sometime about the year 1386, he was living as a " clerk " and lay brother with the monks of St. Mary Overies, Southwark. In

1397, when he was seventy years of age, he married. He had need of a nurse, for in 1400 (the year of Chaucer's death, and probably of Langland's also) he became blind. He died in 1408, leaving his widow well provided for, and dividing the residue of his property among the churches of Southwark, the leper-houses, and a hospital for the blind and infirm.

It is instructive to observe how, simultaneously with this re-forming movement that we have been studying, English Gothic architecture underwent a change. The straight lines and right angles of the Rectilinear or Perpendicular style began to replace and repress the graceful and luxuriant but often weak and even wanton curves of the Decorated style, — a change that symbolizes delicately and beautifully the passage of the sentimental into the moral epoch. The mullions of cathedral windows began to strike right through the tangle of flowing tracery to the mouldings of the window-heads ; transoms intersected mul-lions ; the flat surfaces of walls, buttresses, and towers were ribbed with vertical and horizontal mouldings, and thus marked off into panels ; within, the heads of pier-arches were de-pressed, the triforium disappeared and a plane surface closely ruled up and down with parallel lines took its place. It was like an invasion of architecture by carpentry ; fancy was con-fined by measurement; the style was mechanical, inorganic, — yet something in its regularity, its plain, practical nature, suited the English genius; it was found to be peculiarly fitted for collegiate structures and manorial halls as well as for church-building ; and it became the favorite and characteristic variety of English Gothic. It first appeared in Abbot Litlington's work at Westminster, in the decades 1366–86, — but it was left to William of Wykeham, bishop of Winchester, to develop it with such strength and consistency that it has become in-dissolubly associated with his name. In 1386, Wykeham founded New College, Oxford ; the year following, Winchester College ; meanwhile he was remodelling his cathedral, the nave of which is the crowning example of Perpendicular style. The nave of Canterbury cathedral was also rebuilt in the new fashion at this time. The utmost elaboration of Perpendicular tracery is displayed in the great east window of York Minster, constructed in the years 1403–1408 ; the amazing intricacy of the work fatigues the sense. (A continental example of the triumph of parallelism over flamboyancy is afforded by the marvellous cathedral of Milan, which was being constructed at this very epoch.) During the Lancastrian Period — from 1399 to 1461 — the façades and profiles of several important cathedrals — York, Lincoln, Wells — were rendered more imposing by the completion of their triple towers. That was the palmy period, moreover, of parish-church building : then uprose, all over England, many of those picturesque churches with their square gray towers, that, often embowered in foliage, are such salient and attractive features in the landscape.

The adaptability of the Rectilinear style to scholastic purposes was exemplified at All Souls College, Oxford, — founded by Archbishop Chichely in 1437; at the royal foundation of Eton, in 1446; and (consummately) at Magdalen College, Oxford, founded by Bishop Waynflete in 1459.

Among the minor arts may be mentioned the sepulchral brasses that were multiplied in this period : large plates of burnished metal let into slabs in the floors of churches and mortuary chapels, and engraved with figures to represent those who rested below. The designs are highly characteristic of the time; they are quite conventional in feature and figure, and are almost Byzantine in their stiff symmetry, their straight and clear-cut outlines, and tendency to attenuated forms. The head-dresses are set, the faces flat and staring, and the lines that represent the folds of drapery are sharp and angular, sometimes almost parallel as they fall from the waist downward, to break in stiff folds about the feet with their pointed shoes.

Before we pass to the history and literature of the Lancastrian era, it will be well to review, briefly, the general condition of Europe at the close of the fourteenth and beginning of the fifteenth century. At no other period does the intimate connection that subsisted between the states of Catholic Christendom become more apparent, — the subtle sympathy that bound them together in such a manner that movements originating in any one were soon propagated among the others, so that they all underwent similar changes at about the same time; the working of a like spirit can be perceived at once in all.

In Spain, the ferocious dynastic struggle already alluded to reached its crisis in the year 1369, when Pedro the Cruel was slain by the hand of his half-brother, Henry of Trastamar, — a son of Leonora de Guzman. The new monarch mounted an uneasy throne; he and his descendants were involved in intermittent wars with England and Portugal, — which latter power meanwhile underwent a similar dynastic change. The Duke of Lancaster married Pedro's daughter, and advanced her claim to the crown of Castile. When the papal schism broke out, the Spanish states for a while stood neutral; but French interest brought them at last to recognize the Avignonese pope. England and Portugal, on the contrary, professed obedience to the Roman pontiff, Urban VI; and he granted an indulgence to any who should aid the Duke of Lancaster in his contest with the usurping king of Castile. Henry's son, John I, suffered a severe defeat at the hands of the Portuguese in 1385, which rendered his position so difficult that he had to propose a compromise by which the rival claims to the crown were reconciled; he married his young son, Henry, to the Duke's daughter. His death soon after plunged Spain into years of civil strife; during the minority of the boy-king the great nobles and prelates contended for the regency: among the latter one at least, the archbishop of Santiago, held to the Roman pope. It may be that this fact contains the secret of the political confusion of those years. Peace was attained only when the young king assumed full power, which he enhanced by a bold stroke of statecraft. During those tumultuous times flourished one who was to be their chronicler — Pedro Lopez de Ayala, courtier, chancellor, soldier, and chief, if not the only distinguished man of letters of his nation in that age. He translated into Spanish the works of Livy and Boethius, the "Morals" of Pope Gregory I, and Boccaccio's "Falls of Princes," and wrote a moralizing poem, "El Rimado de Palacio," in which he described, quite in Gower's vein, but with occasional touches of the humor that Gower lacked, the duties of rulers, the corruption of the age, and the need of reform. He died in 1407 — a year before the English poet.

The schism in the papacy was the supreme concern of the period, and it is highly probable that it may serve, to a degree not generally realized, as a clue to the labyrinth of contemporary politics. It should not be forgotten that Urban VI came to the chair as a reforming pope. Catherine of Siena, the spiritual heroine, the most noted and influential woman of her day, engaged herself heart and soul in his cause. But he was sadly unequal to his opportunity ; the severity with which he began his reforms was akin to mania ; false to his trust, he soon abandoned himself to shameful nepotism ; became embroiled with the queen of Naples, and made the conquest of her kingdom the end and aim of his pontificate. Foiled in spite of desperate efforts, he had to flee to Genoa ; there he caused five cardinals whom he suspected of conspiracy against him to be strangled. It was whispered then, and has since been generally believed that his mind was unbalanced. His successor, Boniface IX, was a remarkably able man. At his accession, anathemas were cordially exchanged with his rival of Avignon, from whose obedience he succeeded erelong in detaching the kingdom of Naples. His interference precipitated a revolution in German politics, and indications are not wanting that he was an agent in the dynastic change in England. The peace that Richard II made with France in 1396 drew him into relations, at least of negotiation, with the Avignonese pope Benedict XIII.   This was the time when attempts were made by several governments, greatly to the annoyance of both popes, to induce them to resign.   Boniface had already had occasion to remonstrate with Richard in regard to his ecclesiastical policy.   After the conclusion of the unpopular peace above mentioned, it will be remembered that Richard apprehended certain of his opponents and banished others.   Among the latter was Thomas Arundel, archbishop of Canterbury, whose powerful influence was largely instrumental in raising Henry of Lancaster to the throne of England in Richard's stead.   Immediately after this revolution in the government Arundel was restored to his see by Boniface IX.   Hostilities were renewed between England and France; Henry relied upon the church for support ; and Boniface, as if emboldened by the belief that he had a firmer hold upon the nation than before, revoked certain concessions that he had formerly granted.

The troubled reign of Wenzel, king of Bohemia, and until his deposition in 1400, king of the Romans and emperor-elect, almost exactly coincided in duration with the papal schism. Wenzel was rude even to brutality, and coarse in his pleasures — but perhaps his character was not as black as it has been painted by clerical odium.   He was unable to cope with the turbulence of the great nobles, and though he overawed them once by a stroke of policy similar to that practised at the same period in England and Spain, his partial and temporary success was equivalent to failure, and left him hated and suspected, and in worse condition than before.   But when he joined the king of France in urging the rival popes to abdicate, the measure of his iniquity was full; Boniface retorted by commanding the electors to choose another emperor.   The result was fresh confusion in that age of countless schisms ; there was a division in the college : the electors of the Rhine were in the papal interest, and chose Rupert of the Palatinate ; those of the north and east preferred Frederick of Saxony ; so for a moment there were three shadowy emperors in the field, — but the number was almost instantly reduced by the assassination of Frederick. Wenzel died in 1419 — not without suspicion of foul play.

In the far north-east of Europe profound political changes took place. After the extinction of the Piast dynasty, Jagello, duke of Lithuania, was called to the throne of Poland, and devoted his energies through a long reign to the depression of the power of the Teutonic knights. At Tannenberg, in the year 1410, the order suffered a defeat from which it never recovered ; and thus the glory of another great institution of the Middle Ages passed away.

Meantime, confusion verging upon anarchy reigned in the dominions of the House of Austria. The young duke, Albert IV, died in 1404, entrusting to his cousins, William and Leopold, the guardianship of his son, Albert V, then a mere infant. William's death, in 1406, was the signal for civil strife ; Leopold was involved in disputes with his younger brother, the intractable Ernest, at the head of a powerful faction. The spirit of feudalism broke out once more ; the nobles were all in arms ; for five years the land was desolated with civil war ; commerce and agriculture declined ; robbers infested the highways, — it was the darkest hour in the history of the duchy. It was also a school of hard political experience for the young Albert, who assumed control of the government upon Leopold's death, in 1411. He proved to be a sagacious ruler, restored peace and prosperity to his country, and laid the foundations of the future grandeur of his house.

While the condition of Austria was beginning to improve, that of France was rapidly approaching the lowest degree of

humiliation that her annals record.   Her king, Charles VI,
was demented ; his queen was an evil woman, and exerted a
pernicious influence upon state affairs ; the conduct of government was a prize that was contended for by raging factions
under the lead of the rival dukes of Burgundy and Orleans ;
and the people were wretched.   If anything beside self-interest
guided the policy of Louis of Orleans it was his devotion to the
cause of Pope Benedict XIII : with his help Benedict escaped
from his palace at Avignon, where he had been imprisoned for
years by the royal troops, in the spring of 1403, and shortly
after the kingdom returned to his obedience.   The fortunes
of both pope and duke rose and fell together ; in the fall of
1407 Louis was foully murdered, and Benedict erelong had to
flee into Spain.   For the next seven years the power of the
duke of Burgundy was, upon the whole, in the ascendant.
He favored a conciliar settlement of the papal controversy ;
the city of Pisa, lately conquered by Florence, was offered by
that republic as an eligible site for the proposed synod ; there,
in the year 1409, the fathers met, and, dominated by the
genius of Jean Gerson, declared the rival pontiffs heretics,
schismatics, and perjurers, deposed them both, and elected in
their stead an aged Greek cardinal, who took the title of
Alexander V.   The Roman and Spanish popes, however,
refused to accept the character given them by the fathers at
Pisa ; and for years the church and the world were scandalized
by the intrigues and mutual anathemas of three popes.   Meanwhile, in France, the Orleanist party was reorganized under
the headship of the Count d'Armagnac, by whose name it was
subsequently known ; civil war broke out, and the Armagnacs,
crushed by the Burgundians, appealed for aid in their despair
to Henry IV of England.   The year following he died, and his
son, Henry V, thinking that France in her distracted state was
ripe for subjugation, revived the obsolete claims of Edward III,
and landed with an army at the mouth of the Seine in the

summer of 1415. The Armagnacs now made amends for their disloyalty, and almost entirely by themselves withstood the invader. The duke of Burgundy stood sullenly aloof, and saw his compatriots worsted at Agincourt ; but their ultimate success was assured, for they had identified their cause with the nation's. The siege and capture of Rouen by the English monarch in the winter of 1419, and his imminent advance upon Paris, brought about a temporary cessation of party strife ; but the barbarous murder of the duke of Burgundy at the very moment when reconciliation seemed accomplished plunged his country into an abyss of humiliation ; for his son, the young Duke Philip, opened his arms to the English, and with the coöperation of the queen, and amid the plaudits of the people of Paris, concluded with Henry V in the spring of 1420 the amazing treaty of Troyes, by which the succession to the throne of France was signed away to the English king, to the exclusion of the dauphin. It was many years before the French monarchy, consecrated anew by the vision, heroic action, and piteous death of the Maid of Orleans, resolved the jarring notes of party hatred into harmony, and led France slowly up to power and prosperity again.

At the commencement of the struggle between the Burgundians and the Armagnacs, in the year 1410, died Jean Froissart, the singer and chronicler of a brighter day ; and a few years later another representative of the French literature of the fourteenth century passed away — Eustache Deschamps, author of innumerable ballads and rondeaus. Their younger contemporaries, Christine de Pisan and Alain Chartier, more deeply impressed by the accumulating evils of the time, moralized in prose and verse. Productions characteristic of the period were prose works on morals and manners, which laid down rules of conduct and illustrated the effects of good and bad behavior. But perhaps the most significant product of the age was the " Morality," or moral-play, which made the Devil, the Vice, and the Deadly Sins enact their parts upon the stage, and engaged them in allegorical combat with the Virtues. This development in the drama becomes full of meaning when placed in its proper setting, in the period out of which it sprang.

In spite of this manifest vitality of French literature, it must be admitted that the literary supremacy of the fourteenth century belonged to Italy and England in turn. The names of the great English authors of the last half of that century are the only ones that can be mentioned with those of the great Italians of the first half without a painful sense of incongruity.

It was during the short reign of Henry V that the schism in the papacy was practically healed. The conscience of Europe was thoroughly roused by the enormity of three popes excommunicating and vilifying each other, and was determined to put a stop to it. An ecumenical council — one of the most magnificent assemblies that ever met — was convened at Constance in the year 1414; and then began one of the most impressive exhibitions of moral energy in the history of civilization, — a determined effort to reform abuses, and to bring order out of chaos, the force of which was not spent for more than a generation. The deliberations of the council were guided by the eminent French doctors, Gerson and D'Ailly. Its first important regulation was that the voting should be by nations. It asserted as a fundamental principle that the authority of councils is superior to that of popes. (Nicholas of Clémanges, a learned Frenchman, and a friend of D'Ailly, maintained in a pamphlet published about this time that the authority of the Bible is over all.) The three contending popes were unceremoniously set aside; two of them eventually submitted, but nothing could bend or break the will of the Spaniard, Benedict XIII, — in whose favor a temporary diversion was made by the Armagnacs, then in power, — and he remained in schism until his death.

Meanwhile, the fathers in council proceeded to their task of extirpating heresy, which, they devoutly believed, was accountable for many of the ills that plagued the church. In the severity, the injustice, of their procedure, they were actuated, doubtless, by an uneasy sense that they had gone far along the road of what seemed to many startling innovations in ecclesiastical polity, and that it behoved them to vindicate their unimpeachable orthodoxy. So they made examples of two conspicuous Bohemian reformers, John Huss and Jerome of Prague, who had trodden in Wyclif's footsteps. The writings of Wyclif had long been well known in the University of Prague, and his opinions had been sown broadcast throughout Bohemia. In his preaching Huss had inveighed against the wealth, luxury, and immorality of the clergy, and the abuse of indulgences, — but he had gone no further; at his examination it was attempted to entangle him in errors concerning the sacrament of the altar, but touching that point no fault could be found in him. Nevertheless he was burnt at the stake.

Contrary to the desire of the German delegates, who urged that the promised reform of the church "in head and members" should next be undertaken, the council hastened the election of a new pope, and the choice of the cardinals fell upon a member of the proud Roman family of Colonna, who received the homage of the assembled fathers as Pope Martin V. Reform was bruited no more; and after making arrangements for a future council, that of Constance was dismissed by the new pontiff with fair words, in the year 1417. One little event in the session of that last year — a contest for precedence between the ambassadors of France and England — is of interest to us: the Englishman asserted his right to precede as the representative of a nation that had been converted to Christianity by Joseph of Arimathea, years before there were any converts in Gaul.

Benedict XIII — still maintaining that in him alone was the

true church — died in the year 1424, and the little knot of cardinals whom he had created, and who remained faithful to him to the last, chose as his successor a canon of Barcelona, who called himself Clement VIII. For a time he was supported, on political grounds, by the king of Aragon; but in 1428 he submitted to Martin V — and the schism of half a century was healed.

Terrible religious wars had broken out in Bohemia as a result of the mistaken attitude of the council of Constance towards the reforms of Huss. His followers now went further than he, and demanded that in the communion the cup should be administered to the laity. The revolt was quite beyond the slowly reviving papal power to suppress, and the reluctant pope had to bow to the decree of Constance, and summon a council. It assembled at Basel, in 1431. The above-mentioned controversy over precedence was renewed, this time with the Castilian ambassador; arguments for and against the mission of Joseph of Arimathea were brought forward on both sides, the English adducing "many ancient testimonies" — William of Malmesbury's, doubtless, among the number.

The council of Basel met partly to continue, partly to undo, whether for good or evil, the work of its predecessor. It reaffirmed the supremacy of councils in ecclesiastical matters, and succeeded for a season in humiliating the new pope, Eugenius IV. Its departure from the practice of voting by nations, however, lost it the adhesion of the English clergy, who in convocation determined to obey the pope. The council admitted a deputation from Bohemia, and for the sake of peace acceded to its demands. It also promulgated certain reformatory decrees, which were recognized, for a time at least, in France and Germany. But its influence began steadily to wane from the time when, in its keen conflict with Eugenius IV, who had convened a rival synod, it declared him deposed, and chose another pope. Europe was weary of schisms. The council, weakened by defections to the party of Eugenius, removed, in 1443, to Lausanne; it lingered on, an ever-diminishing remnant, until 1449, when it was glad to accept overtures of peace made by his successor, Nicholas V. The conciliar epoch was over, and the jubilee of 1450 celebrated the completion of the papal restoration.

An earnest, almost pathetic reversion to the antique type of ascetic piety accompanied and adorned this restitution of the old ecclesiastical order. It was an attempt, foredoomed to speedy failure, to retrieve the mediaeval ideal of life which had lately paled before the sunny ideal of the Renascence. It was inspired, without doubt, by a desire to countervail the errors of heretical piety. Within a few years after the papal schism there came into the world a number of pious souls that were destined to be powerful agents in the work of Catholic reformation in the fifteenth century. Bernardino of Siena and John of Capistrano, Franciscans, by their self-denying lives and fiery preaching recalled the primitive zeal of their order. Bernardino refused bishopric after bishopric, believing that by preaching from city to city throughout Italy he could save more souls. John of Capistrano preached at large in Italy, and went on missions into Germany and Austria. A French girl, Colette Boilet, began a reform in the sisterhood of St. Clara, which she carried through successfully in the teeth of angry and contemptuous opposition. She won the regard of Benedict XIII, who appointed her superior of her order. Her reformed rule, first adopted in Savoy, made its way into Burgundy, and at last into Spain and Flanders. Another pious woman, a Roman widow named Francesca, a mistress of the art of self-mortification, and endowed with the faculty of seeing visions, became the founder of a new order for her sex. In the year 1425 she formed a convent which grew so rapidly in numbers and reputation that in 1437 it was erected into an order, that of Collatines, by Eugenius IV. The most vivid lights of this ascetic revival were the sainted archbishops of Florence and Venice, Antonio, later known as Antoninus, and Lorenzo Giustiniani. The former was indeed a noble soul, self-denying in the extreme, but lenient to others, a friend of the poor and the sick, an earnest preacher. He was a Dominican, and before his elevation to the archbishopric was prior of the monastery of San Marco, — among whose inmates in his time was the beatified painter, Fra Angelico of Fiesole, whose frescoes exquisitely reveal the ideal of the devout spirits of his day. Lorenzo Giustiniani, a young Venetian nobleman, had a vision in his nineteenth year that diverted all his thoughts from the delights of a worldly life to the monastic ideal. He tested his constancy by lying all night on knotty sticks, and at last fled to an island monastery to avoid a match that his widowed mother proposed for him, — and never visited his home again until she lay dying. He practised the utmost austerities that one could endure and live. He bore the heats of summer without repining, hoping to escape the more intolerable heat of hell, — and in midwinter refused the comfort of a fire. Called from his convent to the bishopric of Venice, the greatest luxury he permitted himself in his new state was a bed of straw. From the first, his zeal in the performance of his new duties, his cogent preaching, his self-immolating spirit, made the breath of a fresh spiritual life felt throughout his populous diocese, and churches and religious institutions were multiplied. The last eminent exponent of this Catholic reformation was Francis of Paula, on the Calabrian coast. He was much younger than the men and women just noticed, having been born at the very close of the papal schism. At the age of fifteen years he began a hermit's life in a cavern by the sea. Gradually a little community gathered around him; in 1454 a church and monastery were erected; and erelong the brotherhood obtained the pope's approval as the order of Friars Minims. Francis visited Sicily, Naples, and Rome, and passed on urgent invitation into France, where he became spiritual adviser to three successive kings.

The English kings of the House of Lancaster were involved in the perplexities and miseries of the age of schisms; it was left for the rival House of York to participate in the general restoration of order throughout Europe by sovereign authority. Perhaps the most memorable circumstance connected with the history of the Lancastrian line is the decided increase of power that parliament then enjoyed. Freedom of debate was conceded to it, and its right to determine the privileges of its members was recognized. It guarded the public expenditure, and exercised control even over the royal household. These facts are to be viewed in their relation to the significant fact that the House of Lancaster held by parliamentary title purely; not to Henry IV but to the young Edmund Mortimer did the crown belong by hereditary right.

Henry's foreign policy was, naturally, a reversal of that of Richard II; at her father's demand, Richard's child-widow, Isabella, was sent back to France, — but without her dowry; and the treaty between the two kingdoms was ruptured. Henry did not live long enough to take advantage to the full of his neighbor's intestinal conflicts; for great part of his reign he was kept busy at home by warfare upon the Scotch and Welsh borders, and by the menacing attitude of the Earl of Northumberland, head of the great family of the Percys, chief representatives of the feudal nobility of that day, who, having been largely instrumental in raising Henry to the throne, conceived a grudge against him, and, fired with the ambition of a king-maker, conspired to dispossess him, and bestow the crown upon Mortimer. On three several occasions Northumberland rose in arms against his liege ; on the last of these, in the year 1408, he met his death, — but his ally, Owen Glendower, still held out in North Wales.

Scotland had her full share of the portentous crimes and

vicissitudes of those dark times. Her well-intentioned but weak king, Robert III, resigned the conduct of affairs to his ambitious brother, whom, in the year 1398, he created duke of Albany. David, heir-apparent to the crown, a worthless young man, was done to death by his uncle's orders in Falkland Castle, and Robert, fearful of the safety of his remaining son, James, sought a refuge for him in France — but on his way thither, in 1405, the young prince was intercepted by the English, and was lodged in the Tower of London. This last blow broke his father's heart.

By the year 1411, Henry found himself in condition to interfere cautiously in the strife of Burgundian and Armagnac, — but now his health began to fail: he was subject to attacks of epilepsy, and early in the spring of 1413 he died, leaving to his spirited son (with what success we know) the prosecution of his designs upon unhappy France.

Henry V was detained by an alarming demonstration on the part of the Lollards, and by a plot to overthrow his government and raise Mortimer to the throne, before he could make his descent upon the French coast, and emulate, even outdo the achievements of his illustrious ancestor, Edward III. The glories of his brief reign were too transient to initiate a new literary epoch, to do more than cast a passing gleam athwart the sombre history of his house; his dazzling successes left his infant son only a heritage of disaster. The story of Henry VI's long reign is, outwardly, that of the slow decay of English power in France; inwardly, of misgovernment verging upon anarchy, degenerating at last into civil war. For a few years all went well: Humphrey, duke of Gloucester, brother of the late king, was appointed by parliament protector of the realm, and his elder brother John, duke of Bedford, regent in France. A politic act of the new government was the liberation of the Scottish king, James I, after his long detention of more than eighteen years; he pledged himself to preserve peace with

England, and the treaty was cemented by his marriage with the Lady Joan Beaufort, — a cousin of Henry V. Thus the French lost a useful ally. James returned to his native land in the spring of 1424 to begin administrative and legal reforms that promised to open a new era of order and prosperity in his distracted kingdom — but his enlightened designs were cut short by his barbarous assassination in the year 1437.

For the first five years of Bedford's able regency the prestige of the English arms continued unabated : it was even enhanced by the battle of Verneuil in 1427 — a victory that recalled the palmy days of Henry V. But in the same year the young French patriot Dunois achieved his first conspicuous success at Montargis — the first of a series of solid though not brilliant successes that resulted after many years in the utter discomfiture of the English and their expulsion from reconstituted France. In 1428, Bedford began his ill-fated siege of Orleans; the city was defended by Dunois and succoured by Joan of Arc : her vision and his steadfastness regenerated the nation. From that time the tide of English power began steadily to ebb, and the decline was rather accelerated than stayed by the Maid's pitiable martyrdom at Rouen. Bedford's death in 1435 broke the last tie that bound the duke of Burgundy to the English cause, and he made his peace with the French king, who shortly after recovered his capital of Paris.

Meantime, at home, there was angry contention between Humphrey of Gloucester and his uncle, the cardinal-bishop of Winchester, — one standing for a continuance of the war, the other for peace. The logic of events, and such influence as the meek young king was able to exert, favored the latter policy, and in 1444 a truce was agreed upon with France, which was signalized the next year by Henry's marriage with Margaret, daughter of René of Anjou. By a secret article in the treaty the English possessions in Maine and Anjou were restored to the new queen's family.

In this interval of quiet, Charles VII carried out an extremely important measure, — the formation of a standing army; and in 1449 he seized the first opportunity that offered to resume the war.   He sent Dunois into Normandy, and town after town submitted to him; in 1450, Cherbourg, the last possession of the English in that quarter, was wrested from them.

These disheartening reverses, and the waste of taxation in prosecuting so unfortunate a war, added to the unpopularity of Queen Margaret, the suspicion engendered by the cession of Maine, and the penury and monstrous indebtedness of the crown, caused great commotion in England; a popular insurrection broke out that resembled that of 1381.   The general discontent was not allayed when in 1451 Dunois overran Guienne.   The year following, Richard, duke of York, heir to the royal claim of the house of Mortimer, as if representing the national will, demanded a reform in the government.   A temporary diversion was made in favor of the English in Guienne, — but in 1453 the troops of Charles VII closed round them again; they were driven from Bordeaux and Bayonne, and Calais with its environs remained the last shred of their French possessions.

These disasters deranged King Henry's feeble intellect, and parliament appointed the duke of York protector of the realm. But about Christmas-tide, 1454, Henry enjoyed a restoration of reason, and Richard was deprived of his authority.   He forthwith raised an army, and met and defeated the royal forces at St. Alban's in May, 1455, taking the king himself captive.   This was the first of a long series of sanguinary battles in which victory almost invariably inclined to the side of the Yorkists, and in which the genius of feudalism was extinguished.

Again his troubles disordered Henry's understanding, and again the duke of York was made protector.   In 1456 the king recovered, and a hollow reconciliation of the contending parties was effected; for a few years an ominous quiet was preserved. But in 1459 the inevitable conflict between a waning and a rising cause broke out afresh : the Yorkists were victorious at Bloreheath, and the next year at Northampton ; and the duke's title to the crown was admitted by the Lords. The inflexible Margaret, however, gathered an army in the north and won a victory at Wakefield ; Richard fell in the battle, and his head, contemptuously circled with a paper crown, was stuck upon the walls of York. His son Edward, now duke, a good soldier, though but nineteen years of age, partly avenged his death at the battle of Mortimer's Cross, in the winter of 1461, and marching straightway to London mounted the throne, amid the rejoicings of the citizens, as King Edward IV. Immediately after, in conjunction with his cousin, the Earl of Warwick, he established his power by a fearful slaughter of the Lancastrians on the field of Towton.

The poetry of the Lancastrian period was affected by the evil fortunes of the House. It presents to our view the gradual decay of the literary enthusiasm inherited from the fourteenth century. It is afflicted with the garrulity and prolixity of age ; and a deadly blight steals over it with the increasing disorders of Henry VI's hopeless reign. The most attractive quality of the representative poets of the age is, perhaps, their reverent affection for the memory of Chaucer, but their lingering didacticism gives evidence that they derived more from Gower, — whose name they constantly coupled with Chaucer's. Among their most characteristic and readable verses are their confessions of a wasted youth ; the emotion of regret and penitence in these has a ring of sincerity that makes them start out from the mass of mediocre and imitative versification in which they are imbedded.

John Lydgate, monk and scholar, illustrates well the backward look, the longing to have walked and talked with Chaucer, that was his finest inspiration, in the prologue to his volumi-

nous " Story of Thebes." He offers it to us as the last of the
Canterbury tales. He pictures himself as riding in his black
cope on a slender palfrey with a rusty bridle, to visit the shrine
of St. Thomas, and perform his vows after a recovery from
sickness. It befell that he entered the town soon after Chaucer
and his pilgrims had arrived there, and that he sought entertainment at the very inn where they were. The Host
demanded his name, and invited him to join his party; the
following morning, when they were a bow-shot out of town,
he called on Lydgate not to preach, but to tell a tale, "of
effect of joy " :

> " And as I coude, with a pale chere,
>   My tale I gan anone, as ye shal here."

It is the story of Œdipus, and of the unbrotherly struggle of
" Ethiocles and Polimite." It was a parable for its author's
own times ; despite the Host's precaution, Lydgate concealed
under the sweetness of rhyme a homiletic motive ; at the conclusion of the tale he expresses his conviction that Lucifer is
the originator of war.

That mixture of Christian and classic, that vision of antiquity
through the medium of chivalry, which was so characteristic
of the Renascence, is exhibited in this and other of Lydgate's works. The compromise between the royal brothers
by which they agree to reign in alternate years is confirmed
by " othe of Sacrament." Tydeus is the best knight of the
world ; at his marriage all the Barons are present. When they
prepare for war, the worthy Bishop Amphiorax prophesies a
terrible slaughter of princes. Lydgate's " Testament " opens
with praise of the name of Jesus, — who brought many souls
out of hell, in spite of Cerberus ; he is our Samson, our
Orpheus.

The piece last mentioned continues with a pretty but conventional description of spring, to which childhood is compared,

and thus a transition is effected to the main business of the poem — a piteous disburdening of a sensitive conscience by a confession of youthful shortcoming for which Jesus' absolution is implored. As a boy the poet was headstrong and loath to learn ; late at school, chattering and trifling, he would forge a lie to cover up a fault. He stole apples ; no hedge or wall restrained him ; he was readier to pluck grapes off other men's vines than to say matins. He was a wanton ape, scoffing and scorning ; he misused his five senses, — and would sooner count cherry-stones than go to church or hear the sacring bell. He was loath to get up in the morning, to go to bed at night. He was the bell-wether of truants. After he had entered the monastic life, like Lot's wife he often looked back. He took little heed of Benedict's rule, wore a black habit and was a counterfeit, was disobedient, intemperate, the last at choir — until one day he saw a crucifix painted on a cloister-wall and beside it the single word VIDE. From the impression at that moment received he dated his conversion.

For Henry V, Lydgate composed a version of the tale of Troy — a popular subject, as we have seen, among readers who traced the history of their island up to a king of Trojan descent. For Humphrey, duke of Gloucester, he composed another long poem, "The Falls of Princes," based upon Boccaccio's work : a politico-moral subject appropriate to the age. In the writings of his French contemporary also, the didactic Alain Chartier, Lydgate found a congenial spirit.

Bred in an age of schisms, of extraordinary vicissitudes, it is no wonder that he was profoundly impressed by the mutability of the world, the instability of human affairs. "All stands in change like a midsummer rose" is the refrain of one of his poems ; and of another, "All worldly thinge turneth as a ball." Fortune and her wheel play a leading part in his drama of life ; universal history seems to him simply the record of her caprices : where are Pyrrhus, Alexander, and Seneca, he cries, where Rome and Carthage? — it is as Fortune would : she is the disposer. She is a great goddess, the empress of this world, — that is why it is so variable. Death casts down princes from her wheel : witness the fate of Absalom, Hector, Cæsar, Belshazzar, Henry V. A curious piece, of contraries all compact, gives one the impression of a mind confused, without a clue to the labyrinth of life, helpless before the riddle of the world, its oppositions, difficulties, and disappointments : "The more I go, the further behind I am ; the more I seek, the less can I find ; the longer I serve, the more out of mind : is this fortune, or is it infortune? A weary peace, and peace amid the war ; a weeping laughter, a merry glad weeping ; the more I run, the more way I lose ; is this fortune, or is it infortune? A troubled joy, a joyful heaviness ; a sobbing song, a cheerful distress ; trusty deceit, faithful deception ; now light, now heavy, now sorrow, now gladness : how escape these puzzling contrarieties? By faith in God ; Christ's passion shall reclaim us in spite of false fortune." Elsewhere he explains that there can be no "steadfast living" for man, made as he is of the four elements, of four humors that alter with the seasons ; in the midst of this perpetual change it is a relief to lift one's eyes to the constant heavens, to think of the Lord who is eternal, who sits so far above the seven stars in his most imperial palace.

Lydgate's didactic vein crops out with exceeding plainness in his "Dietary," or Rules for Preserving Health, — a compend of popular philosophy : "Rise from meat with an appetite . . . don't grumble at meals . . . beware of rear-suppers ! . . . don't drink between meals . . . too much salt meat is injurious to delicate stomachs . . . be moderate in diet, have compassion on the needy, and live at peace with all men." One of the best of his short poems is his "Counsel to an old man on marriage with a young wife," in which he answers the old man's arguments for such marriage. Another, "On the horned head-dresses of ladies," is a dissuasive from an extravagant fashion of the day. In pieces like these one can mark the natural and easy transition from a didactic to a satirical spirit and style,—exemplified in a fable of two cows, Chychevache and Bycorne, the first of which feeds on debonair wives and is lean, the last on patient husbands, and is fat; in the well-known ballad, 'London Lickpenny,' which gives us an entertaining glimpse into the streets of the capital in that far-off day ; and in an ironical rhyme in which the poet returns to the charge against his times : the world is stable—princes are righteous—knights true—priests perfect—" even as the crab goeth forward "; law is incorruptible—there 's no envy in cloisters—laborers are never idle—women have banished new-fangledness—the hungry are fed, the naked clothed—heretics have left their frowardness—and all 's "as straight as a ram's horn."

In the collection of Lydgate's minor poems may be found one, a love-poem, to the authorship of which he assuredly can lay no claim. It is known that many fugitive pieces of the fifteenth century were attributed to him ; and there is evidence that some anonymous songs and ballads of that time were written by women. The subject of the poem referred to is " A Maiden's Complaint " ; in it we read, without question, a woman's heart ; it is eloquent with passionate yet delicate feeling. "We played and gathered flowers in the mead together as children, he and I, — and love then gave me for my reward a knot in heart of remembrance that will never come undone. And yet I have set my heart where, in all likelihood, I shall never find favor, so great is the difference between his manhood and my simpleness. I shall love him best notwithstanding : would to God that he knew the truth, how often I sigh for his sake ! His countenance, his figure, his bearing are ever present in my sight ; in his absence I can never be happy, without his love I can never be at rest. He is and has been from my tender years my chosen knight, though he knows it not. Imprinted in my inward thought until I die, he shall never depart out of my heart, whose only solace is waking or sleeping to dream of him."

One of the finest ballads of the fifteenth century (though the first draught of it we possess is an inferior version of a later age) is that of "Chevy Chase," — an account of the bold Lord Percy's hunting-party upon the Cheviot Hills, in the midst of which he is encountered by the Douglas and his men; the rival champions fall in deadly combat, and a frightful slaughter ensues. It is impossible to fix the date of this event, so contradictory are the historical allusions in the. poem; it seems like a confused echo of several border battles. It presents to our minds a vivid picture of the lawlessness and bloodshed, the ferocity relieved with rare touches of magnanimity, that characterized those turbulent times. It is an epic in miniature.

In Lydgate's day Moralities, or Moral-plays, were introduced into England; three specimens of such plays, known to belong to the reign of Henry VI, are still extant.

For the canons of St. Paul's, London, Lydgate composed a version of the "Dance of Death," to be illustrated by designs upon the cloister wall. The grotesque subject was exceedingly popular at that epoch, in both verse and painting, throughout Christendom. For the abbot of St. Albans he wrote a metrical life of the patron saint of that ancient and celebrated monastery.

Lydgate was still living, at an advanced age, in the year 1446. About that time, Osbern of Bokenham, Norfolk, an Augustinian friar, wrote in unpolished verse a set of lives of famous female saints for some noble· ladies, his patronesses. Thomas Occleve, a close contemporary of Lydgate's, less of a poet than he but more of one than Osbern, seems like a shadow of the stronger master in his devotion to Chaucer, his retrospective, moralizing vein, his depressing sense of the uncertainty of things, his diffuse and prolix style. In a short poem, "La Male Régle" (Mis-Rule) he makes melancholy confession of youthful indiscretions, which have brought him to poverty and sickness. Youthful lusts led him astray; now he would return to obedience. Venus' family enticed him, wine and "thick wafers"; he was a tavern-haunter. He would go to bed full of liquor, and rise late: he was a mirror of riot. He paid the taverners and cooks at Westminster gate just what they asked, and so was taken for a "very gentleman"; thence home by water he would pay the boatmen well and be called "master," — oh treacherous flattery! Erelong his purse grew light, — excess exiled the coin. Then came sickness to restrain his indulgence, and he found himself in debt. The poem ends with an invocation to the god of health, and in significant proximity to it is another "Au Roy," piteously entreating a flood of royal largess to relieve his distress. Confession and petition are repeated in his long poem, "The Governail of Princes," dedicated to Henry V. This is a free rendering of a mediaeval Latin treatise; it is an "art of government," — another of those politico-moral subjects adapted to the time. In the lengthy introduction he prefixed to it, Occleve bemoans the mutations of the world, the inroads of heresy, the extravagance of fashion, — and the irregular payment of his annuity, by which he is sometimes reduced to great straits; he pays a touching tribute to Chaucer's memory, which he echoes in the body of the work. He lived long enough to direct his worship to the rising sun of York; in an address, doubtless to the Duke Richard, which must have been composed about the year 1449, he recommends himself to the Princess his wife and to Prince Edward, and prays the Trinity for a thousand years of happiness for them all.

In Scotland, the literary impulse exerted by John Barbour had effect early in the fifteenth century in a rhymed history,

"The Oryginale Cronykil of Scotland," written by Andrew of Wyntoun, prior of St. Serf's monastery, Loch Leven. It is in nine books, "in honor of the nine orders of angels," and was called "Original" because it began with the creation. It extends to the death of Robert III, in 1406.

Of Chaucer's immediate followers the Scottish king, James I, was the most poetical. None made the master's works the subject of more loving study, — none so thoroughly assimilated their spirit. His main poem, "The King's Quair" (or Book), is written in Chaucer's stanza, and abounds in reminiscences of his works, — but it is the story of his love — a love that had a happy ending, — and the personal element in it is strong and fresh enough to redeem it fully from the charge of mediocre imitation. It was composed toward the close of his English captivity.

The poet-king pictures himself reading Boethius, and meditating on Fortune's inexplicable power, the insecurity of earthly enjoyment, and his own loss of liberty. Looking from his window (in Windsor Castle) into a fair garden below he hears the birds sing hymns to Love, and wonders what this Love is. Looking again, he sees a lovely lady walking in the garden with her maids : is she the very goddess Nature ? He prays to Venus, and calls on the nightingale to sing, — but the lady goes her way, and his day is turned to night. Suddenly a mystic light streams in at the window, and he is caught up to the lovers' heaven, — Venus has heard his prayer, and receives him graciously. She sends him, with Good Hope as guide, to Minerva, who, on examination, finds that his love is virtuous, gives him good advice (quoting Ecclesiastes), and instructs him in the doctrine of Necessity and Free-Will. The lover then descends to earth, and finds himself in a delicious garden along a river running clear and cold over golden gravel ; he marks the fishes that leap and play in its waters, their scales glittering in the sun like fine mail, — the rows of trees laden with delectable fruit along its banks, — and the divers animals that roam around. At last he discovers a spot encircled with a wall, and within it the great goddess Fortune and her wheel, under which is an ugly pit that never gives up again those who fall into it ; a crowd of folk cling to the wheel, some rising on it, some almost dropping from it, some violently flung off. The goddess sets him on it, and pinches his ear so sharply that he wakes from his dream. Going once more to his window, a turtle-dove bearing a branch lights on his hand — a favorable omen ; and he blesses Fortune's axle-tree and wheel that have whirled him so well. The poem ends, as was customary, with an envoy, and a reference to the "superlative poets," Gower and Chaucer, whose souls its royal author commends to the bliss of heaven in a line that haunts the ear with a fine, far-off, aeolian melody such as distinguishes mediaeval poetry at its best ; he who has never caught it has missed an exquisite satisfaction, a pure and humanizing pleasure.

A very important strain of thought that gave tone to the whole Lancastrian period to a degree scarcely appreciated even by students was that of the followers of Wyclif. During the reign of Richard II they increased so rapidly in numbers that an ecclesiastical annalist could assert that "they were multiplied like suckers from the root of a tree and everywhere filled the compass of the kingdom, insomuch that a man could not meet two people on the road but one of them was a disciple of Wyclif." The accession of the House of Lancaster was inauspicious to their cause ; Henry IV sought to strengthen his precarious title by any means, principally by courting the favor of the clergy, and this he found could be most surely gained by oppressing the Lollards. Hence the famous statute of the year 1400 empowered a bishop to arrest any person suspected of holding heretical opinions, to try him, and if convicted, imprison him at pleasure ; and if, having recanted, he afterward relapsed, to deliver him to the sheriff to be burnt. John

Purvey, the reviser of Wyclif's Bible, bowed before the storm and abjured his heresy ; but a martyr to the cause was soon found in William Sautrey, a priest in London, upon whom the awful sentence of deposition was accordingly carried out. Paten, chalice, and chasuble were taken from him, in token of his degradation from the priesthood ; New Testament and lectionary, alb and stole, taper and church-keys — symbols of the diaconate — were next taken away ; and clad in the simple habit of a layman he was led to the stake and burnt alive. Thus was consummated the first legalized murder for conscience' sake in England. In 1407 another priest, William Thorpe, was convicted of holding Lollards' opinions, and was imprisoned : what finally became of him is not known. In 1410, Thomas Badby, a smith, found in error concerning the capital point of transubstantiation, was burnt to death. And yet, meanwhile, the parliament of the land was sufficiently tinctured with Wyclif's opinions concerning church property to propose the seizure of some of it. Archbishop Chichely actually encouraged Henry V in his warlike projects in order to divert the attention of the people from these questions. The rising of the persecuted Lollards at the beginning of that king's reign has been already mentioned ; their patron Oldcastle, a nobleman, was marked out as a distinguished victim, — but he escaped from prison, and was not apprehended and put to death until four years later.

The decrees of the Council of Constance stirred in England fresh efforts to extirpate heresy. Wyclif's ashes were dug up and vindictively cast into the brook that flows by Lutterworth. An Inquisition was established, with Thomas Netter — confessor to Henry V, and a stalwart defender of orthodoxy — at its head. The learned John Capgrave, provincial of the English branch of the Augustinian order, author of a lost life of St. Gilbert, preserves in his English chronicle many curious items concerning the Lollards which reveal beside his blind and bitter prejudice against the sect.   His chronicle ends about this time, though he lived on to hail the accession of Edward IV.

In 1419, several Lollards were constrained to alter their views.   In 1424, two wandering priests were brought back to the fold.   The same year, James I returned to Scotland — which was honeycombed with the new heresy — to copy there the ecclesiastical policy of his Lancastrian gaolers.   He made friends of the clergy by procuring straightway the enactment of a statute similar to the English one, under which Paul Craw, a Hussite emissary, was burnt at St. Andrews in the year 1432.

At Oxford, in 1427, Bishop Flemyng of Lincoln founded the college named after his see for the express purpose of training young churchmen to combat Wyclifite error.   This shows how widespread and deep-rooted the new doctrines yet were, and how inefficient the Inquisitors had proved themselves in the odious business of suppressing them.   Even if all these indications of Lollard strength were lacking, Bishop Pecock's great work, "The Repressor of Over-much Blaming of the Clergy," composed about the year 1449, would stand as a monument to the persistence of the sect.   But while controverting many of its tenets he manifested so tolerant a spirit toward others, and broached views of his own so novel and startling that he soon came to be regarded as quite as great a troubler of the peace of the church as the sectaries he opposed ; the archbishop of Canterbury condemned his critical opinions, and he found himself confronted by the dilemma of recantation or the fagot. He grasped the former horn and threw his books into the fire. Copies of them were also burnt at Oxford, where they had led astray numbers of the best students. · Now the pope, Pius II, interposed in his behalf ; but only elicited from King Henry VI fuller information as to the grounds of his deprivation, and in 1459 — the year when the civil war broke out afresh — poor Pecock was sent to practical incarceration in a sequestered abbey in Cambridgeshire.   Of his after fate nothing is known.

VI.

It commonly happens that in a vast cycle of the world's history distinguished by definite characteristics from every other there will occur a single epoch, perhaps a generation only, in which those characteristics are so conspicuously summed up that one can put his finger on the place and say: This is the essence of the whole, the focus of every ray. Such a comprehensive period will naturally occur toward the close of a series of ages that have an inner harmony, for the series will display its peculiar qualities more distinctly as it advances. Just such a period, the quintessence of what we call the Middle Ages, now stretches before us for the space of half a century, from about 1460 to about 1510, — including thus the reigns of the Yorkist kings and the first Tudor.

Every age is of course an age of transition, but in the one before us it is especially necessary to couple with this fact, that at the end of the fifteenth century the ideas and institutions of the Middle Ages came to full fruition, their inmost nature standing revealed, this other fact, that there was not one of them which the stream of time was not slowly dissolving away; the mighty fabric of mediaeval civilization was settling down upon its foundations, to be replaced by quite another structure. These facts, if constantly borne in mind, will make many contrasts clear, many puzzling contradictions intelligible. From its very richness and variety this complex era is difficult to comprehend, — more so than any we have yet encountered ; but it will repay any pains taken in its study, for it holds the keys to the next age, the marvellous sixteenth century ; it determined the colossal movements of the Reformation era.

The spirit of feudalism blazed forth with extraordinary brilliancy at the moment of its expiration : never were there more commanding representatives of the feudal nobility than Warwick the king-maker, Charles the Bold, duke of Burgundy, and Ferdinand, duke of Braganza, — yet they fell before the irresistible advance of new ideas, and their falls were the death-throes of a system. Sovereigns and people combined, and between those upper and nether millstones the ancient aristocracy was ground to powder ; it was replaced by a court nobility, — a change indicative of a change in culture equally profound.

Everywhere at this time strong, centralized governments were emerging from amid the confusion of the passing age ; governments that met brute force with deep dissimulation, that overcame the anarchic independence of their vassals by playing off one against another, by sowing suspicion among members of a hostile coalition and detaching them one by one ; by tortuous diplomacy, by employment of mean agents, by disguising stealthy advances to arbitrary power under forms of law ; by ruthless, exterminating cruelty when occasion offered ; by standing armies and the use of ordnance ; by rigid economy in administration, and by encouragement of trade, — thereby gaining the interest of an opulent class and securing a revenue.

The development of a legal spirit, directing particular attention to the details of justice, was a prominent feature of the time. And now, in the decrepitude of the empire, whose "peace," noble ideal as it was, was unhappily seldom more than a dream, the statesmen of Florence perfected a device that was to take its place and exert a tremendous influence upon the destinies of Europe, — the theory of a "balance of power," enforcing peace by common resistance to the aggressions of an overweening foe, — an end often attained only through prodigious wars.

Now, too, intrepid Portuguese navigators were bringing

home knowledge of new lands, and unfolding prospects of a golden commerce to the dazzled eyes of Europe.

To the papacy one more chance was given to retrieve itself, to show of what worth it might be to the nations, — and that chance it made haste to squander miserably. Restored to its place by the religious sentiment of Christendom, encircled with a faint halo by the lives and works of a company of saintly men and women, reformers of discipline, missionaries, preachers, ascetics, visionaries, artists, freed completely from the interference of emperors, the yet more fatal patronage of French kings, it was left to itself for a season to work out its salvation under highly favorable auspices. But hardly had the salutary check of a general council been removed when it began to manifest its deep-seated corruption and to speed upon its downward career; it became the appanage of a few powerful families who used it for their own aggrandizement; the supreme pontiffs themselves were luxurious, some of them revoltingly immoral men, whose highest ambition was to extend their secular sway; and the Christian world was drained of gold by disgraceful means, the German nation being bled above all others, to support their pleasures, their sumptuous courts, and their projects for disturbing the peace of Italy.

Scholastic philosophy now produced its last eminent doctor, Gabriel Biel, lecturer in theology at the new University of Tübingen. He reproduced Occam's doctrine of a Deity incomprehensible by man, whose attributes were mere accommodations to the imbecility of the human intellect and could not be proved to have any ground in his real nature. He made explicit avowal of the doctrine that lay at the root of the religious legalism of the Middle Ages when he defined a meritorious act as consisting of two elements, the free-will of the doer, and divine grace. His fresh assertion of the efficacy of sacraments without regard to the character of the recipient is significant, as is his daring exaltation (connected therewith) of the power of the priesthood. He was an enthusiastic propagator of the doctrine of the immaculate conception.

At the same time the "new learning," coming in in a flood, was rapidly undermining and sweeping away the relics of the scholastic system. Monasticism, another overshadowing institution of the Middle Ages, was likewise disintegrating. Though outwardly it seemed stable, inwardly it was unsound ; the reforming, disciplinary movement of the last age soon spent its force, and its results, partial at best, passed away like a vapor, and left the vast institution to disclose its inherently evil tendencies; it became hideously corrupt. The principal agents in its dissolution were a reviving, eager appetite for enjoyment of life, and a strengthening domestic sentiment.

The astrological and alchemical notions of ages germinated afresh in this fecund period, close upon the dawn of modern science (Copernicus was born in the year 1473). Astrologers were indispensable functionaries at princes' courts ; astrological figures were painted upon walls and ceilings and embroidered upon garments ; almanacs were compiled and were in great request ; the calculation of nativities was pursued with ardor and without restraint, — an ecclesiastic actually presumed to cast the horoscope of Christ. Another could assert that his crucifixion was determined by the influence of the stars, and a Bolognese physician could attribute his miracles to the same influence, and still evade the Inquisition. So far did the thought of the age decline from the ethical common-sense of Gower. Among seekers for the philosopher's stone in this century the most famous was the German, Basil Valentine, — more honorably distinguished by chemical discoveries of real value made during his quest. Divination and magical practices flourished, some of them as disgusting as they were ridiculous. The movements of the lions in princes' menageries were studied with morbid curiosity and superstition, and auguries drawn therefrom. At the bottom of all these notions and practices lay the persuasion that every property, every motion in the universe had some occult significance, some bearing upon human destiny, some correspondence in the frame of man.

The code of prosecutions for witchcraft was now developed with scientific precision and minuteness of detail. The occasion of this was the publication of a bull by Pope Innocent VIII in the year 1484, calling attention to the late portentous increase in the number of witches and recommending stringent measures for its reduction. The year following, accordingly, forty-one miserable beings were burnt at the town of Como alone; and in 1489, the inquisitor Sprenger, having extracted full confessions of the heinous practices of German witches, classified them, and furnished elaborate details of the process of conviction, in his "Witches' Hammer."

Never in the history of the Catholic church had there been so superb a ceremonial, such triumphs of art, as glittered in the last forty years of the fifteenth century; the elaborate rites, centering about the sacrifice of the mass, the ecclesiastical music and ornaments that were so wearisome, even offensive to Wyclif's soul, were zealously cultivated, and restored to more than their pristine magnificence. Evidence of the taste of the time is afforded by the extraordinary demand that there was for Durandus' great work, the "Rationale" of church architecture, ornament, and dedication, vestments, the mass, and other divine offices, festivals and saints' days : it was the first book put into print after the Bible ; a splendid edition of it appeared at Mainz in 1459, and it ran through twelve other editions before the end of the century. The motive of all this was the elevation of the sacramental system above preaching,— extolled by Wyclif and his followers as of superior efficacy ; and so at last we are able to discriminate the point of departure of this from the preceding age : it consisted in a renewed allegiance and devotion to the doctrine of Transubstantiation, that God is received in the consecrated wafer more effectually than through reading or hearing the Scriptures, preaching, or any other means whatsoever. This was the central point of the age ; round it circled the splendid worship and art, the hieratic absolutism, the thought of sin and justification, all the religious life of Christendom. Indissolubly associated with it were the benefits of confession, penance, and priestly absolution — pre-requisites to reception — upon which fresh emphasis was laid. Pilgrimages were resorted to as highly meritorious acts and means of grace, — pleasant likewise, and grateful to a mundane curiosity; indulgences were purchased as easy ways of escape from the consequences of sin. It is worthy of note that the jubilee cycle was now reduced to one of twenty-five years, — so agreeable to one party was that means of expiation, so lucrative to the other. Paul II published a jubilee for the year 1475 — the profits of which, however, he did not live to reap, — and in order to bring its benefits within reach of all he made a remarkable innovation in its observance, commuting the customary pilgrimage to Rome into a visit to some local shrine, and a gift according to ability. His successor, Sixtus IV, reaped the harvest that Paul had sown ; and in 1477 asserted the lawfulness and efficacy of indulgences in ransoming from purgatory the spirits of the dead.

One can hardly doubt that there was a subtle yet real connection between the dogma of transubstantiation and the alchemist's notion of a transmutation of metals; that each stood as an argument for the other. Both were rooted in the confirmed habit of thought of five hundred years.

It is clear that the idea of the institution, the community, corporate interest was in the ascendant, as opposed to the rude individualism of the former age. The church was rehabilitated in her authority, — its impersonation, papal infallibility, did not lack learned defenders. Divergences of opinion in matters of religion were suppressed; in 1478 the Spanish Inquisition was organized anew, and shortly after Torquemada ·began his blood-stained career.   So it came to pass that the experience of more than a century before was repeated, in an intensified form : the intellect and the emotions, denied fair play in the religious sphere, expatiated in the fascinating fields of literature and art.   It is a mistake to suppose that Roman literature was totally neglected during the monastic ages ; most of its greatest authors, Terence, Cicero and Sallust, Virgil, Tibullus, Horace, Livy, and Ovid, Seneca and Lucan, Juvenal, Statius, and Suetonius, were known, at least in part, and probably never ceased to be read somewhere ; but in the fourteenth and fifteenth centuries, through the contagion of Petrarch's enthusiasm, the indefatigable zeal of Poggio Bracciolini, the list was greatly extended ; Plautus, Lucretius, much of Cicero, Catullus, Vitruvius, and Columella, Quintillian, Silius Italicus, and Aulus Gellius were recovered, and early in the sixteenth century much of Tacitus was found in a German monastery ; and all were studied with an ardor and a veneration that it is hard for us to conceive to-day.   Even more notable, and distinctive of the fifteenth century, was the revival of Greek letters.   There was already a strong desire to become acquainted with them, when the precarious condition of the Eastern Empire and the projects for a union between the Greek and Latin churches sent westward a succession of Greek scholars who, finding a warm welcome in Italy, settled there and gave lessons in their language and literature.   The first of these, the learned Chrysoloras, commissioned by the emperor of Constantinople to solicit aid against the Turks, finally established himself at Florence, where he became Poggio's tutor. He was employed by the Roman pope, Gregory XII, to negotiate a union between the churches.   In 1423, Giovanni Aurispa, a famous collector of manuscripts, brought to Venice from Constantinople more than two hundred codices, including

the poems of Pindar, and the complete works of Plato, Xenophon, Lucian, Plotinus, and Proclus. Niccolò Niccoli, a
Florentine, who died in 1436, bequeathed to the republic his
precious collection of eight hundred Greek, Latin, and Oriental
manuscripts. Cosmo de' Medici was a princely purchaser of
Greek, Latin, Hebrew and other Semitic manuscripts, and thus
formed the nucleus of what was later known as the Laurentian
library. Parentucelli, a noted humanist and patron of humanists, who had been engaged to draw up a catalogue of Niccoli's
collection, after his accession to the papal throne as Nicholas
V gathered the extraordinary number of over five thousand
volumes of classical authors, thus founding the famous library
of the Vatican. And now at this most favorable juncture
came the invention of printing, by which the study of these
and other authors was marvellously facilitated ; the triumphs
of this art bring into especial prominence the encyclopaedic
character of the age. A remarkable collection of the earliest
specimens of the art exists in the library that was founded at
Vienna about the year 1440 by the Emperor Frederick III.
The correction of texts of the Latin classics, begun by Niccoli,
was carried on with enthusiasm and success by the poet Angelo
Poliziano, who amended the texts of Ovid, Statius, Quintillian,
Pliny Junior, and Suetonius, and inspired others to do as much
for those of Persius, Martial, and Columella. The concourse
of scholars and ecclesiastics that accompanied the Greek emperor to Florence in 1439, to effect a reconciliation of the
Eastern and Western churches, marks another stage in the
naturalization of Greek culture in Italy. Conspicuous among
them was the cultivated Bessarion, who, with his tutor Pletho,
indoctrinated the Italian mind in the ideal Platonic philosophy,
and, despite the jealous opposition of conservative thinkers,
broke the spell of the mediaeval version of Aristotle. The
domestication of Greek learning may be said to have been
completed by the fall of Constantinople, which drove a host of

literary men to Italy, in the year 1453 — the cardinal date of
the whole century, doubly important in its bearing upon commerce and discovery as well as learning : the imperative necessity henceforth of finding a sea-route to India led to the discoveries of Columbus, the circumnavigation of Africa by Vasco
da Gama.

By the year 1453 the Second Renascence was fully initiated.
The differences between this and the Petrarchian period were
such that it is unscientific in the extreme to confound the two,
to assume that attributes of one pertain to the other also.   One
deeply significant characteristic was common to both : a
divorce of morals and intellectual interests from religion, — a
condition of unstable spiritual equilibrium always provocative
of satire ; but in the fifteenth century the schism was completer
than in the fourteenth.   One patent distinction the later revival
enjoyed, — an infusion of Hellenic thought through the presence and tuition in the Greek language, literature, history,
philosophy, and mythology, of a swarm of Greek ambassadors,
ecclesiastics, and literary refugees of more or less repute who
wandered up and down in Italy.   Again : the first renascence
followed a prolonged endeavor to bring political order out of
chaos that had proved conspicuously successful in several
quarters, fairly so in others ; whereas the second accompanied
a similar endeavor, and emerged amid a welter of conflicting
forces, keeping pace with the reëstablishment of civil and
ecclesiastical authority.   These and other characteristics, such
as the stronger family feeling before mentioned, melt in a clare-
obscure of sentiment more easily felt than defined, differing as
much from that of former periods as Lorenzo de' Medici's
nameless mistress differed from the Beatrice of Dante, Petrarch's Laura, or the Fiammetta of Boccaccio.   The contrast
was as vividly reflected in the arts, in which a revolution
was wrought during the fifteenth century by the study and
representation of the nude figure, the application of the

sciences of anatomy and perspective, and the use of colors mixed with oil.

A notable feature of the later revival of learning was the greater participation in it of the northern nations, shown in the founding of new homes of humanism, the Universities of Freiburg and Greifswald, in the years 1455 and 1456 respectively, of Basel, in 1459, Ingolstadt, 1472, Tübingen and Upsala, 1477, Copenhagen, 1479, and Wittenberg, 1502. In Scotland, the University of Glasgow was founded in 1451; that of St. Andrews was enlarged by the founding of St. Saviour's College in 1459; and King's College, the germ of the University of Aberdeen, was instituted in 1494.

As Italy still led the rest of Europe, so did Florence lead Italy in intellect, varied and harmonious culture, and the art of elegant living. The peculiar position of that republic — then yielding itself to the genial tyranny of the Medici — between the duchy of Milan and the oligarchic republic of Venice on the one hand, and the papal monarchy and the kingdom of Naples on the other, explains how it was that there, in the midst of such mixed political relations, that compelled perpetual vigilance for the preservation of autonomy, there should have been devised that delicate adjustment of forces known as a balance of power. The conquest of Pisa in the year 1406 was probably the most important event in Florentine history; it resulted in the purchase of Livorno in 1421; and Florence, now first possessed of a strip of sea-coast, began a new rôle as a maritime power, — her galleys appeared in the Levant, the Black Sea, and the English channel. This enlargement of horizon was a powerful stimulus to her intellectual life : the sciences of astronomy and navigation had henceforth a practical interest for many of her citizens which occasioned the flourish of mathematical studies that soon ensued and that exerted a profound influence upon the arts. Political consequences of magnitude followed this extension of commerce ; large part of the wealth that flowed from it fell to the merchant princes of the house of Medici and enhanced their power: the recall of the great Cosmo from brief exile in the year 1434 was not obscurely connected with the conquest of Pisa. He remained the first citizen of the republic until his death in 1464, — a position which his grandson, Lorenzo the Magnificent, exchanged for almost absolute sway.

The wealth of Florence exhaled in a refined civilization such as the world had not seen since the golden age of Athenian culture nearly two thousand years before ; and there was about it a subtlety, spirituality, inventiveness, a certain iridescent play of color that contrasts picturesquely with the statuesque repose and beauty relatively perfect within narrower limits of the classic time. It cannot be too emphatically stated that the humanists as a class had no earnest quarrel with the Catholic church, — rather they confessed her authority. They despised the quiddities of scholasticism, the barbarous Latin of which moreover smote harshly upon ears sensitive to Ciceronian cadences ; they had a hearty antipathy to monks and friars, — but none to a cultivated hierarchy, a papacy adorned by such noted humanists as Nicholas V and Pius II. The imposing ceremonial of the church gratified their aesthetic sense ; the common notion of propitiation, quite like that of the ancients, was no offence to them ; nor was the dogma of transubstantiation monstrous to men who revelled in the classic lore of metamorphosis. But while they acknowledged a mysterious dependence upon the sacraments, and yielded to the church all responsibility for their spiritual life, they indemnified themselves by boundless liberty in the region of the human. An ideal of culture, of a perfected personality, of an harmonious play of every activity of mind and body, took possession of the youth of Florence. The charm of the old ideal of knighthood was still potent ; it lingered on as the basis of the new manhood and was enriched by the novel thought of manifold accomplishment; the result was a fusion of mediaeval and classic ideals. The complete man must be expert in horsemanship and all the exercises of a cavalier; he must be a good swimmer, runner and wrestler (a touch of the palaestra here); he must also learn to dance. Beside his native Tuscan a cultivated man should master at least one other language, — and that should be the language of Cicero. He should be versed in literature and be a connoisseur of art; he should sing or perform upon some instrument of music, — lute, harp, organ, or (best of all) the violin. A conception like this seen embodied in one individual enthralls the imagination of an age; it was more than realized in the consummate character of Leo Battista Alberti, — and all who knew him confessed the fascination of his personality. He was athletic, literary, musical; a wit, and a polished Latinist in verse and prose. He wrote an Italian treatise, "La Famiglia," in which he held up a noble ideal of domestic life. He was a mathematician, a student of science and law. He drew and wrote on art. He was a passionate admirer of natural beauty and was often melted to tears by the sight of a fair landscape. His contemporary, Pope Pius II, gave expression to a feeling similar but not so romantic, more in the vein of Virgil and Statius, in his Latin "Commentaries"; in the description of his summer haunt at Tivoli, where, among the ivy-clad ruins of Hadrian's villa, he mused upon the transiency of earthly glory, we have that mingled sense of the beauty of nature and the pathos of the dead past that was a dominant note of Renascent life. This graceful melancholy was nourished by pictures of ruins embowered in dark laurel and funereal cypress, the first of which appeared in the year 1467.

Sex was not recognized in the culture of the intellect; sisters enjoyed the same advantages of education as their brothers; and numbers of highly accomplished women gave tone to the social life of the day. They were conversant with classic literature, both Latin and Greek, and often wrote strong verse of their own ; they could engage in philosophic discussion and correspond with celebrated scholars upon equal terms ; they were skilled in vocal and instrumental music. Graceful and dignified demeanor, facile dialogue, exquisite purity of speech, were cultivated as fine arts.

A day spent in this wise was accounted perfect : first, in the freshness of the morning, a ramble among the hills, the conversation meanwhile threading some Platonic dream ; about the middle of the forenoon, breakfast, accompanied by song and music ; then to a shady garden nook, to listen to the recital of an original poem by one of the company ; after a long siesta through the languid hours, to meet again in the cool of the evening by a bubbling spring or fountain, every one to tell some tale "of effect of joy" or sorrow; then supper, followed by sprightly talk which should yet keep within the bounds of delicacy.

This delightful programme might have been deduced from joyous days actually passed by Lorenzo and his friends at his palatial villa of Ambra, with its woods stocked with Sicilian pheasants and peacocks, its gardens and orchards along the river-side, — or at his other villa at hilly Fiesole, where he especially enjoyed the society of the philosophers, scholars and poets who were his intimate companions. There might be seen the noble Ficino, to whom the Platonic philosophy had become a religion, and who exemplified in his daily walk its refining tendency; Poliziano, his pupil, an eminent scholar, exquisite Latinist, and the first Italian poet since Petrarch; Pulci, wit and poet, author of a voluminous mock-epic, the "Morgante Maggiore"; and thither came a singular product of the Renascence, the omniscient young Pico, prince of Mirandola, who had lately published at Rome innumerable theses, drawn from all the great departments of knowledge, which he was prepared to defend in half a dozen different languages. Poliziano's " Stanzas," written when he was a mere boy on occasion of a grand tournament held by Giuliano de' Medici, evince a delicate, Virgilian appreciation of rural beauty and contain a whole gallery of mythological pictures. His description of the never-fading, Elysian loveliness of Venus' haunt on the island of Cyprus was a first sketch for yet more glowing descriptions of delicious gardens by greater poets of a later day. He also wrote in Italian a tiny lyrical drama, " Orpheus," and a few minor poems. The true nature of Pulci's work has often been a subject of debate; it has been argued that it is wholly satirical and skeptical of established beliefs and institutions. The fact seems to be that it is a jocoserious production, a merry parody of the romances of chivalry still in vogue, heaping deserved ridicule by the way on the religious orders, yet flowering out now and then in passages of genuine emotion.

A sign of the satirical spirit that grew with the growth of political absolutism is afforded by the court fools whose numbers were now multiplied in the retinues of the petty despots of Italy and thence throughout Europe. Those fantastic beings were privileged to mock and gibe without respect of persons, and sometimes, in the guise of jest, to let their imperious masters know what otherwise they would never hear, — just what others thought of them.

The peculiar glory of Florence in the fifteenth century was her art. In architecture a remarkable innovation distinguished the second Renascence, — the introduction of the dome. In the year 1420 Brunelleschi began and left almost finished at his death in 1444 his magnificent dome over the cathedral. Years before he had visited Rome with his boy friend Donatello — destined to prove himself in time one of the greatest sculptors of the world — and had been deeply impressed by the superb cupola of the Pantheon. He returned to Florence filled with enthusiasm for the wonderful works of antiquity and with an ambition to recover the mechanical knowledge of the old

Romans and to rival their constructive feats. Donatello returned to carve many noble statues, among them his ideally beautiful St. George ; after a second sojourn in the papal capital he executed in 1433 his reliefs of dancing children for the choir gallery of the Florentine cathedral. The organ gallery was decorated with like reliefs by Luca della Robbia ; his marble youths and maidens are vocal with the spirit of song ; his children, singing, playing, and dancing, his little naked frolicsome boys, express the very ecstacy of renascent life, and reveal the artist's admiring love of happy childhood. Nothing could picture more vividly the strength of the healthy reaction from monastic ideas.

In 1451 Donatello designed an equestrian statue — the first since the decline of art in ancient Rome. The year following his illustrious compeer, Lorenzo Ghiberti, finished his second glorious set of sculptured bronze doors for the Florentine baptistery.

/   This revival of the sculptor's art was due to the passion for antique and natural beauty already noticed. The rage for collecting statues, busts, fragments of sculpture, vases, coins, engraved gems, was identical in principle with the lust of possessing manuscripts of classical authors. The discovery during the pontificates of Alexander VI and Julius II of the Apollo Belvedere, the group of the Laocoön, the Torso and Venus named of the Vatican, resembled in effect the recovery of a lost work by Cicero or Tacitus. In the early part of the century Cyriac of Ancona, a zealous antiquary, explored the coasts of the Mediterranean, exhuming bits of sculpture, sketching what was too large for him to carry away ; when asked why he spent his time and substance in such pursuits he replied, "To wake the dead!" Cosmo de' Medici left to his son a large collection of gold and silver medals, cameos and gold rings with stones engraved with classic and mythological subjects, inlaid tables from Byzantium, and similar treasures. Such were the beautiful objects desire of which banished, from Florence at least, the old-time eagerness for nauseous relics of saints. The splendid Lorenzo inherited to the full his grand-father's tastes ; the readiest way to his favor was to present him an ancient vase or coin. Along the garden walks and arcades behind his palace in the city he caused his statuary, busts, and other specimens of ancient sculpture to be arranged, and instituted there an academy of art under the direction of Bertoldo, a chosen pupil of Donatello. There that master's methods were transmitted to the succeeding generation ; there Torrigiano studied and the young Angelo learned his art.

We have already observed an improvement in the technics of painting. By the middle of the century the new medium — oil, — first successfully employed by the Flemish painters, Hubert and Jan Van Eyck, — found its way into the studios of Venice and Florence. Somewhat earlier, Masaccio, an artist of extraordinary genius, who died very young, originated the naturalistic style of painting by his noble frescoes (which he did not live to finish) in the Brancacci chapel of the Carmelite church in Florence. In one of these a youth who kneels to an apostle who has wrought his miraculous recovery is represented entirely naked, — the first figure of the kind in modern art.

The Brancacci chapel became a school for future artists ; Filippo Lippi studied there, and his son Filippino finished Masaccio's frescoes.

The next nude figure of note was that by Botticelli of Venus floating over the sea in her shell. But all previous efforts in this line were puny and immature as compared with Signorelli's ; in his frescoes at Orvieto, executed upon the threshold of the sixteenth century, that great master revealed a consummate knowledge of anatomy and a Dantesque imaginative power that mark him as the forerunner of Michael Angelo.

A pioneer in the application of mathematical science to the arts of design was Paolo Uccelli, a pupil of Ghiberti. He prosecuted with enthusiasm the study of perspective and made its principles generally known. A younger contemporary of his, Antonio Pollajuolo, was an expert both in perspective and anatomy.

When we turn to the inventive side of the art we are struck by its widening range of subjects and its increased capacity to express emotion, from the tenderest human feeling to the terrific and sublime. The irresistible inclination of the age made it inevitable that art should at last overstep its scriptural and ecclesiastical limits and enter the field of classical and mythological illustration. Botticelli led the way; his "Birth of Venus" has just been mentioned; another interesting work of his among many in this style is his attempted reproduction of the "Calumny" of Apelles, from a passage descriptive of the original in an ancient author. The magnificent series of pictures by the great Paduan master, Andrea Mantegna, illustrating "The Triumph of Julius Cæsar," is well-known. Pinturicchio's "Sibyls" at Rome remind us of Angelo's, and those of the "Three Fates," and those of Da Vinci's terrible Medusa.

Pinturicchio's name recalls his masterpieces at Siena (in executing which he enjoyed the collaboration of the young Raphael) — frescoes illustrating the leading events in the life of Æneas Sylvius (Pope Pius II) — representative of the new departments of historical and portrait painting that flourished with the reviving idea of earthly renown. Families and communities were desirous of preserving likenesses of their illustrious members. Another important feature of renascent life we may connect with his name: delight in beauty of landscape, charmingly shown in the backgrounds of some of these pictures.

The deepest inspiration, the motive power of this great epoch of art was, however, a renewed devotion to the Virgin Mary. A causal connection subsists between the feminine ideal and all high art; the perception of the divine in womanhood, in motherhood, exerts a refining influence, bestows a new sense of beauty. Without the Athena of Phidias, the Hera of Polycletus, the Mary of Giotto and Raphael, those artists and the epochs they dominated would have been other and far less than they were. In the fifteenth century pope and council were at one in forwarding the cultus of Mary : the council of Basel promulgated anew the doctrine of her immaculate conception, and Sixtus IV forbade dispute about it and authorized its celebration. This action was symptomatic of a fresh wave of popular devotion, generated in part by way of reaction against Wyclifite and Hussite disparagement of the cultus. Even the laughing Pulci grows serious and devout when he invokes Mary, as he does in opening several cantos of his work ; at its very beginning he adores her as daughter, mother, and spouse of God (that is, of the persons of the Trinity respectively) and entreats her to illumine his mind, inspire his style, and guide him through the whole progress of the work. Thus she became to him what the Muse was to a Roman poet.

The painters of the age set forth their ideal of womanhood in innumerable Madonnas. Representations of the man Christ were remarkably rare : their place was usurped by the Madonna and infant Jesus. The invasion of devotional art by the realistic spirit is shown by this, that whereas previously the Virgin was represented veiled and the child swathed, toward the close of the century she was pictured with uncovered head and the child naked. Scenes from her life were painted by Ghirlandajo upon the choir-wall of Santa Maria Novella. A memorable development of the doctrine of the immaculate conception was the novel cultus ôf Ann, mother of the Virgin ; the devout sentiment of the age soon raised her to a position close by her daughter, as we see her portrayed by the Bolognese master Francia. In such a subject we can perceive beside the working of domestic sentiment, of a sense of the beauty and goodness of human relationships, which was manifested yet more strongly and perfectly in those beautiful groups, the " Holy Families " that first appeared at the end of the century.

A further awakening of emotion, an effort to compel feelings of pity, pain, and terror by representations of the mortal sufferings of the Redeemer, are widely apparent in the art of the time. The tragic series of " Stations of the Cross " was transplanted into Europe by a pilgrim from the Holy Land in the year 1477. Now for the first time we find the Saviour represented as falling under the weight of his cross. The awful scene of the crucifixion was depicted with great power by Mantegna and the Venetian master Bellini; and now at that supreme moment the triumph of natural feeling over faith was betrayed by the swooning of Mary, — in some examples she even falls as if dead. By reason of its pathos the " Pietà," — the mother lamenting over the dead body of her son — was an oft-attempted subject : it was nobly and tenderly treated by Francia and Fra Bartolomeo. Perugino's sentimental conception of the ascension offers a significant contrast to the fervent faith revealed in Giotto's upward soaring figure : his Saviour seems to pause between earth and heaven, and looks down with a pensive, almost affected grace upon the friends he is leaving below.

Finally, we have to notice an invention that was to art what printing was to literature, a means of multiplying copies of pictures as the other multiplied books, — the art of engraving on copper. To Baccio Baldini, a Florentine, who acted upon the suggestion afforded him by impressions of goldsmiths' work, the credit of the invention seems to be due ; he was assisted with designs by several of the eminent artists lately mentioned.

The substance of these last few pages is intended whenever henceforth we have occasion to allude to the influence of Italy upon other peoples. It is futile to talk about that influence unless it is clearly understood what is meant by it.

In Spain, during the long and troubled reign of John II, considerable progress was made in domesticating the study of classic and Italian literature by Juan de Mena and the Marquis of Santillana. The latter introduced the sonnet into Castilian literature, and, though not a scholar himself, was a generous patron of scholars, and urged on translation of the Latin classics ; the former was a devoted student of the Italian poets, and in his famous 'Labyrinth' modelled himself upon Dante. The conquest of Naples in the year 1443 by the royal humanist Alfonso V of Aragon was an important factor in making the intellectual movement in Italy better known in the Peninsula. At that epoch, too, flourished the Catalan poet Ausias March, whose delicate love-poems composed some during his lady's lifetime, some after her death, confessed the fascination of Petrarch's muse.

The main interest of Spanish history through the first half of the century centres in the person of one of the most famous of royal favorites — Alvaro de Luna. His influence over the cultivated but somewhat frivolous king seemed like witchcraft; it was offset by the implacable hatred of the great nobles. In part, doubtless, to divert their attention from his internal administration of the government, the favorite engaged John II in a campaign against the Moors of Granada ; it was highly successful, and the conquest of that delightful province might have been anticipated by many years but for the disaffection of the nobles; their intrigues against Alvaro culminated at last in tedious civil wars that gave opportunity for a retaliatory invasion by the Moors. Alvaro's pride finally outwore the king's infatuation : his sudden fall from the pinnacle of power and speedy execution in the year 1453 added another example to the moralist's long catalogue of Fortune's caprices. A year later John II followed him to the tomb and was succeeded by his son, Henry IV, who in the recent disturbances had joined the ranks of the rebel lords. In his careless, pleasure-loving temper Henry resembled his father, but was yet weaker ; he was governed by favorites and mistresses and the manners of his palace were a scandal to Spain.   In order to humble the lords — his late associates — he advanced persons of low origin to positions of honor and influence, — but the result was a repetition of the wretched broils of his father's time.   In 1463 Henry and Louis XI had a conference at Fuentarabia ; the French king had offered his services in settling matters in dispute between Castile and Aragon, — but his decision pleased neither party.   Shortly after civil war broke out in Castile ; beside the nobility, many large towns fell away from their allegiance ; Henry's conduct had disgusted all classes, and in his person the monarchy was subjected to extreme humiliation.   His crown was at last offered to his young sister, Isabella ; she put it by for the time, and Henry, having submitted to his enemies' hard conditions, was allowed to end his pitiable career upon the throne.   In 1469 took place one of the famous marriages of history — a union destined to bring order out of this political and social chaos and to weld the weak and warring states of Spain into one compact and powerful monarchy — the marriage of Isabella with Ferdinand of Aragon.   From the first their union was regarded by all who longed for order as the hope of their distracted country, the pledge of good government to come — a pledge amply redeemed by Isabella when she acceded to the throne upon her brother's death in the year 1474.

The strange character of Louis XI impressed itself deeply upon his age and has been revealed for all time by his secretary and confidential adviser, Philippe de Comynes, whose "Memoirs" are doubtless the best-known and most considerable work of the period.   Less therefore need be said about him than his darkly commanding position would justify ; all we need do is to indicate, with a few brief touches, his historical connections.   Like Henry IV Louis had, as heir-apparent, joined the rebels to his father's authority ; like him, but with more success, he as king made use of mean agents in his subtle stripe with the feudal aristocracy. His confidants and tools, Olivier le Dain and Tristan l'Hermite, remind one too of Catesby and Cochran, the base instruments of his young contemporaries, Richard III of England and James III of Scotland. To the extension and elevation of the royal power and the ruin of feudalism involved therein Louis bent all the energies of an intellect fertile in resource, tireless in operation, and unscrupulous as to the means employed. In the science of politics the despots of Italy were his tutors; the wonderfully successful career of an elder contemporary, Francesco Sforza, who by a master-stroke of craft and cruelty had made himself duke of Milan, especially excited his admiration. He mastered perfectly the art of managing others by self-interest and fear, of dividing opponents that he might overcome them separately. He played upon the weaknesses and passions of his victims and would flatter one to his face while by secret, far-off agencies he was preparing his destruction. And when he had an enemy in his toils nothing could exceed his malice and cruelty. The mingled guile and ruthlessness of his nature and the singular success with which his policy was crowned exerted a sort of fascination, the fascination of terror, over the minds of his contemporaries. Some years elapsed, however, after he came to the throne in the summer of 1461 before his character appeared fully in this light: at first he was more openly aggressive and ambitious; the great representatives of French feudalism took the alarm, banded themselves together, and gave him check in battle at Montl'héry, — and with that his career of cunning began ; he resolved henceforth to avoid appeals to arms and to meet violence with skilful negotiation, deceit, and corruption. After the battle he seemed to yield everything they asked to the confederated lords, but it was only to find time to practise upon them, break up their league, and isolate his great adversary, Charles the Bold, who in 1467 became duke of Burgundy and for the next ten years — the middle period of his reign — gave Louis' energies abundant employment. The way in which the king recovered the ground he had lost, his dealings with the French dukes and with Charles, the personification of overgrown feudalism, remind one of nothing so much as of Reynard the Fox, and the tricks he played upon the bear, wolf, cat, hare, etc., in that great poem of the thirteenth century which was now enjoying a renewed popularity. The redoubtable league of little Swiss republics proved at last a serviceable tool to the most absolute monarch in Europe : the city of Berne, instigated by Louis, rushed into a war with Charles, drew with it the other cantons, and inflicted upon the rash duke a series of crushing defeats that culminated in his death upon the field of battle early in the year 1477. It was left for Louis, in the seven remaining years of his reign, triumphantly to gather in the fruit of his dextrous policy. His exultation at the fall of his powerful rival, however, caused him to forget the caution that was necessary in prosecuting one of his favorite projects, the marriage of his son to Charles's daughter Mary, heiress of Burgundy : he allowed his rapacious, treacherous disposition to appear so plainly in his dealings with her that the young duchess, disgusted and indignant, threw herself into the arms of the imperial faction, and in August, 1477, wedded Maximilian of Austria, — and Louis had the mortification of seeing the wealthy provinces of the Netherlands transferred as an hereditary possession to the House of Hapsburg. This was the second marriage of rare consequence in that period. It was the chief success attained by the emperor Frederick III — Maximilian's father — in his reign of more than half a century (one of the longest in history), in the course of which he suffered every ignominy.

Frederick is a conspicuous example of the way in which the princes of his time rallied around the rehabilitated papacy : none of them surpassed him in devout submission to it, — and he had his reward. He surrendered to Eugenius IV the privileges that the council of Basel had secured to the German church ; and some years later, when his incapacity and neglect of imperial interests had so disgusted the electors that they began to think seriously of deposing him, Pius II came to his support and held him on the throne. He carried on his private studies, astrological and medical, careless though the empire fell to pieces under the blows of the invading Turks. In public affairs he pursued a Fabian policy of inactivity, — but under a phlegmatic exterior concealed far-reaching designs for the aggrandizement of his house which were realized at the end of his reign, after the Burgundian match.

The founding of German Universities has been mentioned as evidence that the wave of humanism was travelling northward; in the year 1467, Desiderius Erasmus, destined to become the great exponent of northern humanism, was born in Rotterdam. In France, during the conflict between Louis XI and Charles of Burgundy, there occur several indications that the future triumph of the Renascence was preparing : Terence was done into French for the king, and a fresh translation of Ovid's " Metamorphoses " was made, while for the duke Quintus Curtius' life of Alexander and Cæsar's " Commentaries " were translated. In the year 1483 a romance based upon the Æneid appeared in print.

In 1465 died Charles, duke of Orleans, — a poet whose work belongs to the past generation, when Louis XI was yet Dauphin, but who may be placed here because he illustrates well an intellectual attitude that greatly furthers political absolutism like Louis' — a tendency of cultivated minds, enamoured of beauty and pleasure, to abstract themselves in stormy periods from all interest and interference in public affairs, and to create for themselves worlds apart where, as Charles himself urged, they can think at their ease, and banish care and sadness. In the present case, this attitude of mind excites no wonder : the duke of Orleans had had his full share of the tribulations of his disastrous time.   Taken captive at Agincourt and detained long years in England, when he was allowed to return he secluded himself in his château at Blois amid a world of music and song, and practised poetical composition in the pretty, artificial forms then in vogue.   Among his gay and dainty little verses those on the changing seasons of the year are especially pleasing.   The representative poet of the reign of Louis XI was one much younger than he, and of a condition of life as different as could be imagined — " a poor little scholar who was called François Villon " — the poet of the Paris streets. A spendthrift and libertine, he was acquainted with all the profligacy, penury, squalor, and misery of the worst purlieus of the Paris of his time.   Yet he was bred for better things and had something of an education, — and the contrast between what was and what might have been made him wretched. When he thought of it he spoke out with a passion of regret or a settled sadness that brought into French poetry a new and thrilling note of personal experience and appeal.   The upshot of it all was his resignation in thought to a cheerless fatalism, — he would make the stars responsible for his faults : " I am a sinner, I know it well," he cries, "and what the planets have made me I shall be."   In other moods an experience like his gives rise to satirical reflections ; much of his work is instinct with that spirit of satire that was characteristic of the period and grew sharper as the century grew older.   A notable expression of it is the cynical " Fifteen Joys of Marriage " — an attack on women — a prose work ascribed to Antoine de la Salle, who is believed also to have had a hand in composing a famous set of prose tales, the " Cent Nouvelles Nouvelles," — which Louis XI richly enjoyed.

The taste for dramatic representations continued unabated, and gave rise in this period to new forms of art.   The old mystery-plays now rolled up into series of huge bulk, and the great

number of clever farces that have been preserved from the end
of the fifteenth century proves that these were a favorite form
of popular diversion.

Such, in sum, is the historical and literary setting of the
dynasty of York.

The years of Edward IV's reign — 1461 to 1483 — exactly
coincided with those of his French rival, Louis XI. The two
halves of the fifteenth century do not offer a contrast more
vivid than that that Edward offered, in aspect and character, to
the poor king whom he displaced — a man weak in feature,
intellect, and will, whose virtues fitted him rather for a cloister
than a throne. Edward was a youth of nineteen years when he
assumed the crown. He was the handsomest prince of his
time : Comynes assures us that he was the handsomest man he
ever saw. He was vigorous, a good fighter, devoted to pleasure,
luxurious, lascivious even, and cruel on occasion, as men of his
stamp generally are. His accession signified the triumph of
the principle of legitimacy, of natural right, over parliamentary
enactment, by which the House of Lancaster held. Royal
authority was now in the ascendant ; parliamentary power
declined. Edward had large possessions in his own right and
was further enriched, after his success at Towton, by the
estates of a host of attainted lords and gentry ; parliament,
moreover, helped him tó greater independence and diminished
its own consequence by granting him the customs (now increasing in productiveness) once for all, for the term of his life. As
a result of this and of the peace with France it was rarely
summoned during his reign. To balance this constitutional
regression there came about a signal development of law, its
practice and interpretation, — a condition of things characteristic of strong reigns : Louis XI ever sought to give his
arbitrary acts a color of legality. In 1461 the first solicitor-
general of the crown was appointed ; in 1471 the first attorney-
general. In John Markham, a consistent Yorkist, Edward

found a useful ally, and he was appointed chief justice of the Court of King's Bench ; but because he would not go the length the king wished in straining the law to suit his ends he had to make way, toward the middle of the reign, for a more pliant tool of power, Thomas Billing, who balked at nothing so it pleased the king.   The latter part of the reign was adorned by the labors of the learned jurists Sir John Fortescue and Thomas Littleton.   In 1481 Littleton's famous treatise "On Tenures" was printed.   It was couched in the old French of the law-courts and was divided into three parts, treating respectively of tenancies in general, — of the rights and duties of lords and tenants, — and of means of acquiring and surrendering rights in land.   It was the first work of the kind in England, and so clear were its definitions, so thorough its analysis, so systematic its arrangement, that it aroused real enthusiasm in the profession, — an enthusiasm that may be gauged by the fact that William Hussey, Edward's attorney-general and last chief-justice, got it by heart.   Fortescue was a faithful Lancastrian.   He had been Henry VI's sergeant and chief-justice, and after the battle of Towton, in which he took part, he fled with Margaret and her little son to Scotland and suffered attainder.   He accompanied the queen in her wanderings upon the continent as tutor to the prince, for whom he composed, in Latin, his "Praises of the Laws of England." After the extinction of the male line of the house of Lancaster in 1471 he gave in his submission to Edward IV and his attainder was reversed.   About this time, probably, he wrote his treatise, in twenty short chapters "On the Governance of England."   In this work he had the courage to use English.   He begins by drawing a comparison between absolute and constitutional monarchy and their effects as exhibited in France and England respectively, — goes on to show the necessity of an ample revenue for the king, greater than that of any subject, — discusses the means of raising it, — and winds up with a recommendation (acted upon later) to form a body of councillors who should advise the king in financial matters especially.

We have spoken of the increasing value of the customs : it sometimes seems as if the most significant feature of the revolution that raised the house of York to power is that it was a victory of the townsfolk, artisans, traders — of what is called the middle class. Great advances were now made in commerce and manufactures : English merchants began to compete with the men of the Hanse towns even in the Baltic Sea : for the encouragement of home-industry a highly protective statute was passed in 1463 by which importation of woollen and leather goods and specified articles of hardware was forbidden. For the farmer's benefit a corn-law was also passed forbidding the importation of wheat when it was under a specified market price. Artisans and manufacturers prospered in this period — their work was well paid for, their hours of labor were few; rural laborers on the contrary suffered, their day was long, their wages were low. Little by little the farm-lands of England were being converted into pasture, into enormous sheep-walks, to supply the great English staple, wool, — in constant demand in foreign markets.

It was some time before the nature of the new monarchy was fully disclosed; at first it seemed allied in policy as well as by blood and fellowship in arms with the great house of Neville and its head, the popular and powerful earl of Warwick, the full-blown flower of the feudal age. We have not in our possession every link in the chain of events that led up to the inevitable crisis, the mortal conflict between the new monarchy and the old feudalism on Barnet field. Edward's marriage with the beautiful young widow, Elizabeth (Woodville) Grey, made known in the fall of the year 1464, is commonly held to have begun the breach, which was widened by the favor shown the new queen's relatives and by another marriage, that of the king's sister Margaret and Charles of Burgundy — brought about by the Woodville interest in 1467. On both occasions Warwick was planning a French match, for he favored alliance with Louis XI; in the latter instance he was cruelly discredited, for he had already begun negotiations with the French king.   The antagonism of sentiments and ideas grew keener; in the summer of 1469 Warwick gave proof of his power, actually making the king his captive — but soon released him.   It is unnecessary to search for the disgusts that hurried on the final catastrophe: Edward was restive under his great vassal's overshadowing influence and Warwick divined that the king's policy was inimical to his whole system. In 1470 he rose again; but this time Edward was prepared and the earl had to take refuge in France.   There his affiliations underwent a radical change; he turned Lancastrian, was reconciled to Margaret of Anjou, and contracted his daughter to her son, to whom he pledged the crown of England after the demise of Henry VI.   Surprising as this change of connection was, we yet feel that there was an inner fitness in it; it was the desperate embrace of the Lancastrian and the feudal cause, destined to sink together.   With aid from Louis XI which he hardly needed, so popular was he, Warwick landed in England in September; in a few days he was at the head of a large army; Edward was deserted and fled with his brother Richard on fleet horses to Lynn just in time to escape on a ship bound for Holland where he arrived with no other possessions than the clothes he wore.   Warwick now had Henry VI proclaimed and reigned in his name for half a year.   But in the spring of 1471 came the amend : with some little help from his brother-in-law, Charles the Bold, Edward returned, nominally to recover his duchy, really to try his fortune once more; finding the way clear he pushed on to London and was warmly welcomed by the citizens.   Turning back he encountered Warwick at Barnet and in the sanguinary battle that followed the great earl fell. Edward promptly marched across the kingdom to meet Margaret of Anjou who had landed in the west, defeated her at Tewkesbury and caused the prince her son to be slain. Immediately after Henry VI perished in the Tower, — and Edward was sole master in the kingdom. His restoration was the triumph of London and of trade : the Hanse merchants had contributed toward it and as a reward he confirmed their privileges in London and granted them beside factories at Lynn and Boston. Another point deserves notice, — his victories were won with gunpowder. By this time the long-standing prejudice against that medium was wearing out ; its use was pretty well understood and was henceforth constant — and the relics of feudalism were wiped away.

The sun of York was now supreme in an unclouded heaven and the king, freed from every rival, every apprehension, in the pride of youth and conquest and a power greater perhaps than any of his predecessors had ever enjoyed, gave himself up to the pursuit of pleasure, and tournaments, hunting-parties and banqueting were the order of the day. A type of the new nobility was the head of the family of Howard which now rose into prominence : Edward created him duke of Norfolk and showered offices upon him. But the particular ornament of the court, — the mirror of courtesy, of elegant tastes and chivalrous manners, — was the queen's brother, Anthony Woodville, Caxton's patron ; and second only to him came the lord Hastings. As an instance of the refinement, the intellectual atmosphere of the court, we note that the first royal poet-laureate in England was appointed in this reign, — a writer of Latin verse named John Kay. A scarce perceptible dawn of 'new learning' began to spread as a slender succession of scholars returned from Italy, some of them bringing manuscripts. Thus the downfall of scholasticism was heralded ; but the humanists were not numerous or influential enough to stamp the age, — it was Caxton rather and the mediaeval themes over which he labored that gave it its literary character. In 1477 he introduced the art of printing into England, — an event sufficient of itself to make the reign illustrious.

We have seen English used for the first time in the discussion of problems in political philosophy by Sir John Fortescue; he was preceded by several years in this serious use of the mother tongue by Bishop Pecock, — against whom this very indictment was brought by his enemies, that he wrote in English. As a result he is vindicated to-day with acclamation and his enemies are put to confusion, — their memories are only revived to be covered with contempt and consigned again to oblivion while his " Repressor " stands forth a model of argumentative composition and without question the most considerable work produced in England in the course of the fifteenth century. At first it seems difficult to place him : he was rejected by the Lancastrians and his case was not bettered by the revolution that put Edward IV on the throne : in 1476 we find that king, who in such matters took his cue from the opinion of those about him, commending the authorities at Oxford for suppressing Pecock's works and bidding them withhold the degree of doctor in divinity from some theologian who was believed to have been infected with his obnoxious ideas. But the fact that his books were circulating at the university and making many converts during this reign makes their examination fitting at this point ; the title of his principal tractate, moreover, is a helpful indication, — it was intended to "repress " the Lollards, to put a stop to their fault-finding with the church clergy, — an end pretty effectually realized by Edward IV : it is a remarkable fact that after his accession the Lollards subsided, disappeared beneath the surface ; the church was heartily Yorkist and held to the monarch a relation of close and mutual support. More than all we feel in the bishop's work the breath of the new epoch ; he occupied in truth a transitional position. His fate was that of most comprehensive minds, — to be misunderstood and abused on all sides, — proof enough of the independence and originality of his views. His tolerance — extraordinary in that age, — his willingness to see what was good in the contentions even of his opponents, his desire to do justice to all parties, — his recognition of the claims of the papacy, the English church, and the Lollards, — brought it to pass that he was suspected and hated by all. His work was of deep significance, for it was instinct with that fine humanity, that respect for ancient usages which yet does not preclude all timely change, that loyalty to Scripture, that large reasonableness, fairness in discussion, soundness of mind and heart, that came to be known later as the spirit of Anglicanism, — a truly catholic spirit.

Beside his " Repressor " Pecock wrote in English a grammar of morals which he called his " Donet " and a " Treatise on Faith " in which he met the Lollards half way, admitting that Scripture is the rule of faith. He also wrote " Of Matrimony " and projected a work on logic.

His relation to the ages of religious thought that we have traversed may be stated thus. It will be remembered that in past centuries the reason had been held to be a useful organ of religious knowledge, competent to prove some if not all of the fundamental doctrines of Christianity; that later it had been discredited and the authority of the church had been declared the ground of faith ; and that finally the Bible had been set over against that authority as the sole depository of unadulterated truth. It was left for Pecock at the close of these ages to combine the results of all and to set forth with varying degrees of clearness and consistency, the reason, the Bible, and the church as the threefold root of religious knowledge. Thus he curiously exemplified in his theological culture the composite character of the age ; but as has been shown by reason of its strenuous reaction against Wyclif's ideas the age was one-sided and intolerant in regard to the Bible and so could not appreciate Pecock's liberal attitude ; and though his defence of the constitution of the church and certain of its popular practices was agreeable to some it displeased others by its moderation, — and all took alarm at his appeal to the reason.

The " Repressor " falls into two main divisions, the first part general, clearing the ground and establishing principles, the second particular, applying those principles to some special usages chiefly objected to by the Lollards.   It begins by setting forth three radical errors of theirs : (1) That no ordinance is of God that cannot be found in the Bible (some are so "smart and wanton" as to ask of any usage they dislike, "Where groundest thou it in Holy Scripture ?"); (2) That any humble Christian can discover the true sense of any passage in the Bible ; (3) That when that sense is thus gained one should not listen to any argument about it.   Then follows the doctrine of the reason ; it is not the office of Scripture to establish any law or truth that reason may discover.   The Moral Law is of equal authority with Scripture : upon it temperance, justice, and reverence toward God are based ; it is the law " of kind," of nature, — the "doom" or judgment of natural reason, — written in men's souls by the finger of God ; it is the 'print and image of God,' not grounded on the Bible but presupposed by it, to be dutifully kept by men though there were no Bible — as was the case, for instance, before Abraham's time. The principles of morals are not founded upon any words of Christ but were presupposed by him.   Whenever there seems to be a conflict concerning a point of morals between the outward letter and the law within the heart the former must be harmonized with the latter for that is of absolute obligation. And the larger part of God's law is written on the heart ; acquaintance with moral philosophy, therefore, is necessary to Christians.   Let none disparage or seek to diminish that " inward Scripture."   Next, as to the Bible ; it certifies to truths

intuitively derived, publishes anew the moral law, and estab-
lishes beside points of faith, some of which are laws (as, for
instance, baptism), and some not (as historical facts). Pecock
would not forbid the laity to read the Bible ; he pays by the
way this fine tribute to Wyclif's version : the Scripture in the
mother tongue is delectable and sweet and draws men to devotion and love of God, — hence it is esteemed beyond reason.
Many lawful things are not ordained or even mentioned in it,
— as articles of clothing, cooking, clocks, *translations of itself*,
shaving, laughing, singing, quoit-throwing, ale and beer-making
(much worse than images !). " Vain, disputatious women appeal
to express statements of Scripture : how, then, dare they wear
kerchiefs or wash and anoint themselves ? They may not
adduce the example of Susannah for that is an apocryphal
book !" The Lollards' argument from the sole authority of
Scripture is thus reduced to absurdity and they are brought
back to reason. From laymen's conflicting interpretations and
quarrels over the sense of Holy Writ is deduced the need of a
learned ministry ; and from the divisions among the sectaries
is drawn a powerful argument for the authority of the church.
" You Bible-men differ, — some of you are called Opinion-
holders, some Neutrals ; you are full of schism, — ought you
not to admit the doom of reason and return to the catholic and
general faith and lore of the church ? "

In the second division of his work the bishop applies himself
to a defence of eleven points in the constitution or practice of
the church which were commonly brought in question by the
Lollards. It is interesting to learn that these were the use of
images, pilgrimages, property in land, the hierarchy, ecclesiastical laws, religious orders, invocation of saints, costly church
ornament, the mass, taking of oaths, and maintaining the lawfulness of war and capital punishment. He opens his defence
with a philosophical classification of the whole body of
knowledge according to its derivation (1) from reason, which

is Philosophy, (2) from revelation, by testimony, apprehended by faith, — that is, Theology. Further, all truth may be classed as either "speculable" or "doable" (practical); and the latter may be distributed into actions approved, forbidden, or left undetermined by faith and reason, — that is, actions lawful, unlawful, or indifferent — and those of the last class may generally be considered lawful. Any who deny these distinctions are out of the pale of argument. Herein the bishop forces into clear relief the nature of the difference between his and the church's view of the Bible and the Lollard view; they may be distinguished as broad and narrow; according to the former all usages are lawful that are not forbidden by Scripture, — according to the latter none are lawful that Scripture does not enjoin. One by one the points above mentioned are passed in review; the procedure is simple, — it is to bring each to the dual test of reason and the Word of God. The first matter in dispute is the use of images; it is usual but not apposite to refer to the second commandment as condemning these; in fact it condemns idols only, not images used as "minding signs." These are approved by Scripture, — God himself commanded the brazen serpent to be made, the cherubim, the bosses and images of the Temple; Christ used money stamped with Caesar's image. Crucifixes therefore are lawful. Reason, moreover, does not forbid them, for no one in his senses worships them or supposes that any divine virtue inheres in them ; nor are they to be put out because some abuse them to superstition, for other good things are subject to abuse, — the Bible in English for instance ! To use "seeable, rememorative signs," such as the sacraments are is both permissible and helpful ; they assist the memory like a knot in one's girdle, — they are like portraits of dead or absent friends. Pilgrimages when tried by Scripture and reason are not found lacking, — the women who visited the sepulchre very early in the morning were pilgrims, — and though these too are liable to abuse yet when rightly used they quicken devotion. But the Lollards contend that the Bible and preaching are better reminders than images and pilgrimages and that living men are better representations of Christ "than is any unquick stock or stone graved and orned with gold and other gay paintures" and that God is equally present everywhere so that one place is no holier than another. But this is not true: "God chooseth to give his grace one place before another, therefore that place is holier." Such a spot was Bethel, — and Jacob said, dreading: "How gastful is this place!" And out of the bush God said to Moses: "Undo the shoes off thy feet for the place in which thou standest is holy land." Again, the Bible is a "hearable" not a "seeable" sign of the Lord, and a glance of the eye brings to mind much and long matter more quickly and easily than hearing and reading do — and there are many who cannot read. Finally, an image must resemble its object and nothing else, and no living man can represent Christ as truly as a crucifix does. Here is the conclusion of the matter: "whatever reason deemeth to be done is moral law of God and his pleasant service even in case it cannot be found specially witnessed to by Holy Scripture." A digression on the origin of idolatry follows; Pecock thinks it began in the worship not of dead men but of the stars. The third point, as to ecclesiastical rights in land: some of the laity declare that those who defend them are in a state of damnation. Yet such holdings are not condemned in either testament: the Levites were endowed with forty-eight cities; and if Christ's example of poverty be of universal obligation so also should his celibacy be. Human law does not forbid endowments. The bishop has a fling at Wyclif's doctrine of dominion: "a clerk — verily to say a heretic"— asserts that if the clergy misapply their property the temporal lords may take it away: but the evil deeds of an unfaithful servant should not prejudice his innocent heir for otherwise bad kings might be similarly deprived.

Further: some of the laity say that all ranks above the priest-hood — bishops, archbishops, patriarchs, the pope — are anti-Christian; yet they are not forbidden by reason or Scripture, — remember the Jewish high-priest and Christ's appointment of Peter. The remaining points are briefly treated, — the method of disposing of them had been amply illustrated and the bishop was growing tired of the discussion. Some call religious orders devilish; yet they are not prohibited by Scripture. It is objected that they were not instituted by Christ, — neither was the Lord Mayor of London. The habits of the brothers are "seeable signs," like liveries, and in their "lordly mansions" they are given to hospitality. The bishop's last retort sounds somewhat flippant: it was in truth a flash of not unjustifi-able indignation at the perversity of his opponents' temper, — one cannot call it reasoning. It is clear that the pristine evangelical fervor of Wyclif's followers had declined and that the sect was muffling itself in a mantle of legalism, a carping literalism, — the veriest formalism, and that of an ugly kind. It was just as well that it should lift its voice no more.

In writing his book Pecock evidently had access to many documents long since lost or destroyed. The "Repressor" is thus a precious record of a highly important controversy.

We turn now to the civilization of the age upon its domestic and material side. And here we are exceedingly fortunate in possessing a mass of correspondence that brings the times of Edward IV before us with the vividness of lightning. The letters of the Paston family present us pictures of real life so broad and animated and full of detail that they transport us into the period with an immediacy quite unprecedented. This remarkable collection begins well back in the reign of Henry VI but is most intimately associated with the following reign for it attains its greatest interest and volume during the time that Sir John Paston figures upon the scene. He was the same age as Edward and the companion of his revels; and after his death at the end of the year 1479 the correspondence loses its vivacity and gradually dwindles away. In the epistles of the sportive knight we get an inkling as to the license in speech and manners of the boon companions of the king. A rueful remark of his after the battle of Barnet shows us what men of the world inferred from the recent course of events as to the divine government in general : it seemed to them sheer caprice : "God hath showed himself marvellously like Him that made all and can undo again when him list, — and I can think that by all likelihood shall know Himself as marvellous again and that in short time." The fact that Sir John had turned Lancastrian after Edward's flight the year before gives point to the sentiment. In her correspondence extending over forty years his mother, Margaret Paston, sustains the reputation of her sex in the art of letter-writing ; he furnishes the high-lights, the glimpses of a courtier's life, — she puts in the shadows, and some of them are black indeed, — the vexations, difficulties, and dangers of a country gentlewoman's life in the epoch of the Wars of the Roses. We commiserate her anxieties, — the constant hard times, the difficulty of getting in the rents, the neighborly quarrels, the general insecurity; we shudder at deeds of violence committed on property and person, at mention of the thieves that prowl by the highways, at fearful visitations of the plague. Looking through these letters and the documents found among them we can see the cottages of the peasantry in a wretched state of disrepair: well for the poor people if they can get rushes from the lord's marsh and windfallen sticks from his trees to mend them with ! — and little wonder that in these forlorn haunts, living on unwholesome and often scanty food, they suffer from fevers, scurvy, and leprosy. Up at the hall if it be late autumn we can see them laying in the winter's supply of beef; can watch the swing of the butcher's axe, the liberal use of the salt-bushel, and see the salting-tubs and barrels

ranged in the larder; if it be late in the winter we note the
arrival of a horse-load of herring and some eels as a Lenten
supply.   Passing through the kitchen we mark the yawning
fireplace well-furnished with its "great brass pot," caldron,
spits, flesh-hook, pot-hook, and other utensils, mortars and
pestles both brass and stone; and in the buttery may inspect
the gallon bottles, leather pots, wooden trenchers, pewter
basins, ewers, and candlesticks, the silver spoons and dishes,
some chased and bordered with gilt, the precious pottlers
enameled with violets and daisies, the salt-cellar "like a bas-
tille" gilt with roses.   The living rooms seem to our eyes
scantily furnished; save for the formidable array of armor and
weapons at its upper end — bassinets, gauntlets, cuirasses,
cuishes and greaves, cross-bows, spear-heads, swords and
guns — used moreover not long since to protect the manor from
assault, — the great hall has nothing in it but a long table,
some chairs or benches, and a pair of andirons, tongs and fire
shovel.   The walls are lined with arras and pieces of tapestry
curiously embroidered : one has on it a hawking-scene, another
a group of archers shooting birds with cross-bows, another, a
lady harping by a castle, another, a savage with a child in his
arms, — these last being subjects drawn, no doubt, from old
romances.   The bed-rooms have one or two chairs each, a fire-
pan, tongs and bellows, — but the one piece of furniture is the
bed, with tester and curtains of linen or say (a necessary
defence against draughts), fine sheets, fustian blankets, silken
coverlets and down-pillows cased in green or purple silk or the
rare magnificence of red velvet.   Next we may inspect the
wardrobe — the splendid gown of cloth of gold, velvet and
woollen gowns purfled with fur, black and purple girdles "har-
nessed with silver," jackets of blue, russet, red and black velvet
and figured satin, damask, deep green, scarlet and purple
hoods and black and scarlet hose.   The wardrobe of a young
student of good family is as follows : a short musterdevelers

gown, — other short gowns, green and blue, the latter made out of a silk dress, — one of murrey silk made only a year ago and one of russet silk furred with beaver "was made this time two year." The walk of letters was not all of flowers to this youth; his mother or grandmother writes to ask if he is "doing his devoir in learning" and adds, "if he do not well nor will not amend pray [his tutor] that he will truly belash him: so did the last master and the best that ever he had at Cambridge."

Family relations were harsh and unlovely, bearing the impress of the feudal system: "homage" was rigorously exacted of the young as is indicated by the "lowly terms" of address to be met with in the Paston letters: a daughter begins a humble letter home with "Right worshipful and my most entirely beloved mother"; and Madame Paston writes with some asperity to Sir John because he has omitted a customary form: "I think ye set but little by my blessing; if ye did ye would have desired it in your writing to me." Children were felt to be troubles to be "bestowed" as early as possible; it was usual to send them to serve in families of distinction to be taught good manners; daughters were then disposed of to the first fair bidder or even offered — as time wore on — with a bonus, and if the heart of one revolted from a match arranged by her parents it was of no consequence — except perhaps a merciless beating. In one of her epistles Mistress Margaret urges her husband to look out a good marriage for his sister for his mother is fain to be delivered of her: let him inquire about widower Knyvet's livelihood. John Paston, a light-hearted, careless boy, was often in disgrace; we have a "lowly" letter of his to his displeased father and one from his mother on the same occasion pleading for him: "Vouchsafe to be his good father for I hope he is chastised." Erelong he ran away and joined Edward IV; his father was very angry and visited his indignation upon his mother: she writes, "I durst not let him know of the last letter that ye wrote me because he was so sore displeased with me at that time." More than a year passes and this cry is wrung from her: "I understand that ye will not that your son be taken into your house: for God's sake, sir, a pity on him, and at the reverence of God be ye his good father, and have a fatherly heart to him — and the blessed Trinity have you in His keeping." How pitiable this paternal anger seems, seen in the deep light of four hundred years!

Romances (among them Guy of Warwick, the Green Knight, and the Belle Dame sans Mercie), chronicles, and lives of saints formed the staple reading of the household. For pastimes they had, indoors, chess, cards, "playing at the tables," music (harp, lute, and song), "disguisings," —and the ladies had, of course, their embroidery; out of doors, they pursued the venerable amusements of hawking, hunting, and jousting. What a far-away, romantic sound has the following piece of news in one of the Paston letters! — it rings in the ear with a mournful music as out of an infinite past. "There is one come into England, a knight out of Spain, with a kerchief of pleasance iwrapped about his arm, — the which knight will run a course with a sharp spear for his sovereign lady's sake."

Having finished our progress through the hall we may next visit the chapel of the estate and admire its appointments — all the property of the lord of the manor, — the altar-cloth "with the Trinity in the midst," the silver-gilt crucifix, silver candlesticks, pyx and cruets, chalice and paten, and pax (a small plate with a raised crucifix on it to be passed round and kissed during mass), the antiphoners and missals with silver clasps, — the alb, tunicle, cope and other vestments. While we examine these we are aware that the lady of the manor has sunk on her knees before the altar and is rapidly running over her rosary of "chalcedony beads, gaudied with silver gilt." On a Sunday we might hear a sermon on Lydgate's text: "this world is but a thoroughfare and full of woe."

Last of all, and the closing scene of this old-world history, we are permitted to attend the funeral obsequies of the father of the family. We catch his parting sigh: " For the more hasty deliverance of my soul from the painful flames of the fire of Purgatory, let them faithfully deal my goods." We mix in the crowd of priests, friars, bell-ringers and torch-bearers — whose lights so fill the church with smoke during the dirge that the windows have afterward to be taken out to purify the air. We share the funeral baked meats, beef, mutton, pork and capons: there are also fish and eggs in abundance, barrels of beer, and a "roundlet of red wine." In the deserted church a solitary light is burning over the newly filled tomb, which will finally be closed by a memorial slab with a flat brass figure inlaid.

It is interesting to know that during the most prolific years of the Paston correspondence a similar revelation of home life in distant Florence was being made in winsome Italian by Alessandra degli Strozzi, in her letters to her exiled sons. All we need do to correct any exaggerated estimate we may have formed of the Paston letters as literary productions is to put the best of them side by side with hers : the English examples have the charm of perfect sincerity, of unconscious self-revelation, but only rare and accidental touches of any literary value ; Madam Strozzi's have also that indefinable charm, and her letter on the death of her youngest son is an exquisite production, rising a whole Apennine above the Paston lowland : it is a pure and perfect blend of tender human affection and divine faith.

The most eminent literary man of the Yorkist era was William Caxton, merchant, printer and translator. Because he produced no original work one is apt to overlook his claim to regard in the history of literature. The work he did was of great importance in his age ; he was its representative man of letters ; it was an age not of creative energy but of culture,

and he responded perfectly to its demands.   He was versed in
Latin and French and put his knowledge to account in multi-
farious translations ; and as he was guided in his choice by the
desires of his cultivated public the list of books he published
is a faithful register of the taste of his time.   Until his fiftieth
year he was known only as a man of affairs and a courtier : in
1465 he was made superintendent of the colony of English
merchants at Bruges, and he was employed by Edward IV to
negotiate a commercial treaty with the duke of Burgundy.   In
1471 he finished with the Duchess Margaret's encouragement,
his first translation, the " Recuyell [or collection] of the Histories of Troy."   The work was soon in such demand that
enough copies could not be supplied in manuscript and Caxton
was glad to put it into print some three years later.   By that
time he had finished his second piece of literary labor, a translation of a work belonging to the end of the thirteenth century
— " The Game and Play of the Chess Moralized " — in which
under the figure of the pieces of the game and their func-
tions — king and queen, knights, rooks, "alphins," and
pawns—the duties of various ranks in the social order are set
forth.   After this was printed he left Bruges and established
himself and his press at Westminster where he brought out in
1477 " The Dictes and Sayings of Philosophers " — the first
book printed in England.   The translating had been done by
the accomplished Anthony Woodville.   Henceforth until his
death fifteen years later Caxton kept the reading public supplied
at the rate of three or four publications a year.   The most
significant thing in his list of productions is an omission :
there is no Bible or portion of the Bible in the mother tongue
to be found in it.   A Latin psalter he did print, and the
" Hours " according to the use of Sarum.   Another striking
feature of his work is that beyond a version of Tully on Old
Age and Friendship it betrays hardly a trace of the revival of
interest in classic authors.   Some of it is distinctly practical

and didactic, as for example a French and English vocabulary for the use of travellers, a Governal of Health, and books of Courtesy and Good Manners. The popularity of Lydgate's minor works is attested by numerous publications ; and we find translations of Alain Chartier's letter on the vexations of court life, Christine de Pisan's Moral Proverbs and Feats of Arms and Chivalry, and one of those moral treatises belonging to their time, a Chevalier's advice to his daughters. Quite early in his career Caxton published an edition of the Canterbury Tales and followed it up with other of Chaucer's works, — his version of Boethius, Parlement of Fowls, and Troilus and Cressida. He also printed Gower's Confessio Amantis. Going further back in our history we find him selecting for translation and publication an English Chronicle, Reynard the Fox, the Golden Legend (lives of saints), Bonaventura's Mirror of the Life of Christ, — and finally touching the spring of the literature in Malory's great compilation, the Noble Histories of King Arthur and some of his Knights. The worthy old printer rounded his career appropriately with the sequel to the story of Troy, bringing out his translation of the French romance drawn from the Æneid ; in his conclusion he appeals to a rising literary light, "Master John Skelton, poet-laureate of Oxford," to amend the work where necessary.

From this review it appears that the result of Caxton's labors was to create a library of mediaeval literature for English readers. His work was to gather up the literary treasures of a closing cycle. That is the right way to envisage it, — as resulting in a real mediaeval encyclopaedia.

It is a fact worth noting that the writings of Edward IV's reign were almost without exception in prose, — and of that prose Sir Thomas Malory became by long practice the principal master: it attained its highest relative beauty in his Morte d'Arthur. Rhymed romances, however, were still so popular as to warrant the production of new ones; as an example of these and not from any inherent merit, — as an illustration also of the witchery of Geoffrey of Monmouth's legends, potent enough to convert many a fugitive tale into a satellite of the Arthurian system, — we may give an idea of "Sir Launfal," a version of a French original made by an otherwise unknown rhymer named Thomas Chester. Launfal was one of Arthur's knights. He disapproved of the king's marriage with the Irish princess Guinever; and at the wedding feast she marked her displeasure by bestowing gifts on all but him. He forsook the court forthwith and haunted the woods about Caerleon, until one day two lovely damsels came on him in his poverty and conducted him to the splendid pavilion of their mistress, the Lady Tryamour. She showed him peculiar favor, gave him a magic purse in which whenever he put his hand he should find a piece of gold, gave beside a charm against the dangers of the tourney, a steed named Blanchard, and a page to wait on him, — enjoining him at the same time never to speak of her in the presence of others. Thus equipped and attended he returned to Caerleon where he lived right royally for a while and was victorious in many jousts. His fame flew afar, and Sir Valentine, the champion of Lombardy, sent him a challenge. Launfal journeyed thither, defeated the haughty hero, killing him in the conflict, then slew his would-be avengers and returned to Arthur's capital in a blaze of glory. Guinever now made advances to him which he rejected scornfully and in his indignation forgot the due government of his tongue, declaring that his lady's ugliest maid was as fit to be queen as she. The furious woman went straight to the king and reported his insolence, adding a foul slander thereto. Meantime Sir Launfal feeling in his purse found no gold, saw his page spurring away on Blanchard, and bitterly repented his disobedience to his mistress's command. Summoned to Arthur's presence and bidden to produce his incomparable mistress he was in a desperate strait — when on a sudden ten beautiful maidens appeared, each fairer than the queen, and after them the dazzling Tryamour. She cleared the happy knight from Guinever's calumny and breathing on that wicked woman turned her blind; then rode away with her lover and her maids to the magic isle of Oleron. "Thus was Sir Launfal borne away to faëry and never seen more by mortal men."

The spell of Arthurian legend and the Sancgreal was laid with fresh power upon the England of Caxton's day. It is a significant fact that in Wales there had been in progress for fully a century a revival of song largely connected with Glendower's war of independence. Some time in the reign of Henry VI a voluminous and singularly dull rhymed version of the familiar story had been produced, destined speedily to be effaced, together with all previous versions, by Sir Thomas Malory's rendering, completed, as he tells us, in the ninth year of the reign of King Edward IV — that is, in 1469 or the winter of 1470. Though in prose this work, unlike the poem just mentioned, is anything but prosaic; it is in fact a prose-epic; into that mould was poured the aspiration of an age that would otherwise have found vent in poetry. Malory caught the naïve narrative manner and poetic charm of his French originals ; his concluding book especially — the Morte d'Arthur proper — has in both style and subject the true epic cadence. And so it came to pass that an enchanted wind of high and chivalric romance blew through those money-getting days of Edward IV, and the mystic light of the Grail silvered them, touching with exquisite refinement and spirituality an age in which the body was re-asserting itself imperiously and the senses were grossly indulged, — but that glamour could stir strange yearnings even in the sensual breast. And the old knight's prose-epic has remained one of the chief legacies that the Middle Ages have bequeathed to after-times: its theme universally known, itself more widely read and loved in the land of its birth than any other composition of those periods. It has been a great poetic factor, richly nourishing the imagination, awakening perennially the sense of wonder.

Those tales of the Round Table are the doubly distilled essence of the four centuries during which they were in process of elaboration; they are a compend of the ages of chivalry, feudalism, and Latin Catholicism, — the embodiment of what we call the mediaeval spirit, its sensuality and asceticism, its ferocity and loyalty, its superstition and spirituality. Their real hero, Sir Launcelot du Lake, is its consummate type, — and second only to him comes Sir Tristram de Lyoness. These rival champions form, with Arthur and Guinevere, Mark and Isoud respectively, two triads of souls deeply sinned against and sinning, in each triad an imperfect marriage, a love perfect and passionate yet guilty when it might have been holy, — such is the simple and tragic motive of the double action in this vast aggregation of romances. It may not be called immoral for not the representation but the justification of immorality is immoral and that is not suggested here. Upon the treatment of the theme our judgment must be based and then the tales of Tristram and Launcelot will be acquitted of any solicitation to illicit love ; a heavy sense of a law broken weighs upon the spirit of the actors, and in the suffering, penitence, and agony of the guilty ones, even to the rending asunder of soul and body, poetic justice is duly meted out. Many episodes in the working out of the plot cannot be thus acquitted save as they are truthful reflections of a moral lawlessness rife in those times, largely consequent upon enforced and unhappy marriages unworthy of the name. Beside, a frank submission to the demands of the senses was undoubtedly a latent characteristic of the Middle Ages, often erroneously supposed to be peculiar to the Renascence, — a fact that should be sufficient warning to those who seek to make rigid separation between those periods, ruling any touch of Renascent life out of its legitimate connection with mediaeval history. The most vehement expression of this riot in the blood is an incident in Tristram's career, when a fresh wound, bleeding freely, cannot assuage his raging lust.

The ferocity, the lust of fighting of those knightly ages is expressed in what are perhaps the most tedious passages in the volume — descriptions of battles in which knights "hurtle like wild boars," one smiting down one and another another in wearisome repetition until the ground is covered with blood.

A propensity to magic runs through the whole romance as was inevitable in an age that practised it and explained everything beyond common experience as the result of magical influence. The prominent parts played by the wizard Merlin and Arthur's witch-sister, Morgan le Fay, come instantly to mind : in a highly imaginative passage the Fay, being pursued and nearly overtaken, turns herself and her steed into a great marble stone. Other enchantresses are Dame Brisen and the Lady of the Lake. The diabolical mantle that the unnatural Fay sends her brother the king, his sword Excalibur and other enchanted or fated brands, suggest a strain of Saracenic magic imported at the time of the Crusades. Violent love and hatred are the result of witchcraft, as in the case of Sir Pelleas and the lady Ettarde, practised upon by the sorceress of the lake; a classic example is the philtre shared by Tristram and Isoud, "whose love never departed after for weal or woe." Works of art are a product of subtle craft, as the twelve gilded statues of kings that Merlin made with the figure of King Arthur above them all, his drawn sword in his hand. The sovereign enchantment is that of the blessed Grail, which heals deep wounds, dispels madness, and spreads the board with delicate viands.

The landscape through which the knights course on their quest is solemn, grand, and vague, as befits the breadth and mystery of the action; there are no touches of minute observation, but the large, primitive elements of natural scenery are ever present — mountain and valley, lake and river, wood and sea; almost always an old chapel, abbey, or castle may somewhere be discerned, and the May sun or the moonlight of romance irradiates the scene.

Of the crowning glory of nature — the human form — a fine appreciation is displayed that only needed a little quickening to turn into the passionate admiration felt by the artists of the Italian Renascence.   Thus Sir Galahad's beauty moved all who saw him (and whoever would behold his semblance, an ideal knight " without villany or treachery," may go to Florence and in the St. George of Donatello see it immortalized in stone). A unique touch occurs in the romance of Tristram, where the king, riding in the forest, discovers a " fair naked man " sleeping by a spring, his sword lying on the grass beside him, — it is his nephew, Sir Tristram, who has gone distracted through suspicion that Isoud is deceiving him.   The suggestion of shining water, the gleam of steel on the soft green grass, the tint of flesh, and the figure of the king on horseback, pushing through the boughs of the forest, — these few simple elements make up a picture of rare beauty.   Enjoying this perception of the beauty of the nude male form — without which the highest art can never be — it is somewhat remarkable that that generation gave birth to no fine painting or sculpture; the absence of these indicates a conspicuous defect in the English genius.   The final gorgeous efflorescence of English Gothic architecture was indeed then preparing : in this the artistic impulse of the time found satisfaction.   It was certainly nourished by Malory's narrative, which constantly blossoms out into passages of high pictorial value that make it in truth a mine for artists.

A few extracts will help to illustrate what has been said and will afford a taste of the enchantment of the tale.

" So they rode till they came to a lake the which was a fair water and broad. And in the midst of the lake Arthur was ware of an arm clothed in white samite that held a fair sword in the hand. ' Lo,' said Merlin, ' yonder is the sword that I spake of.' With that they saw a damsel going upon the lake. ' What damsel is that?' said the king. ' That is the Lady of the Lake,' said Merlin, ' and within that lake is a rock and therein is as fair a place as any on earth and richly beseen; and this damsel will come to you anon and then speak ye fair to her that she will give you that sword.' " . . .

" Right so there came by the holy vessel of the Sancgreal with all manner of sweetness and savor but they could not readily see who bare that vessel. But Sir Percivale had a glimmering of the vessel and of the maiden that bare it, for he was a perfect clean maiden. And forthwithal they both were as whole of hide and limb as ever they were in their life days." . . .

" And then the king and all estates went home unto Camelot and so went to evensong to the great minster, and after that to supper, and every knight sat in his own place as they were toforehand. Then anon they heard cracking and crying of thunder that hem thought the place should all to drive. In the midst of this blast entered a sunbeam more clearer by seven times than ever they saw day and all they were alighted by the grace of the Holy Ghost. Then began every knight to behold other and either saw other by their seeming fairer than ever they saw afore. Not for then there was no knight might speak one word a great while and so they looked every man on another as they had been dumb. Then there entered into the hall the Holy Grail covered with white samite, but there was none might see it nor who bare it; and there was all the hall fulfilled with good odors and every knight had such meats and drinks as he best loved in this world. And when the Holy Grail had been borne through the hall then the holy vessel departed suddenly that they wist not where it became. Then had they all breath to speak and then the king yielded thankings to God of his good grace that he had sent them. ' Certes,' said the king, ' we ought to thank our Lord Jesu greatly for that he hath showed us this day at the reverence of this high feast of Pentecost.' " . . .

" And at the last he came to a stony cross which departed two ways in waste land ; and by the cross was a stone that was of marble but it was so dark that Sir Launcelot might not weet what it was. Then Sir Launcelot looked by him and saw an old chapel and there he weened to have found people. And Sir Launcelot tied his horse to a tree and there he did off his shield and hung it upon a tree and then went to the chapel door and found it waste and broken. And within he found a fair altar full richly arrayed with cloth of clean silk and there stood a fair candlestick which bare six great candles, and the candlestick was of silver. And when Sir Launcelot saw this light he had great will for to enter into the chapel but he could find no place where he might enter ; then was he passing heavy and dismayed. Then he returned and came to his horse and did off his saddle and bridle and let him pasture ; and unlaced his helm and ungirded his sword and laid him down to sleep upon his shield before the cross." . . .

" ' But my time hieth fast,' said the king unto Sir Bedivere ; ' take thou Excalibur my good sword and go with it to yonder water side and when thou comest there I charge thee throw my sword in that water ' . . . So Sir Bedivere departed and by the way he beheld that noble sword that the pommel and the haft was all of precious stones and then he said to himself, ' if I throw this rich sword in the water thereof shall never come good but harm and loss.' And then Sir Bedivere hid Excalibur under a tree ; and as soon as he might he came again unto the king and said he had been at the water and had thrown the sword in. ' What saw thou there?' said the king . . . ' Sir ' he said, ' I saw nothing but the waters wap and waves wan.' ' Ah, traitor untrue !' said King Arthur : ' But now go again lightly for thy long tarrying putteth me in great jeopardy of my life. For I have taken cold, and but if thou do now as I bid thee if ever I may see thee I shall slay thee with mine own hands, for thou wouldest for my rich sword see me dead.' Then Sir Bedivere departed and went to the sword and lightly took it up and went to the water side ; and there he bound the girdle about the hilts and then he threw the sword as far into the water as he might, and there came an arm and a hand above the water and met it and caught it and so shook it thrice and brandished, and then vanished away the hand with the sword in the water. So Sir Bedivere came again to the king and told him what he saw. ' Alas ' said the king, ' help me hence for I dread me I have tarried over long.' Then Sir Bedivere took the king upon his back and so went with him to that water side ; and fast by the bank hovered a little barge with many fair ladies in it, and among them all was a queen, and all they had black hoods, and they wept and shrieked when they saw King Arthur.

'Now put me in the barge,' said the king, and so he did softly. And there received him three queens with great mourning and so they set him down, and in one of their laps King Arthur laid his head ; and then that queen said, 'Ah, dear brother, why have ye tarried so long ?' And so then they rowed from the land. Then Sir Bedivere cried, 'Ah, my lord Arthur, what shall become of me now ye go from me and leave me here alone among mine enemies?' 'Comfort thyself' said the king, 'and do as well as thou mayest for in me is no trust for to trust in. For I will into the vale of Avilion to heal me of my grievous wound.'"

With such dirgelike music the Morte d'Arthur draws to its close, and not there only, but through the whole complex of romances as well may be heard a like æolian strain, swelling and dying away and rising again with the wind of inspiration.

For poetry of form as well as substance we must cross the northern border, for such was produced in this era by one man only in Britain and he a subject of James III. Robert Henryson, schoolmaster at Dunfermline, in his bright and picturesque Scotch verse both openly confesses and unconsciously reveals the sway that Chaucer's genius exerted over him ; he was though no servile follower: he linked his work to the master's by writing a "Testament of Cresseid," intended as a supplement to Chaucer's "Troylus," but in the act gave evidence of his independence of spirit, for in his sequel he proposed to correct what he deemed amiss in the moral of his original by inflicting upon Cressida a fit punishment for her faithlessness. His "Robyne and Makyne," a comic pastoral, is the first of its class in British poetry. Makyne, a lovelorn country lass, has long teased with her affection the insensible Robyne ; just as she, weary of his hardness of heart, is beginning to catch his spirit of indifference he begins to relent and erelong grows ardent — but she is now heart-whole and cold ; the moral is, " He that will not when he may, when he will shall have a nay." But it is by his clever fables, thirteen in number, that Henryson is best remembered ; the demand for such reading was general in his day, — Caxton printed a version of the fables of Æsop. Two of Henryson's — " The Dog, Sheep, and Wolf," and " The Wolf and Lamb " — are palpable hits at the rich and powerful for their oppression of the poor people, the commons.   For his " Chaunticleir and Fox " Henryson was indebted to the Canterbury Tale told by the nun's priest.   His beautiful prologue to the fable of the Lion and Mouse is an excellent example of his descriptive powers : his delicate observation of nature supplies a notorious want in contemporary English literature, — indeed, he is often startlingly modern in his sensitiveness to external impressions.

During the reign of James III a prolix narrative poem on the national hero, William Wallace, was produced by a Scottish minstrel popularly known as Blind Harry. This effort was suggested, doubtless, by the success achieved by Barbour's " Bruce," — to which it serves as an introduction.   It is inspired by a bitter hatred of the English.

In the time of Edward IV, apparently, the old mystery-plays were matured into the form in which we now possess them. Among the Wakefield or Towneley mysteries are two lively pictures of rustic manners — the " Cain," and the Second Play of the Shepherds. Cain is naïvely represented as an English boor of the fifteenth century; he is a burly brute, lustful, greedy, irascible, envious — an incarnation of all the deadly sins : a full-blooded " Iniquity" as compared with that old abstraction, the Vice of the moral plays.

Chaucer's canon's yeoman's tale may be read as an introduction to this age which was infected fully as much as his with a rage for alchemical pursuits. To the first half of

Edward's reign belongs an imposture called "The Book of Quint-Essence " — a panegyric on that purest of substances, the "Water of Life," incorruptible, and imparting incorruptibility, able to restore old feeble men to the strength of youth : a walnut-shell full of it is a panacea for every ill. To make it, "distil one thousand times," etc., etc. George Ripley, a Carmelite friar, was a celebrated alchemist ; he dedicated his rhymed "Compound of Alchemy " to the king. Incited by his success, another of these philosophers named Thomas Norton produced an "Ordinal of the Chemical Art," also in verse, which he presented in 1477 to Archbishop Neville, his patron — brother to the fallen Warwick. Roger Bacon was Norton's paragon, — a fact that we may record as one among many indications of a certain sympathy between this age and that of Edward I.

A cursory view of the condition of the mainland of Europe at the end of the century reveals an extraordinary development of the principle of centralized government so forcibly expounded by Louis XI. Nowhere is this more striking than in the Spanish peninsula, where political affairs had long been in a state of distraction amounting almost to anarchy. Now, under the resolute control of Ferdinand and Isabella, the Hermandad, or league of towns for mutual defence, was developed into an effective police for the whole kingdom ; the nobility even was subjected to its jurisdiction ; and crime and disorder were repressed. Justice was everywhere unflinchingly administered and a revision of the Castilian law-code was taken in hand. Not less remarkable were the financial and economic reforms, — by which the state of the coinage was improved, and the royal revenues were largely augmented, — and the industrial awakening, extraordinary for Spain, that ensued upon the restoration of credit : trade and agriculture revived, and the roads — now freed from robbers — were put in better condition.

A step symbolical of the changed relations of the feudal

aristocracy and the new monarchy was taken in the year 1476, when at the death of Rodrigo Manrique, grandmaster of the famous order of Knights of Santiago, Ferdinand assumed the headship. The incorporation of the masterships of the other military orders with the crown followed in due course and was erelong made perpetual by a papal provision.

Manrique's death was the occasion of one of the noblest poems in Spanish literature — the sonorous "Coplas" or stanzas of his son Don Jorge, a young hero who died on the field of battle three years later. Beginning with some solemn reflections on death's universal empire over the race, the relentless sweep of time, and the transiency of this world's pleasure and glory, the monody passes to a few particular instances of the power of death and change drawn, in a manner that reminds us of one of Villon's ballads, from recent Spanish history, and concludes with a tribute of filial love and pride to the memory of Don Rodrigo, a typical Castilian cavalier, brave and devout. Solemn as the poem is it is yet nowhere gloomy for it is relieved by a perfect faith in a brighter and an enduring world.

In 1492 the protracted war of conquest waged against the Moors of Granada to which Spanish zeal gave the character of a last Crusade and which afforded an opportunity for a final glorious display of mediaeval chivalry was brought to a conclusion and made amends in some measure for the losses that Christendom had lately sustained at the other end of the Mediterranean. Later in the same year the discoveries of Columbus gave to Castile and Leon a new world.

At this period the dramatic pieces of Juan de la Enzina were being performed, — an edition of them was published in 1496. They are remarkable for the light they throw upon the process of transition from the ancient mysteries to the comedy of real life. In 1499 was published a clever play called "Celestina" from the tricky woman who is the leading character; it was written by a law-student at Salamanca named Rojas.

Beside the creation of these new forms in the drama active work was done in translating popular romances. It is interesting to note that about the same time with Malory Spanish translators were busy with French versions of Arthurian fiction : a Spanish "Merlin" and "Artus" appeared in print at the turn of the century. Then, too, was completed a translation of the Portuguese fiction, "Amadis of Gaul," and bulky as it was it proved so fascinating that numberless additions were grafted upon it.

Feudalism was annihilated in Portugal and the monarchy made absolute by John II, who reigned from 1481 to 1495. Louis XI was his model. Like Ferdinand and Isabella he made use of the representatives of the people in his contest with the feudal nobility and when his end was gained calmly dispensed with their services and stood alone and supreme. The first year of his reign he struck severe blows at the power of the great nobles by setting on foot an inquiry into their titles to their estates and by ordering the suppression of their courts of justice. The duke of Braganza, the proudest of them all, — for nearly a third part of Portugal was in his fee, — led the way in opposing these measures : he was summarily arrested, tried, and put to death in the year 1483. A relative of his, the duke of Viseu, stepped into his place, — and was stabbed to the heart by the king's own hand the year following; a hecatomb of his confederates was then sacrificed and the ruthless work was done. The king could now turn his attention to cannon-founding, ship-building and the progress of his mariners along the African coast, and to the encouragement of the study of classic literature.

The policy of Louis XI was carried to its triumphant consummation when Brittany, the last feudal area in France, was annexed to the crown by the marriage of his son Charles VIII to its Duchess Anne in the year 1491. The French power thus consolidated was now the most formidable in Europe, but a rival speedily appeared in Spain, aggrandized by the conquest of Granada : the two powerful states began to try conclusions with each other and the theatre of war was hapless, divided Italy. Imperial prerogatives were endangered by French aggression there and Maximilian of Austria, emperor-elect, was hence involved in the struggle. At the same time united England under the strong government of her Tudor kings was ready to begin her rôle in the new political system of Europe. A novel aspect was thus given to the face of Christendom: the great powers, united within, began to direct their energies outward, came into manifold relations with each other, formed league after league, now for the partition of Italy, now to counterpoise an overgrown and threatening power : the history of the next twenty-five years is one of incessant, confusing, kaleidoscopic changes.

In 1494 the ambitious young king Charles VIII, his head full of fantastic ideas of conquest, descended upon Italy to enforce his claim to the sovereignty of Naples. His course was like a triumphal progress and excited such apprehensions that Milan, Venice and the pope, Spain and Austria formed a confederacy to cut off his retreat. Charles had to leave Naples in haste and fight a battle against great odds in order to save himself; his conquest was transient but the impression it made sufficiently long-lasting ; one consequence of it was that the French carried home with them fruit of the Renascence.

In 1496 took place a profoundly important union, the complement of the famous marriages formerly noticed, that of Philip, son of Maximilian and Mary of Burgundy, and Joanna, daughter, and eventually heiress, of Ferdinand and Isabella. In the last year of the century there was born to the young pair a son upon whose head were to be heaped coronets and crowns.

At this epoch Louis XII, who had just succeeded his young cousin Charles upon the throne of France, bringing to it a decidedly questionable claim to the duchy of Milan, made an easy conquest of that rich province and then entered into a nefarious alliance with Ferdinand of Aragon for the partition of Naples. The kingdom was speedily overrun by their armies but in the division of the spoils the allies quarreled; the French were defeated in several desperate engagements and their forces wasted by disease; and at the end of the year 1503 the perfidious Ferdinand remained in sole possession. Untaught by this reverse, Louis immediately, and it must be said wantonly, projected with Maximilian a partition of the territories of the republic of Venice. Thus was formed the league of Cambrai, to which the pope and the minor princes of Italy acceded, and in a short campaign in the spring of 1509 the republic was despoiled of its possessions on the mainland. From this sorry triumph, however, Louis reaped no advantage, for the pope — the belligerent Julius II — suddenly veered round and negotiated with Spain, England, Venice and the Swiss the Holy League for the purpose of driving the French out of Italy — an end that was soon successfully accomplished.

An astonishing figure dominated Florence in the last decade of the fifteenth century — the last and greatest of that line of preachers of repentance the origin of which we have seen — the eager Dominican friar, Girolamo Savonarola; an extraordinary apparition like a Hebrew prophet of old rising in the midst of renascent Italy to convict her cultured ones of sin and startle them to contrition, to cast a lurid light upon the vices of a great city, to denounce the skepticism and immorality that were infecting the literature and art of the Renascence, to proclaim the necessity of a reformation in the church, and to establish a momentary theocracy under which gay Florence grown devout took Jesus for her king. In other lands as well eloquent preachers arose to inculcate righteousness and call the people back to a spiritual religion — and the attentive crowds that assembled to hear them showed that they satisfied a widely felt need. The Breton-born Franciscan brother, Olivier Maillard, whose life overlapped Savonarola's by some years, preached in many parts of France and in Flanders, exhorting to holiness of life, rebuking the sins of every class, sparing not those in highest place : his sermons lacked the intense glow of the great Dominican's but he was an earnest and persuasive preacher in the allegorical style then in vogue and his exceedingly direct and familiar address to his congregations, the satirical touches, anecdotes, and scraps of verse with which his discourse was enlivened, his frequent improprieties in matter and manner, simply enhanced his popularity. Another eloquent Franciscan, Michel Menot, a slightly younger contemporary of his, far outdid Maillard in these homiletical extravagances, — examples of which were afforded in German literature by the sermons of Geiler of Strassburg, in which we find the same true piety and zeal to do good with a like quaintness of illustration, allegory, amusing and satirical anecdote. An instance of Geiler's appeal to the public taste is the fact that he drew texts for a number of sermons from Sebastian Brandt's " Ship of Fools " — an extremely popular and not ungenial satire that issued from the press of Basel in 1494.

Two versions of that Leviathan of fables, " Reynard the Fox," demand notice, one in Dutch prose — the one that Caxton used, — the other in Low German verse based upon the first. That mordant satire upon all lofty pretensions, with its ridicule of royal authority, personated by King Lion, its mockery of religious profession by the Fox's sanctimony, manifests the sharp, quite disenchanted vision of the common folk. Denying with a grin all that is knightly, romantic, ideal, and spiritual, it is to the Morte d'Arthur as nadir to zenith, — but both must be attentively perused by any who would apprehend the Middle Ages in their entirety. The Morte d'Arthur was bandied back and forth between England and France, Reynard, between the Netherlands, France and Germany; and it may be doubted whether any other two productions can give one as clear a notion of the spirit of those times.

Of the many German artists of that day we may mention one of the most eminent, Peter Vischer of Nuremberg, because of his conception of King Arthur presented in bronze at Innsbruck. It is a noble figure and the helmeted face, especially as seen in profile, is severely beautiful. Vischer's work otherwise deserves our attention as indicative of the transition from Gothic to Renascent art.

During the fifteenth and first quarter of the sixteenth century, while Denmark was exercising an hegemony over the other Scandinavian states, final transcriptions of almost all of her old ballads were being made. Through the veil of the language of this later age it is not difficult to see how these interesting little poems can be arranged in groups corresponding to the grand divisions of European literature in the centuries we have traversed. Thus some of them are based on legends of saints; one remarkable ballad pictures the soul of a rich man just dead as seated on the body's breast bewailing and accusing it: others are poems of tender sentiment, the supreme type of these being the beautiful and pathetic tale of the loves of Axel and Walborg; others again are humorous, among them a delicious parody of the turgid style of the romances of chivalry, quite in the spirit of Chaucer's Sir Thopas or Pulci's Morgante.

The fall of Richard III on Bosworth field in 1485 and the elevation of his rival to the throne as Henry VII put an end to the Wars of the Roses; thereby was effected indeed a profound dynastic change but no real revolution. The policy of the new king was a continuation of that of Edward IV whose daughter he married. He projected a war with France and got subsidies for it from parliament which, according to a precedent set by Edward, he reinforced by "benevolences" or loans exacted from wealthy subjects — and then sold peace at a high price to the French king, making heavy profits on all sides by the transaction. He promoted commerce, making treaties with Florence, the Scandinavian countries and Riga. He provided John and Sebastian Cabot with ships for their voyage over the western ocean; and in June, 1497, they discovered the North American continent in the neighborhood of Newfoundland.

The key to Henry's character and system of government is a simple one, — avarice. Studying the vicissitudes of the past generation he perceived that Henry VI was poor and unfortunate, his successor rich and fortunate, — and he inferred a causal connection between those terms. So he decided that to ensure his dynasty and the nation against a return of those disorders the one thing needful was money, and he cast about to accumulate it in a manner that suggests that the task was congenial to his nature. His policy of repressing the great lords chimed with it; parliament had passed a statute reducing their large retinues to safer limits and the king was keen in discovering through his agents any breach of the law and inexorable in exacting the penalty. Ingenious instruments of his rapacity were found in the lawyers Dudley and Empson; and no device by which sums of money could be extorted and which could bear a semblance of legality was left untried by them. These exactions were popularly represented by the dilemma known as "Morton's fork" from the king's minister, Cardinal Morton: it was said that none could escape being impaled upon one or the other of its horns, for if he lived splendidly he was asked to give the king of his superfluity, if economically, to contribute of his savings. By these various artifices, by a pacific policy that traded upon the expectation of war, by the device of benevolences, by fines and forfeitures and by a rigid parsimony, Henry managed to amass an enormous treasure and to keep himself quite independent of parliament. He is to be reckoned among the astute sovereigns of that day.

The ridiculous pretensions of Simnel and Warbeck and the measure of credit they gained are curious examples of popular credulity, the unsettled state of men's minds and the prevalency of plots and imposture in that period. Warbeck's attempt had at least one substantial result, for under color of repelling the Scottish king's invasion in his behalf Henry wrung fresh subsidies from parliament. The utter failure of the plot revealed beside to foreign powers how firmly the king was seated on his throne, and he was now able to negotiate brilliant matches for his children, of unforeseen consequence. In 1501 he married his son Arthur — a name that yields historical evidence of the power of romance — to the princess Catherine, younger daughter of Ferdinand and Isabella. The frail young prince died in the following spring but the king provided a substitute for him in his second son, Henry, then in his twelfth year, — for otherwise the princess would have had to return to Spain and with her her precious dowry. Soon after Henry gave his eldest daughter Margaret in marriage to the king of Scots, James IV, and thus secured peace on his northern frontier.

We have seen how exquisitely the changing sentiment of ages is registered in architecture; fresh and striking illustrations of this law now confront us. The principal monument of Edward IV's time is the beautiful church of St. Mary Redcliffe at Bristol — one of the finest churches in England not a cathedral, — a peculiarly attractive specimen of the perpendicular style. But the crowning artistic glory of Henry VII's reign and of the age is the vaulting known as fan-tracery, superbly exhibited in the three royal chapels of Windsor, Cambridge, and Westminster. In the system of fan-vaulting each section is in idea a half of a spreading cone up the surface of which

splay numerous ribs all of the same length and same curve, like
the fingers of a bent fan.   The concave-sided lozenges left in
the roof between the crowns of the vaulting segments are filled
with elaborate tracery or droop in pendants.   The effect of the
whole, especially as seen in St. George's chapel, Windsor, is
rich, elegant and buoyant.   The inception of the new style
has been thought to belong to the last years of Edward's reign ;
thus the Divinity school at Oxford is referred to the year 1480
— but it is roofed in the manner of the next century.   Both
St. George's chapel and that of King's college, Cambridge,
were begun by 1479; it was left for Henry VII and his son
to finish them; and so we have an architectural parallel to
what was said above regarding Henry's policy: he built upon
the foundations Edward laid.   The nave of St. George's was
vaulted in 1490, its choir in 1507.   A pleasing specimen of the
style is the "new building" at the eastern extremity of Peterborough minster, begun as a receptacle for relics quite early in
the century but not completed until this and the following
reign.   Bath Abbey is another example.   To the year 1502
belongs the tiny chantry of the lamented Prince Arthur at
Worcester; and then his father's sumptuous mortuary chapel at
Westminster was begun.   Here, arching ribs spring from the
wall free for a space, pushing forward and piercing complete
and highly decorated cones.   They resemble arms holding
torches and with the whirling flounces of tracery, the astonishing pendants in the middle seeming to rest on air, exert a
truly bewildering effect.   It is the very flamboyancy of vaulting,
the dolphin-death of Gothic architecture.

Considerable progress was made in the revival of classical
learning during the reign of Henry VII.   Thomas Linacre, a
fellow of All Souls', Oxford, went to Bologna in 1485 to perfect himself in Greek as an aid to advanced medical study
and putting by the mediaeval versions of their works read
Aristotle and Galen in the original.   He visited Florence

(where he met Poliziano), Rome, Venice and Padua. William Grocyn, a fellow of New College, learned Greek of an Italian resident at Oxford; in 1488 he went to Florence and spent two years in Italy studying. He was followed by one Latimer in 1489; and both returned to Oxford to teach what they had learned in the favored haunts of classicism.

John Colet was born in London in 1466. In 1483 he entered Magdalen College; there he studied Greek and read the works of Plato. After ten years he visited Italy and herein the wide difference between him and the scholars just mentioned appears: they returned thence polished humanists, — he returned with something more than learning — with religious convictions greatly deepened and a grave sense of the necessity of a reform in the faith and morals of the clergy.

It has been suggested with a large measure of probability that he owed to Savonarola this deepening of his religious consciousness; it is certain that he was in Florence during the great preacher's supremacy, — and a soul like Colet's could not fail to be moved by that impassioned eloquence. In 1497 we find him back at Oxford imbued with the teaching of St. Paul, delivering lectures on his epistle to the Romans, not in the jejune style of the scholastic scribes with their endless patristic references, but fresh, helpful, rich in suggestion, vibrating with the note of personal experience. The hall was crowded whenever he lectured; it was felt that a new spiritual force was manifesting itself at the University.

A disciple and friend of Colet was the young Thomas More, son of a justice of the court of King's Bench. He had served as a lad in the household of Archbishop Morton (afterward Cardinal), and was distinguished even then by his intelligence and uprightness of character. In 1492, at the age of fourteen years, he was entered at Oxford: in 1496 at Lincoln's Inn. When he was about twenty years old he underwent a severe religious experience and sought peace through the ascetic discipline still in vogue among earnest souls: he wore a harsh shirt of hair next his skin, scourged himself, and slept on the bare floor. While in this mood he made the acquaintance of Erasmus, then on his first visit to England, who, though eleven years his senior, felt an instant attraction to the young Englishman and the two became fast friends. The great scholar exerted a wholesome influence, without doubt, upon More's sensitive nature, helping him gently out of the thorny thicket of his spiritual anxieties into the flowery path of letters again. Erasmus moreover now ripened into intimacy an acquaintance he had formed with Colet upon the continent some time before. It is a charming group, an intercourse delightful to think upon, that of these three scholars and sympathetic, ardent souls — especially in an epoch otherwise singularly barren in literary attraction. More became the fairest type of an English humanist. It is a pity that he and Colet did not trust more than they did the capacity of expression of their native language : had they done so their fame — and Colet's in particular — would now be greatly enhanced.

Kay's successor as poet-laureate royal was Bernard André, a scholar from the south of France. About the middle of Henry's reign he composed a panegyric in French verse, "The Twelve Triumphs of Henry the Seventh," in which that monarch and his brave exploits were compared with Hercules and his labors. About that time, too, the slender ranks of English humanists received an accession in the person of Polydore Vergil, a native of Urbino, who, having been despatched to England by Pope Alexander VI to levy Peter's-pence found his situation there so agreeable that he decided to remain and was erelong rewarded by preferment in the church.

A native scholar of considerable celebrity was John Skelton, to whom, it will be remembered, Caxton looked up and whom even Erasmus extolled. According to a custom of the time he had received the degree of poet-laureate from the University of Oxford for his skill in Latin versification. In a rhyme of some length, pleasing in spots, entitled "The Garland of Laurel," and addressed to some ladies who had worked a wreath, the insignia of his rank, upon his court gown, he vindicates his title to the poet's crown, adducing a number of his poems. The king was his patron: he was appointed tutor to Prince Henry and had the honor of producing a "morality," since lost, before his majesty and the court at Woodstock. When he had reached middle age he took orders and was presented with a living in Norfolk; his biographers seem to suppose that at this time his character underwent a sudden change and that from a scholar he became the coarsely abusive satirist that his name now first suggests. But in his earliest known effort, a dirge for Edward IV, we find the moralizing tone, the note of disenchantment, of disgust with the world, that proclaims the embryo satirist; and if we had his poems in chronological order they would no doubt reveal that his temper grew more savage as the character of the times became plainer. In the piece just referred to he quotes St. Bernard to the effect that "a man is but a sack of stercory and shall return to worm's meat," — and upon that hideous text great part of his production hangs. Skelton had a morbid sense of the loathsomeness of physical decay, disease and death ; in a repulsive poem he held up a grinning death's head to the age as a picture of the end of all its strength and splendor. An oft-printed piece of his, "The Tunning of Elinor Rumming," is a superlative example of nauseous realism.

The testimony of Alexander Barclay, translator of Brandt's "Ship of Fools," is that the England of his day was given over to "Lewdness and Folly." Brandt's famous satire had by this time been translated into several languages. Its conception was furnished by the chariot shaped like a ship and peopled by droll figures, the "naval car" that is believed to have given its name to the carnival, at which it used to be a principal show, being dragged along in procession. Brandt fancied its passengers and crew to be representatives of over a hundred classes of fools; his motive was to expose the myriad deviations from common sense that make men ridiculous. Barclay's free English version with alterations was produced in 1508 and printed the following year. He explains that its title might have been " The Satire, or Reprehension of Foolishness." The book was illustrated with quaint German wood-cuts, among them two representations of that antique machine, long a poetic property, — the wheel of Fortune. Amid the crowd of fools we note the bibliophile, the superannuated man of fashion, the young man who has married an old woman for her money, the petulant woman, the fat-witted person who cannot understand a joke, the boaster, the gambler, and some choice specimens of the fool in orders — the ignorant priest, the covetous bishop.

In marked contrast to these specimens of satire indicative, whether coarse or dull, of some deep-seated disorder in the social framework — a schism fast becoming too grave to be borne between what was and what ought to have been — is the placid rehabilitation of mediaeval ideals in Stephen Hawes' " Pastime of Pleasure." To an Oxford education Hawes added the polish of travel in his own country and in France. He was something of a linguist and was especially conversant with French. He was a student of literature, a critic even after his kind: thus he would draw comparisons between Chaucer and Lydgate, magnifying the excellences of the latter bard. Lydgate he adopted as his master, his patron saint in letters; for his memory he showed an extraordinary veneration and affection. In paying his tribute of respect to the three lords of English song he despatches Chaucer and Gower in three stanzas while he devotes ten to Lydgate. Here we have the unmistakable sign-manual of the literary dilettante, of one who would establish an esoteric cult in poetry by reversing the popular, the vulgar estimate, who seeks distinction by an amiable eccentricity of judgment, an affectation of special insight. Hawes was in fact the representative man of letters of the reign, the exponent of its culture; he was its product, for he was yet young when towards its close he composed his principal work. He was an ornament of the court, being in great request for his talents in composition, conversation and recitation from the elder poets — for he had a capacious memory. The king made him his Groom of the Chamber.

"The Pastime of Pleasure" was produced in 1505–1506 and printed in 1509. Although the author, in accordance with a long-standing fashion, prays to Venus for success in love and to Mars for the meed of enduring fame, and though this desire of fame is felt to be a potent motive in its composition, the poem is yet essentially mediaeval in general design and detail. Its groundwork is that of the romances of chivalry: it is the quest of a knight, Grand Amour, toward union with the feminine ideal, La Belle Pucelle. It is allegorical in intention as these titles indicate and exceedingly didactic — mediaeval characteristics both. Its characters are those of a "morality": thus Grand Amour in his quest encounters an ugly dwarf, False Report, slays the three-headed giant Falsehood, and is instructed by Counsel. In its execution it develops into a little cyclopaedia of mediaeval culture, for the typical knight must be a master of all the sciences: Grand Amour is bidden by Doctrine to perfect himself in the studies of the trivium — grammar, logic, and rhetoric, — and of the quadrivium, — arithmetic, music, geometry and astronomy. His course in the school of Rhetoric occasions quite an interesting analysis of that art as taught in Hawes's day: its parts, we learn, are Invention, Disposition — or arrangement of narrative or argument, Elocution — that is, choice of words, expression (well exemplified by Lydgate !), Pronunciation, and Memory. In the tower of Music its patroness sits surrounded by a heap of instruments — tabors, sackbut, dulcimers, rebeck and soft recorders, — and we are treated to a little essay on the moral influence of the art: it banishes evil thoughts and gladdens the heart. Under Astronomy several sciences are included. We are taught first of all that omnipotent God, the "chief astronomer," has made Nature to be his vice-gerent. A treatise of mediaeval psychology follows: the five external "wits" or senses are five gates through which information streams in upon the first of the five internal senses, the "Common wit" or understanding; the other four are Imagination, Fantasy ("finishing" the matter afforded by the former), Estimation (whose function it is to comprehend space, time, cause and effect), and finally Memory. Hawes here takes occasion to explain that his "native language is obscure." A bit of physiology comes next, for under the "high influence of the planets" falls the discussion of the four elements and four humors.

His tuition finished, Grand Amour proceeds to the Tower of Chivalry and forth thence to slaughter giants with his sword Clara-Prudence and finally to pierce with it a metallic monster, Malice, — after which feat he is received by Pucelle in a hall paved with precious stones, its windows of crystal, its walls covered with arras, its roof "of marvellous geometry." There they are wedded by Church-Law. In another passage, descriptive of Fortune's hall with its "curiously branched roof," Hawes reminds us that he belonged to the epoch of fan-tracery: like it his work is studied and ornate. He has some passages that are full of color, — notably the description of Doctrine's palace. His characteristic lines lending themselves easily to quotation read like echoes of the proverbial philosophy of his day:

> "After an ebb there cometh a flowing tide" . . .
> "After the day there cometh the dark night:
> For though the dayë be never so long
> At last the bell ringeth to evensong."

His literary enthusiasm finds expression in a highly characteristic line, in praise

> " Of famous poets many years ago."
> " Farewell, sweetheart, farewell, farewell, farewell,"

— if read with ever fainter breath, a vanishing effect, a dying
fall, will give a just impression of the pensive sweetness long
drawn out, the attenuated grace of Stephen Hawes. His was
a mild St. Martin's summer of mediaeval poetry; he was the
darling of the ladies of the court of Henry VII.

Part of the verse-production of this reign as of previous
ones was anonymous and popular, taking the form of ballads.
It is cause for regret that as in the case of the Danish examples most of them have been preserved to us only in the
adulterated versions of a later time. One entertaining specimen, among the best of its class, may be safely ascribed to the
earlier portion of Henry's reign — the ballad of the Nut-brown
Maid, composed presumably by a woman to vindicate the constancy of her sex in love. The maid's lover subjects her
affection to a series of severe tests; he pretends that he has
committed some breach of law and must away to the greenwood
for refuge: she promises to accompany him and is not deterred
by his clearly drawn picture of the discomforts and dangers of
woodland life. Finally he declares that he is already provided
with a sweetheart in the forest who is fairer than she and
whom he loves better, — but the maid stands even this searching test triumphantly :

> " ' Though in the wood I understood ye had a paramour,
> All this may not remove my thought but that I will be your ;
> And she shall find me soft and kind and courteous every hour,
> Glad to fulfil all that she will command me, to my power;
> For had ye, lo ! an hundred mo, yet would I be that one,
> For in my mind, of all mankind, I love but you alone.' "

This supreme surrender overcomes her lover who comforts
her telling her that he had only said it to prove her and re-

veals what he had hitherto concealed, that he whom she has won for her husband by her enduring love is an earl's son and no banished man.

As regards domestic life in this reign we are provided, but slenderly as compared with Edward IV's time, with the correspondence of some Yorkshire gentlefolk that serves as a continuation to the Paston letters, beginning where they leave off — but it is by no means as voluminous or as interesting as that famous collection. The centre of the new correspondence was Sir Robert Plumpton, warden of Knaresboro' Castle ; and his wife, the Lady Isabel, held to it a relation similar to that that Margaret Paston held to the earlier series. We are afforded a vivid glimpse of the straits of one among the many families that were drawn into the toils of Richard Empson, the king's agent ; he began proceedings against Sir Robert in 1497. "The great man E[mpson] sits for assessing of fines for knights," — fines, that is, levied upon persons who might receive knighthood but who sought to avoid the attendant trouble and expense — and his correspondent goes on to warn Sir Robert : "Your adversaries intend surely to attempt the law against you." Erelong we hear Lady Plumpton complaining that she can neither borrow money nor sell wood upon the estate for everybody knows that she is eager to sell and next to nothing is offered for the largest trees — and meanwhile there is Lenten stuff to buy. None can tell what the land would bring for the title is insecure. "We are brought to beggar-staff." Later, her husband sends her warning: "If any precept come from the sheriff to take your cattle obey ye it not. No cattle should be taken thereby but your husband's cattle and he hath none — and so may ye make the bayly answer."

A curious but by no means exceptional instance of affection traded upon is offered by a kinsman of the Plumptons who considers whether it might not be as well to give his sister in marriage to a gentleman who loves her so devotedly that he would probably take her with a smaller dowry than any other would demand.

Leaving Yorkshire we cross the northern border once again. The young king of Scots, James IV, handsome, pleasure-loving, popular, was enjoying an influence rare for the crown in his distracted country which had lately been rent by discords worse than ordinary. Under his energetic administration which reflected the spirit of the age Scotland enjoyed a respite from strife and a measure of prosperity. James had splendid tastes, in especial a passion for architecture ; the palaces of Stirling, Holyrood, Linlithgow and Falkland were built, restored or decorated in his reign. He loved music and song : minstrels, rhymers and scholars were welcome at his gay court and gave it a finer lustre. Its greatest literary ornament and, indeed, the chief of Scottish poets throughout the two-hundred years' course of independent Scottish literature, was William Dunbar. Formerly a Franciscan friar he had discarded the frock to become a dependent of the king whom he served in several foreign missions. He flattered the taste of the age by his allegorical poems — which are unusually successful specimens of their class. His "Golden Targe" opens with a pretty description of May — impaired as was inevitable then by classical allusions. The "Targe" is the shield with which Reason defends the poet for awhile against the darts of Beauty. Dunbar's finest production in this vein, his best-known work and one that possesses a permanent charm, is the graceful epithalamium he composed for the king upon his marriage with the Tudor princess Margaret. "The Thistle and the Rose" is its symbolic title : it is instinct with light and color — the best and most characteristic properties of Scottish poetry.

Removed by a whole hemisphere from such play of fancy and sentiment are the satirical pieces that Dunbar penned in an altered mood : indeed, but for the well-known vicissitudes of mood to which the human spirit is subject it would be hard to believe that species of writing so different could proceed from the same author. In his versified report of the confabulation of some female ribalds, "Two Married Women and a Widow," there is a cynical display of an almost savage lust, of hypocritic cunning devoted to the service of animal instinct, that uncovers an abyss of moral evil in the social life of Scotland as the Middle Age was drawing to a close. (The king himself was a notorious libertine.) Another tale of coarse humor and intrigue, "The Friars of Berwick," may be ascribed to Dunbar; it is quite in the manner of the baser element in the Canterbury Tales.

We have from him a Scotch version of the "Dance of the Seven Deadly Sins" — and surely that grotesque subject has never been treated with more force, originality and grewsome realism. He addressed to the king many rhymed petitions for places in the church; and repeated disappointment appears to have inspired a series of despondent, moralizing poems that remind one of Lydgate's favorite themes : "the world is false and unstable," and "all earthly joy returns in pain." He wrote "Of the World's Vanity," and "Of the Changes of Life," and once when he was sick and in fear of death composed a lament for the famous poets of Britain from Chaucer's to his own day. A like occasion, a like mood doubtless inspired his "Confession" of all sorts of sins : a line in it tersely expresses the religious attitude of his age and of a character such as his : —

> "I trow in the kirk, to do as it commandis."

Submissive as he became he could not escape accusation of heresy; in a "Flyting" or humorous dispute in verse his contemporary and literary friend, Walter Kennedy, charged him with being a "Lollard laureate, a lamp of Lollards," — doubtless because of his shrewd hits at the priests and the religious orders. Kennedy was of noble birth, well-educated, and had travelled upon the Continent.   He composed some devotional poems, a "Passion of Christ " and a " Ballad in Praise of our Lady " wherein he blesses her from top to toe and begs her intercession for " KENNEDY her man."

Another noble author and of greater distinction was Gavin Douglas, whose " Palace of Honor," addressed to King James, is one of the polished, artificial allegories then in vogue at court — a dream of adventure on a May morning among myth-ological personages, classic heroes and poets, including a course over classic geography.   As may be imagined, it is tedious reading to-day ; yet it contains some gorgeous coloring and reveals its author's genuine and undiscriminating passion for the antique : it is thus a monument of the spread of renascent sentiment into remote Scotland.   Of that sentiment Douglas was the one exponent in his day and corner of the world.   By it he was nerved to accomplish his great feat—a translation of the Æneid into the Scotch dialect, in heroic couplets.   He prefaced every book with an original prologue, the seventh and twelfth of which are gems of natural description.   In the former we have a picture drawn from his own observation of the effect of winter wind and cold upon the sea, upon streams and fields, cattle and men ; in the latter, the converse of this, — the effect of the spring sun upon the atmosphere, the sea and land, cities and meadows, trees, flowers, birds and beasts, and finally upon man.   Many passages in these are almost startlingly modern in delicacy and accuracy of observation, in the light with which they are irradiated and the color with which they are imbued.

At the very close of our period printing was introduced into the northern kingdom and the new literature was thus put into wider circulation by Walter Chepman, a cloth-merchant of Edinborough.   Under the king's patronage, Chepman set up a press in his house and furnished the capital, a junior partner, Andrew Miller, who had learned the art in France, doing the printing.   In the autumn of the year 1507 they received a royal patent "to imprint books of laws, acts of parliament, chronicles, mass-books and legends of Scotch saints, and all other books that shall seem necessary." Poems, romances and ballads, in the judgment of the shrewd partners, seemed evidently to belong to the last class and issued from their press before the heavier kind of literature specified in the patent. In 1508 the first book printed in Scotland was put upon the market: it comprised some popular romances of chivalry, the "Gest of Robin Hood," the "Maying" of Chaucer, the "Golden Targe," "Book of Good Counsel to the King," "Two Married Women and the Widow," and "A Lament for the Makers" (*i.e.*, poets), all by Dunbar, and the "Flyting" of Dunbar and Kennedy. Then appeared a breviary, in parts, completed in the summer of 1510; of other works that may have issued from Chepman's press nothing is known. The defeat and death of James IV at Flodden demoralized the nation: the light of literature paled and a press could no longer be supported.

VII.

WE now approach one of the mightiest periods in human history — the era of the Reformation; an era crowded with great characters and great events, confused with conflicting aims; it is at once one of the most tempting and difficult of subjects, — it seems inexhaustible, oceanic.

In the first half of the sixteenth century there appeared in Europe a constellation of crowned heads, effulgent, almost absolute in might and glory, foremost among them being Henry VIII, Francis I, and Charles V. Off in the extreme south-west reigned a most opulent king, John III of Portugal, — the richest sovereign in Europe, for his treasuries were filled with the gold and silver of the Indies and his capital, Lisbon, which had attracted to its capacious port the eastern trade formerly enjoyed by the cities of Italy, was now become the principal mart of the world. In the extreme north-east there rose a strong and beneficent king, Gustavus Vasa — founder of the greatness of Sweden. All these monarchs were practically absolute within their several dominions; only among themselves was any effectual constraint put upon each other's power and pretensions. The collapse of feudalism was complete.

The supreme political factors upon the continent of Europe were four in number, and three of them were marshalled against one — the emperor Charles V. It is necessary to bear in mind the tremendous power of Spain throughout this century: the union of Castile and Aragon and the resulting conquest of Granada had created a potent nationality cemented by a sombre religious enthusiasm, — and Spain was suddenly lifted to the first place in Europe. At the same time streams of precious metals poured in upon her from the new world — but

this was not an unalloyed blessing: the Spaniards came out of
the Middle Ages with a knightly contempt of labor, — they got
gold by fighting, and it enervated the realm at last: the industrial movement of the preceding generation, slight enough as it
was, subsided under the blight of the American conquests and
erelong ceased.   For the time being, however, the strength
and influence of Spain were vast, — sufficient of themselves to
give her young king a commanding position in the polity of
Europe.   Charles was beside king of the Two Sicilies; Austria and the Netherlands were in his domain; in the year 1519
the crowns of Lombardy and the Empire were united upon his
brow: thus he had the whole continent in his grasp, — his was
the widest sway since Charlemagne.

This prodigious power was a menace to the liberty, to the
very existence of the other states of Europe; Charles was more
dreaded than the pitiless Turk; Francis I made it his life-
work to struggle with him — and with the coöperation of the
Protestant princes of Germany and of Suleiman II managed
to make head against him and to maintain a precarious balance of forces.   Such were the four political factors of the
Reformation era.   A singular spectacle! — a Catholic king of
France, German Protestants and a Turkish sultan forced into
combination against the power of Charles V.

The transition from feudalism was accomplished; that from
mediaeval Catholicism was now in progress.   It is commonly
taught that the Middle Ages came to an end with feudalism,
— but that was only one and on the whole a lesser feature of
those ages; while the mediaeval church yet stood, with its
system of education, morals and worship, its monasteries and
nunneries, cardinalate and papacy, it is erroneous to say that
the Middle Ages were over.   That could not be said, either,
until their municipal life was extinct; until the civic activity
of old, the freedom of the city republics of Italy, the power of
a great institution like the Hanseatic League had also passed

away. Never had the mediaeval church seemed more magnificent than in the first quarter of the sixteenth century under the splendid pontificate of Leo X; we can now see that its institutions that then seemed impregnable were in reality but hollow shells only needing a touch to crumble away. The principal interest of the history of the first half of the century lies in the mighty religious revolution that went forward despite many checks in the north of Europe. It was a conflict of north and south, — of Teuton, Saxon, Norseman against Roman, Celt and Frank, — of the more moral against the more ideal, — of the English and German languages against the universal Latin, — of the ideas of Wyclif, Huss and the Lollards against those of the succeeding age; and not of Wyclif and Huss only but also of the reformers of a century or two before their time: of the almost forgotten Waldenses, of Friar Berthold and Robert of Lincoln. The historian would err greatly who neglected the thought and work of those early leaders of the reformation, of a strenuous evangelicalism that was never totally extinguished throughout the Middle Ages and that emerged with power at their close. And so we behold a tremendous conflict waged over all Europe with alternate failure and success between evangelical doctrine, the Scriptures and preaching on the one hand, and on the other the sacramental and sacerdotal system of the mediaeval church. The tide of reform flowed and ebbed and flowed again; there were eager forward movements and violent reactions: it was a giant oscillation that cradled a new world into being — and it went on with the greatest ease, evenness and success under the strong hands of Henry VIII and Gustavus Vasa.

In the capital of Christendom itself the faith of former time was dead: skepticism was so general and daring that the fifth Lateran council, held by Leo X, thought it expedient (to Luther's great disgust) to promulgate anew the doctrine of

the immortality of the soul against the philosopher Pompo-
nazzi, who had denied that it could be proved by reason or
out of the writings of Aristotle. From the same synod issued
a fresh assertion of papal supremacy and shortly, with almost
cynical disregard of the awakening conscience of Europe,
there was published by the Curia a greatly enlarged and scien-
tifically classified inventory of sins with the prices of accompanying pardons. Yet in the days of Leo X Italian humanism
put forth its consummate flower, — not as winsome, fresh and
fragrant as in the time of Lorenzo his father, but full-blown
and gorgeous: rarely in the annals of mankind has there shone
such a galaxy of genius and talent as then graced the courts
of Rome, Florence, and Ferrara. Leo's secretary was the
cultivated and fastidious Bembo, who piqued himself on the
classic purity of his Latinity and the almost equal elegance
of his Italian style. He encouraged the use of the vernacular
by men of letters and gave them an example of refined rhetoric
in the elaborate discussion as to the nature of love held by
"gli Asolani." Of greater importance for universal literature
was the dramatic poet Gian-Giorgio Trissino: his tragedy of
"Sofonisba" achieved such conspicuous and instantaneous
success that it secured for its author the favorable notice of
the pope, who appointed him to be one of his ambassadors.
The work appeared in the year 1515: it was the first of its
kind in Italy that gave evidence of spontaneity of native
genius: there had been nothing before but feeble imitations
of the antique. As is natural in nascent drama, "Sofonisba"
is a tale of turgid passion couched in a style that is by comparison weak and frigid: it is full of long, studied and declama-
tory speeches: but its significance can be gauged by this, that
they are cast in *blank verse*. The origin of so important a
form is of such interest that Trissino's reasons for using it are
worth citing; in the dedication of his tragedy to Pope Leo he
explains that he uses Italian so as to be popularly understood

and blank verse because it is best suited to express emotion : rhyme, which suggests careful thought, is not adapted for emotional utterance, which as it is not must not seem studied : moreover, blank verse has a certain dignity. This last remark is weightier than it seems : there can be no doubt that the new poetic medium originated in an endeavor to catch the effect of the inimitable unrhymed measure of the ancients. And so Trissino has the credit of having devised this simple, flexible and henceforth indispensable form — one of the most precious legacies of the Italian Renascence to modern literature. There is evidence, however, that before him others were experimenting in this line ; the credit of prior invention would seem to belong to Giacomo Sannazaro, a Neapolitan, — in the fourth eclogue of his " Arcadia," published fully ten years before the " Sofonisba," there occurs a considerable passage in blank verse. The work is otherwise of importance, for it heads the list of those classico-romantic pastorals that were exceedingly fashionable for many generations, — pictures of an ideal country life in the open air — colloquies of Platonic shepherds and shepherdesses on mountain lawns or in flowery fields by running streams under green boughs.

Giovanni Rucellai, a cousin of the pope and his ambassador to the court of France, was the next distinguished writer to employ blank verse, in a didactic poem of fifteen hundred lines inspired by one of Virgil's Georgics, — " Le Api "— " the Bees." He also produced a tragedy, "Rosmunda," for his cousin's entertainment.

Meanwhile in Florence the sinister Macchiavelli had just published his manual of a portentous political science which was yet nothing more than the practice of the rulers of Italy in his day : they had succeeded in effecting a divorce of government and morals quite as complete as that already achieved between morals and religion. When a state has been conquered, says Macchiavelli, every scion of the reigning family should be killed off, or, if it has been accustomed to govern itself, it should be effectually ruined and then garrisoned. A successful usurper should establish his power by a general massacre. A prince may abide by his engagements when convenient; he should seek a reputation for honor and *talk* much of good faith; he should also be accounted liberal and to this end should be lavish of the possessions of his enemies but scrupulous as to laying fresh taxes upon his people. Macchiavelli breaks out in admiration and commendation of the triumphant craft of Caesar Borgia: he was his political paragon. A characteristic discussion is that as to whether it is better for a ruler to be feared or loved; the misanthrope concludes that human nature is so changeable, selfish and contemptible that it is better to be feared: punishment is the surest means of control.

"The Prince" merely spoke out the open secret of all the tyrants of Italy. When he had finished it Macchiavelli turned to his profound "Discourses upon Titus Livius."

The greatest poet of the age flourished at the court of the Estes at Ferrara. There in the last century, in his "Orlando Innamorato," Bojardo had told over again the story of the favorite hero of mediaeval romance in verse that was too rude for a later, more refined generation. The subject was worked over in a bright style by Francesco Berni, — but the final and incomparable version was Ariosto's. In the year 1516 appeared forty cantos of his "Orlando Furioso"; six supplementary cantos were added later; the first complete edition was pub-published at Ferrara in 1532. The following year the poet died.

It is to be noted that the incidents, the theme of this great poem — the fury in love and warfare of Charlemagne's paladin, Roland — are thoroughly mediaeval; though touched with the finer taste, fancy and sensuousness of the Renascence it is yet a tale of chivalry.

This was the period of the utmost glory of Renascent art, — of the exquisite school of Milan under da Vinci, Luini and Ferrari, — the sumptuous school of Venice under Giorgione, Palma and Titian, — of Correggio at Parma, del Sarto and the rest at Florence, and Bazzi at Siena; it was typed in the magnificent reception that Pope Leo gave to the reconstructed college of cardinals in apartments of the Vatican just decorated by Raphael. But there was a spirit that deeply felt the difference between what was and what ought to have been, and in the wonderful figure of "the Slave" the indignant Angelo compressed the speechless agony of his great soul over the enslavement of his native land.

His tutor Torrigiano spent several years in England making the famous tomb of Henry VII and his queen that may be seen in his fan-vaulted chapel at Westminster. Another Italian artist named Benedetto was engaged by Wolsey to execute a tomb for him at Windsor.

The gabled halls of Brasenose College at Oxford, begun in the year 1512 (the year that Torrigiano arrived in London), are interesting relics of the collegiate architecture of Henry VIII's reign. At the same time the beautiful tower of Magdalen was rising. The intellectual ambition of the time found expression in many scholastic foundations: Margaret, Countess of Richmond, mother of the late king, had just established two colleges at Cambridge; at Oxford, Bishop Fox began to build Corpus Christi, Wolsey endowed a Greek lectureship, and in 1524 suppressed an old priory and erected Christ Church upon its site. We have in this church a fine example of fan-tracery vaulting; English architecture was still Gothic and mediaeval.

Scholasticism still cumbered the ground, but the vehement efforts its partisans made to sustain it, their loud vociferations, showed that the system was in its last stages. Feeling ran high between the disciples of the old and the new learning;

the quiet cloisters of Oxford rang with their debates which not seldom ended in blows. The old order was changing, giving place to new.

One would have an inadequate idea of the age of Henry VIII who did not perceive under its external brilliancy the pathos that attends the decline and fall of great and once beneficent institutions. A profound pathos invests the decay of old ideals — but God fulfils himself in many ways lest one good custom outgrown should corrupt the world. And the grief is generally forgotten in the midst of the magnificence of the age. It was the last effulgence of mediaevalism — the last intense crimson and golden glow of the long mediaeval day. But there was a light within that light; the sunset of the Middle Ages paled before the new sun of modern times, and the color of the former half of Henry's reign faded out into the broad white glare of the latter part. So it was with the century: it began mediaeval, it ended modern.

We have in Henry VIII a striking illustration of the popular belief that fathers transmit their peculiar qualities to their daughters and mothers to their sons, — for his character is illuminated by reading into it that of his maternal grandfather. With Edward IV we are already acquainted; his daughter Elizabeth (queen to Henry VII) inherited from him her fine figure, beautiful countenance and engaging manners, and transmitted them, together with his appetite for pleasure and magnificence and — most important of all — his determined will, to her son. Henry was seventeen years old when he came to the throne and a burst of popular rejoicing, long pent up under the severe represssion of his father's reign, greeted the handsome young prince at his accession. His was certainly an attractive, indeed a superior character. His physique was fine and he was fond of all knightly exercises. He was a good scholar, especially in languages, and had refined tastes — loved painting and music, which he practised a little himself;

he composed some masses that were sung in his royal chapel. He was moreover well instructed in mediaeval divinity and polity and piqued himself somewhat upon his attainments in that line ; he was an expert in theological discussion. The force and fascination of his personality may be estimated by this, that he retained, if not the early affection, at least the admiring awe of his people all through his long reign of nearly forty years.

He was crowned with his queen, Catherine of Aragon, in June, 1509, a few days before his eighteenth birthday. He and his people were at one in their willingness to make a sharp distinction between his and his father's administration : Empson and Dudley, the instruments of the old king's rapacity, were cast into the Tower and erelong beheaded, and his chancellor and minister, Archbishop Warham, a man of mediocre talents whom Henry never regarded with particular favor, was eclipsed and at last edged out by Thomas Wolsey.

The young king hastened to waste the treasure so painfully collected by his father in tournaments, splendid entertainments and wars. He continued the time-worn, ancestral policy of hostility to France, invaded that country in the summer of 1513, and achieved a glittering success in the Battle of Spurs. The year following, however, perceiving that he was being tricked by his father-in-law of Spain, he veered round, made a peace with the French king which he cemented by the gift of his sister Mary in marriage, and began a series of negotiations that culminated in the pageantry of the Field of the Cloth of Gold in the summer of 1520. His position was a novel one for an English king ; in possession of a copious treasure, at the head of an insular kingdom, strong, compact, and happily freed from the burden and embarrassment of continental dependencies (which it was well that he could not recover), Henry was able to play a distinguished part upon the theatre of European diplomacy and to pose as an arbiter between mighty opposites.

In Wolsey the king found a minister after his own heart. Of affable manners and splendid tastes, fond of architecture, fine gardens, spectacles and shows, yet of extraordinary capacity for public affairs, Wolsey was unique in English history in the number of great offices that were heaped upon him in successive years. Beginning as royal chaplain and almoner, he was summoned to the king's council, was appointed dean and then bishop of Lincoln, and was almost immediately afterward elevated to the archbishopric of York. The next year — 1515 — Pope Leo made him a cardinal at the king's own request and the great seal of the chancellor, taken from Warham, was conferred upon him. In 1517 the pope, still acting under pressure from the king and as a special favor to him, invested Wolsey with legislative powers over the English church. He was now the lordliest, most magnificent prelate that England had ever beheld, — the final, full-blown type of an ecclesiastical statesman of the Middle Age; he held to the church the same relation that the great earl of Warwick held to English feudalism. And that very year Martin Luther posted his theses against indulgences on the door of the castle church at Wittenberg.

Strange as it may seem, a weighty motive of this accumulation of high offices was a desire of reform: a feeling was gaining ground that something must be done to reform the corrupt church. Archbishop Warham had attempted the task in a feeble way and found it too great for his powers; he was thrust aside and Wolsey was invested with unlimited power over the church. For as papal legate he was superior to the archbishop of Canterbury and moreover could do what no bishop could— he could inspect, control, suppress monasteries. To effect a disciplinary reform of the clergy both regular and secular— such was in large measure the motive of these combinations.

In the early years of the reign, in the midst of the jubilant rebound from the repression of former years, Lollardy rose to the surface; prosecutions for heresy were renewed, the principal point involved being transubstantiation; in the year 1511 the movement excited general attention and alarm, — several Lollards were forced to recant, some preferred to suffer death.

The Lollards of London flocked to hear the evangelical preaching of the dean of Saint Paul's, John Colet — altogether the most significant character in the English church at that day. He deplored schism and advocated a reform within the church: his was a voice coming from within, like conscience, calling upon the body to repent — and when such warning voices die unheeded the retribution and the only remedy is schism. His prophetic, apostolic character was manifested in his self-denying life and simple attire. The king respected and admired him for with all his earnestness he was free from taint of fanaticism. When the spread of heresy impelled the summoning of convocation in the winter of 1512 Colet was chosen as preacher; it was the opportunity of his life and in a stirring sermon, in Latin, he proclaimed the duty, the necessity of immediate reform. He attributed to the evil lives of her ministers the patent corruption of the church; the impurity of priests, he said, is the most grievous heresy. He took his text from the twelfth chapter of St. Paul's epistle to the Romans and admonished the assembled bishops and clergy in fearless tones not to be conformed to the world in pride of place, feasting and pleasures of the senses, pursuit of rich benefices, worldly business and distractions, but to be reformed to humility, temperance, charity and a spiritual life. And the reform must commence with those of highest station: the bishops should be spiritually-minded men, clear of all simony, should reside in their sees, abstain from everything unbecoming their high office and carefully strain out unworthy applicants for orders: thus the reformation would be extended to the priesthood and through it finally to the people.

Colet's sermon made a deep impression; it was translated into English and purely practical though it was the bishop of London brought against the preacher a charge of heresy; he was however protected by a powerful sympathizer — the archbishop of Canterbury, — and the year following was invited to preach before the king. The whole country was looking forward to the war with France upon which the king had set his heart — but Colet in the courage of his convictions condemned that war. The king's conscience was touched; he sent for the preacher and for more than an hour they conferred together in the palace garden. From that hour none of Colet's foes ventured to assail him.

A picturesque event was the pilgrimage that Colet and Erasmus took together — a last pilgrimage to Canterbury. The two friends found the relics exhibited, the mouldering rags and bones, repulsive to a degree, and were completely convinced of the inefficacy of pilgrimages as a means of salvation.

In the fall of 1515 the great preacher had an opportunity to inculcate sound politics in the sermon he was asked to deliver upon the occasion of Wolsey's installation as cardinal. His friend More had just embodied a social ideal in his "Utopia." The brightest minds of the day were much exercised over the political and economic situation.

Colet's attitude toward the schoolmen was antagonistic: he condemned Aquinas for having adulterated the simplicity of the Gospel with philosophical refinements. Toward the new learning upon its purely literary side he was no less hostile; he exhorted his hearers to shun pagan culture as a vain and worldly thing and to beware of the books of heathen philosophers unless they would become associates of demons. Herein his Montanistic strain is revealed; such a narrow and partial outlook contrasts painfully with Erasmus's genial, catholic suggestion: "Perhaps the spirit of God is shed abroad more widely than we think."

Colet was a reformer and of too earnest a spirit to jest and enjoy. His business was to call men back to the Bible, especially to the writings of St. Paul, whom he esteemed as the "wisest of men." He was uncompromising in his Augustinianism : man is by nature evil, ignorant, utterly without the divine; the world is like the restless sea and men are as fish beneath its surface, in a state of death and darkness, — they have to be drawn from it to see the light. In this body of ours, so vile, dark and mortal, a pure, bright and deathless soul may yet dwell. And God knew before those who should be fitted for his mysteries, — those who cleave less closely to this world; they are called and chosen out of the mass according to his wise and holy will; their minds are illumined by his presence, their wills corrected. For the divine artificer moulds men as wax, moves them as stones, and so constructs his church. The thought of one Spirit in many persons is a favorite one with Colet.

With such postulates as to our nature the union of the divine and the human becomes a serious problem. Colet's view of the Incarnation was that the iron of Christ's humanity was attracted and upheld by his divinity as by a magnet.

His teaching on the subject of marriage proves that he still belonged to the monastic age : marriage is God's condescension to man's weakness; it is not good in itself and is but the lesser of two evils ; if one can do without it he ought to. "If only all the faithful had remained chaste the heathen would have supplied new material for the church, and when all the heathen were converted the kingdom of God would have come, and if all men had thus come to an end — what end more desirable to this pilgrimage? But man's weakness delays Christ's return !"

In his project of a disciplinary reform within the church Colet was ably and ardently seconded by Erasmus, who brought to the cause a finer scholarship and a trenchant weapon of

satire and gave the idea currency upon the continent. In his
" Praise of Folly " Erasmus launched out in unsparing satire
upon luxurious popes and bishops, lazy and ignorant monks
and friars and quibbling schoolmen — nor did he fail to score,
in passing, those princes who careless of the public good sought
only their own pleasure.   The book attained a European
circulation ; indeed, Erasmus recalls Petrarch by the dicta-
torial position he occupied in the republic of letters.   In 1516
appeared his revision of the Greek text of the New Testament
— a monument of critical scholarship.

A like reformatory movement was in progress in France
inspired by a like enthusiasm for Biblical studies.   Lefèvre
d'Étaples, of the University of Paris, commented upon the
New Testament in the original, dwelling especially upon the
epistles of St. Paul, applied himself to amending the text of
the Vulgate and even ventured to translate the Gospels and
Pauline epistles into the vernacular.   Conservative Spain too
felt the stir of the new Biblical scholarship: at the University
of Alcalà, lately founded by the austere Cardinal Ximenez, and
under his patronage, the learned Lebrija got out a famous
polyglot edition of the Scriptures.

If Colet commanded the respect, more, the veneration of
Erasmus, More drew forth his admiring affection — and surely
he is one of the most lovable characters in history.   The subtle
blend of seriousness and humor that made him so winning
comes out in the " Utopia," in which deep thoughts far in
advance of the age are mingled with many a playful fancy.
The beings of that Platonic dream held that reasonable pleasure
is accordant with the will of God ; they therefore condemned
the ascetic life as cruel to one's self and thankless to the
Creator, — as though one would not be indebted to him and
so refused all his gracious gifts.   In Utopia was no persecution
for conscience' sake, for they held that a man cannot force his
religious beliefs and that various forms of worship might

proceed from the same God, who might inspire different men different ways and be pleased with that variety. A novel liberality! It is a pity that More did not entrust the work to his native language for it would then have enjoyed a wider and longer circulation. His " History of Richard III " shows how well he could write in English, though its style — doubtless because it was a first essay at historical composition — is still too much in bondage to Latin syntax. It is bright and interesting reading and is set off with speeches in character, in the manner of Thucydides, — the argument of the queen-mother in sanctuary at Westminster is acute and spirited. At the end of the description of Jane Shore occurs the author's mournful comment : " Men use, if they have an evil turn, to write it in marble ; and whoso doth us a good turn we write it in dust."

In Germany the first tide of reformation was at flood in the year 1520, when Luther, his thought having been clarified by controversy, began to realize his spiritual kinship to Huss and was forced, however reluctantly, to the conclusion that even an ecumenical council might err. In his address to the German nobility he assailed the papal supremacy and speedily followed this by a thorough-going criticism of the sacramental system of the mediaeval church, to which he attributed her various maladies and upon which the papal supremacy seemed plainly to be based. He rejected all but three of the seven sacraments and repudiated the dogma of transubstantiation.

The German knights put forth their last strength in behalf of Luther's reform, and the union was symbolized by the literary labors, the satires and ardent appeals of Ulrich von Hutten, one of their noblest representatives. But upon the threshold of the third decade of the century a marked reactionary sentiment manifested itself and at the Diet of Worms the ban of the empire was pronounced against Luther and his adherents, his writings were burnt and all future dissemination of his teaching was forbidden. Had the decree been enforced it would have gone very hard with him and the cause — but the fall of Belgrade into the power of the Turks that same year created a timely diversion. In France the reaction attained sufficient strength to drive d'Étaples from the kingdom and to wring a retractation from his pupil and protector, the bishop Briçonnet. In England it was signalized by the entry of the king into the lists of theological controversy; by a "Defence of the Seven Sacraments against Luther" he won from the grateful Leo the title, "Defender of the Faith." In his book Henry assumed perforce the position of bishop Pecock when attacking the Lollards, — namely, that much is lawful which is not expressed in Scripture; and in the judgment of the reactionary party he achieved success. Whatever the effect of the work may have been upon the continent, for England it was of real moment, for in it Henry put himself on record as a devoted Catholic and from that position he never receded. Having once assumed it all his pride, all his obstinacy of will, not to speak of his convictions, held him to it, and through life he remained a consistent mediaeval Catholic in all that concerned doctrine, a determined upholder of the dogma of transubstantiation. So now for several years reform languished; Colet was dead, and the only apparent use that Wolsey made of his legatine commission was the suppression of a few monasteries.

Henry's book and Luther's reply — in which he handled his royal opponent pretty roughly — had this important consequence, that a decisive breach was thereby effected between the great reformer and Erasmus. The latter cordially assented to Henry's thesis; their relations were otherwise of the friendliest; and Erasmus, scandalized by Luther's incivility, now came out as a representative of the reaction. He examined the reformer's writings, found the weak spot he sought in his doctrine of predestination and published a severe animadversion upon it. A truculent German monk named Murner rushed into the fray in the king's behalf with a book bearing the sensational title, "Is the King of England a Liar or is Luther?" — and his singular defence must have been gratifying to Henry, for he invited him to visit England.

Murner was a universal satirist, sparing no class, no dignity, equally bitter against the hierarchy of the old church, the monks and friars, and the reformers. Such general discontent is indicative of some deep-seated malady in the social frame. A like raucous note was raised in England by John Skelton, who grew more abusive as he grew older and the times worse. In the short, rattling lines of his "Colin Clout," running through odd lists of rhymes, he rails at bishops, priests, friars, schoolmen, Lollards and Lutherans! His ire was especially excited by the unprecedented grandeur of Cardinal Wolsey, to whose administration he ascribed all the misfortunes of the reign. "Why come ye not to Court?" is a ferocious attack upon "linsey Wolsey, who rules all the roost with bragging and boast, with pomp and pride; who nods and becks in the Star Chamber and regards lords no more than potsherds, — all the barons fear the butcher's dog." This coarse personal satire so roused the cardinal that its author had to flee from his vengeance to Westminster sanctuary.

Skelton composed the best moral-play of the period — designed without doubt as a salutary warning to King Henry VIII. It shows how Magnificence, seduced from Moderation by Self-Will and Craft, loses both Liberty and Felicity and becomes a prey to Adversity, Poverty and Despair; he is saved by Hope, Redress, Circumspection and Perseverance, who instruct him in genuine mediaeval fashion as to the mutability of things.

In "The Manner of the World nowadays" Skelton probed many a social sore spot of the age. (He always had a curious taste for mortality, the grotesque, and the loathsome.) "So many good sermons and so few devotions saw I never; so well apparelled wives and so ill of their lives — widows so soon wed

after their husbands are dead, — so proud and so gay, so rich
in array and so scant of money, saw I never; so many places
untilled, so many beggars, such increase of thieves, — all
England decays." This pessimistic outcry — in which we catch
clear echoes of Piers Plowman of old — had only too much
reason in the existing frame of things. The kingdom was in a
deplorable economic condition. The mediaeval system of
cultivation — by which a farm was divided into three fields,
one growing wheat, another beans or peas, while the third lay
fallow — was fast wearing out. Food was dear; the prices of
wheat, pork and poultry doubled during the middle of the
reign. As the profit on English wool was high the passion for
sheep-farming continued and was shared by both spiritual and
temporal lords; lands were enclosed, small farms were blotted
out and holdings grew ever more extensive. The evicted
tenants flocked to the towns where they helped to swell the
pauper and criminal classes. As villages were deserted their
churches fell into disrepair and were used as folds for the sheep
that pastured in the burial grounds. The whole Isle of Wight
was turned into a vast sheep run. In the cities poverty and
suffering were great and general; the streets were filthy, the
houses unventilated and noisome; the old-time guilds that
controlled labor and its materials were rapidly declining, manufactures decayed, and there were constant complaints of
trickeries practised in trade — of light weights, small measures
and adulterations. The divorce of ethics and economics was
as marked as that of ethics and politics, or religion. And when
the hard struggle for subsistence was made harder by heavy
taxation and a forced loan to build the king's ships and carry
on his wars the popular discontent came near exploding in an
armed insurrection.

War had been declared with France — for the political and
military corollary of the religious reaction was a drawing away
from the French toward a Spanish alliance. Of this war there

remains a literary memorial of worth, for the king, wishing to kindle the enthusiasm of his subjects by reviving the recollection of the great deeds of their forefathers in the glorious wars of old, gave Lord Berners as a task the translation into English of Froissart's Chronicle — a task which he accomplished with much graphic power. The emperor attached Wolsey to his cause by holding out to him a golden lure — the popedom, — in the attainment of which summit of his ambition he promised to use all his influence over the college of cardinals. Charles and Henry now entered into a nefarious confederacy to partition France; Henry was to revive his obsolete claims to the crown of that country and in the division was to have its western half. But the emperor never intended to lend his power to the aggrandizement of his ally's, and after the terrible defeat of the French at Pavia and the capture of their king, Charles made his own terms with him in utter disregard of Henry and let him go. He had just shown how lightly he regarded his compact with Wolsey by permitting a scion of the Medici family to be raised to the papal chair as Clement VII. If Wolsey in his resentment now put it into the king's head (as Catherine always supposed) to offer a mortal insult to the emperor by repudiating his queen, Charles's aunt, he bitterly atoned for it later, for that troublous divorce was the rock on which all his hopes were wrecked. Catherine was several years older than the king; all their children had died in infancy save Mary, now a sickly child of some ten summers; and Henry interpreted their loss as a divine judgment upon him for having married his brother's widow. His longing was for a male heir; it was impossible for men to see clearly then how far removed England was from any danger of a return to the distressful condition of the Wars of the Roses; Henry really dreaded another succession war and thought it essential to his dynasty and the welfare of the kingdom that he should have a son, — and Wolsey was commissioned to negotiate a divorce, which implied a revocation of the papal dispensation for the marriage. The matter — first bruited in the year 1526 — was a consequence of the breach with the emperor already determined on.

Copies of William Tyndale's version of the New Testament, just printed at Cologne, were burnt in London that year and it was forbidden to bring others into the kingdom. In Scotland a distinguished martyr to the reformed opinions was found in the young Patrick Hamilton — but his death at the stake marked the culmination of the reaction: its force was now spent and combinations favorable to renewed progress were forming. In Germany the Lutheran princes leagued together and at the Diet of Speyer secured the right of administering religious affairs in their respective dominions. This result was achieved through the emperor's alarm at a fresh irruption of the Turks; by their terrible victory at Mohacz the ancient Catholic kingdom of Hungary was annihilated : the king and his principal lords fell on the field of battle and a famous mediaeval state, which had been a bulwark of civilization against the Turks for more than a hundred years, came to an end, losing its independence. The following year, 1527, the reformation was carried out in Sweden by Gustavus Vasa, who met the churchmen in diet at Westerås and bade them choose between him and the pope. Henry and Francis, scandalized at the sack of Rome by the imperial forces, consummated a treaty that paved the way for an onward march of reform in their dominions. It was of no avail to Wolsey that he obtained a bull from Clement VII authorizing the suppression of some more monasteries : that trifling measure could not avert the great catastrophe: he could not arrange the divorce and he felt that he was doomed. As a prince of the church his lot was cast with Rome; the question lay between a text in Leviticus and a papal dispensation which he could not but believe to be valid; he did his best to please the king, failed, and was banished from the court. Henry seized his palace of York-place (Wolsey had before presented him with his other palace of Hampton Court) and ordered him to retire to his archbishopric. But his enemies were not satisfied with his fall from power; they wanted his life; and in the autumn of 1530 they prevailed upon the king to summon him to London on a charge of high treason. The old cardinal, broken down, that is, in body and spirit, though not old in years, started to obey the king's command but was prostrated upon the journey; at an abbey by the road he took to the bed from which he never rose again, — and with him mediaeval ecclesiasticism expired in England.

A new set of characters appeared upon the stage: Thomas Cromwell, formerly one of Wolsey's servants, destined to be for the next ten years the minister of the most absolute monarchy that England had ever known; Thomas Cranmer, who had suggested an appeal to the universities of Europe concerning the divorce case and who was shortly to be made archbishop upon the death of Warham; and Anne Boleyn, who had some time since supplanted her mistress, Queen Catherine, in the king's affections and was soon to replace her upon the throne. Interest led her to ally herself with the reformers.

In 1531 came the humiliation of the clergy, who were forced to pay an enormous sum to obtain Henry's pardon for having submitted to that legatine authority of Wolsey which he himself had procured. Convocation, overawed, passed a resolution that the king was supreme head of the church of England. In 1533 he was married to Anne Boleyn, and Cranmer, now archbishop of Canterbury, adjudged the marriage with Catherine to have been invalid. It was a triumph of the Protestant principle of appeal to Scripture as against the authority of a pope. The new queen was now crowned with sumptuous ceremony and in September gave birth to a daughter who was named Elizabeth. In 1534 the obsequious parliament, echoing the definition of the terrified convocation, declared the king supreme head on earth of the church of England. This royal supremacy was precisely analogous to the principle lately established at Speyer.

While these events were transpiring in England the prospects of Protestantism were brightening upon the continent as well. The Augsburg Confession was followed by the League of Schmalcald, by which the Lutheran princes opposed a firm front to the emperor, — and in 1532 Suleiman and his Turks appeared before the walls of Vienna. Charles was compelled to reconcile himself to the Protestant princes and signed with them the religious peace of Nuremberg by which he granted them free exercise of their religion within their own territories. A prosperous period ensued: state after state joined the Protestant cause, — Würtemberg in 1534, Brandenburg and Saxony in 1539: by the latter year Bavaria was the solitary principality in Germany that remained solidly Catholic.

In France the reformers enjoyed the sympathy of the king's sister, Margaret, queen of Navarre. Francis too favored them at first, willing to use them as instruments against his rival the emperor, but by the year 1535 he began to feel anxious at the progress that reformed ideas were making in his kingdom; some of their representatives moreover were either fanatical or were falsely accused of having posted some daring placards that appeared upon the walls of Paris, even upon the king's palace doors; several persons were arrested therefore and burnt at the stake. And yet Francis concluded that year an alliance with the Turkish sultan, subordinating religion to policy. At the same time that he was allied with the infidel he was burning reformers in Paris and encouraging them in Germany.

News of these martyrdoms came to John Calvin in his retreat at Basel and he began forthwith his master-work, the "Christian Institution," in which he regarded the whole circle of Christian doctrine from the point of view of justification by faith: the result was a clear, logical, severely systematic treatise. He composed it in Latin and soon translated it into French for the benefit of a larger public. Luther had recently completed his translation of the Bible into German and an Italian version had appeared at Venice, the work of Brucioli, a capable Greek and Hebrew scholar. Cultivation of the popular speech was everywhere a feature of the Reformation.

The most eminent Hebraist in England was Robert Wakefield, for whom a lectureship in Hebrew was founded at Oxford. In 1535 the king commanded that Greek should be taught in all the colleges there, and this definitive triumph of the new learning was celebrated by the students by a general immolation of the works of the schoolmen. But Henry did to death that year the new learning's fairest representative, Sir Thomas More. He fell a sacrifice to the royal supremacy in religious matters, and the following year the king got Tyndale burnt at Antwerp as a sacrifice to the mass. Such was the policy, as tortuous as that of Francis I, by which Henry daunted his subjects.

The monasteries represented the ancient polity in an especial manner and consequently the tide of reform as it rose was bound to break about those old institutions; with the collapse of papal authority they too were doomed. In 1536 Henry caused his submissive parliament to institute a commission of inquiry into the state of the monasteries and in consequence of their report nearly four hundred were suppressed. In 1537, to make relic-worship more ridiculous, the frauds perpetrated at various shrines were exposed; Becket was declared a traitor, his ashes were cast out, his shrine was demolished — and two great chests full of jewels from it escheated to the king. In 1538 it was ordered that throughout England every statue that had been worshipped should be pulled down. And now the turn of the remaining and greater monasteries came — and the pope, out of all patience, published the bull of excommunication that he had ready some years before but had delayed at the entreaty of Henry's ally, the king of France.

One who looks into the literature of those ten years must be amazed to note the awe approaching adoration in which the English held their king. He made, interpreted and executed laws to suit himself; parliament and bench were as putty between his fingers; although for form's sake he made use of his subservient parliament it came at last to this, that his proclamations had the force of law. He was invested with the attributes of the highest secular and ecclesiastical authority and to the majority of his subjects he appeared as a kind of earthly divinity. Never has the doctrine of regal irresponsibility been more boldly expressed than by William Tyndale, the spokesman of that iconoclastic decade: "The king is in this world without law and may at his lust do right or wrong and shall give account but to God only." This apotheosis of earthly sovereignty sprang from the thought of the divine, upon which it was grounded, of which it was the visible analogue. Tyndale clearly reveals the connection: God is absolute, inscrutable: we may not ask why he saves one and not another; "God hath power over all his creatures of right, to do with them what he list; he will be feared and not have his secret judgments known." And God rules the world through kings: "he that resisteth the king resisteth God"; even an evil king is a benefit of God, for "it is better to suffer one tyrant than many." Such is the passive "Obedience of a Christian Man" inculcated by this Protestant Macchiavelli, and his defence is that only so could the yoke of Rome be broken.

In Tyndale the English Protestant appears in plain colors. He was a disciple of Colet but his radicalism registers the rise of the tide of reform far above the limits his master would have assigned. He disparaged sacraments, ceremonies, consecrated buildings; of the first he rejected all but two, baptism and the Lord's supper — and the latter he defined as a memorial of

Christ's everlasting sacrifice but not itself a sacrifice. Confirmation he declared to be "a dumb ceremony" reserved by bishops to increase their power — but "the wagging of a bishop's hand is not blessing." In like manner he ridiculed auricular confession, pilgrimage, saint-worship and priestly celibacy. The spirit that razed Gothic shrines and shattered statues comes to light in his dictum, God is in all places alike: what careth he for the temple? "The temple wherein God will be worshipped is the heart of man" and no place is holier than any other. God's absoluteness, man's nothingness were the poles of his thought. Original sin he defined as birth poison remaining in all men in this life; the freedom of the will and the gospel of works seemed to him the most odious heresy. "That faith only before all works and without all merits but Christ's only justifieth, is proved by Paul"; that the outward deed justifies and makes holy is the error of "the pope's sect." He vindicated his translation of the Bible; the papists, to quench the light, call it impossible, unlawful, heretical to translate the scriptures — but "will ye resist God? Hath he not made the English tongue? Why forbid ye him to speak in the English tongue then as well as in the Latin?" He charged his opponents with wresting Holy Scripture from its plain meaning by their doctrine of multiple senses and allegorical interpretation, whereas "it hath but one simple, literal sense," — and brushed aside the old and common argument about its difficulty: "a man without the spirit of Aristotle may by the Spirit of God understand Scripture." His fling at the light literature of the day is characteristic, Puritanic: "the priests permit the reading of Robin Hood, Bevis of Hampton, Hercules, Hector and Troilus, with a thousand histories and fables of love and wantonness and of ribaldry as filthy as heart can think, to corrupt the minds of youth withal, clean contrary to the doctrine of Christ and his apostles." He magnified preaching as the great duty of churchmen and defended it from the charge that it was accountable for grave public disorders: not preaching the gospel but the evil life of ecclesiastics causes disobedience and insurrection. Wyclif is justified: "he preached repentance unto our fathers not long since, and they repented not. What followed? — the French and civil wars that made the land a wilderness." Such was his prophetic philosophy of history. His practical teaching is of interest. He sought to recall the daily and economic life of man to its moral and religious basis: "Let every man of whatsoever craft, whether brewer, baker, tailor, victualler, merchant or husbandman serve his brethren as he would do Christ himself, and so his occupation pleaseth God." All occupations, either washing of dishes or preaching the word, are alike if done with the spirit of God. His teaching concerning the family is marked by a curious contradiction: all generation, all life is of God, he says, — and in the next breath bids children remember that they are their parents' good and possession (a piece of bad logic from which has ever sprung most of the misery of the world). A child should dread its parents — for "when they are angry with thee God is angry with thee and his vengeance will not depart from the disobedient till they be murdered, drowned or hanged. The marriage of children pertaineth unto their elders" by the fifth commandment — a truism then, yet one to which all romance gives the lie. "The husband is to the wife in God's stead" and the master to the servant: "his commandments are God's." All heads up therefore in marital and paternal absolutism — the analogue in the family to the regal in the state and the divine in heaven. By a contradiction similar to the above Tyndale bids his autocratic king remember that the people are God's and not his.

Thomas Starkey, sometime Henry's chaplain and intermediary between him and his relative, Reginald Pole, reflects the king-worship of the hour. He wrote an apology for the royal supremacy and the king's second marriage — for in saying " My kingdom is not of this world " Christ designed to leave all such things to the governance of man and worldly policy! This exegesis did not convince Pole; he sent his kinsman an insulting book upon the points in dispute, identified his interest with that of the papacy, visited Rome and was raised to the cardinalate. It was a terrible blow to his agent, Starkey, to whom it was "great grief if the king should not be good lord to him and gracious." His disgrace begot in him a "contempt for this life and its vain pleasures." To recover favor he wrote and dedicated to Henry an imaginary but instructive "Dialogue" between Pole and a royalist named Thomas Lupset, one of Colet's pupils. It treats in an interesting manner of the origin of civil life and of existing economic evils. Pole, it would appear, was a determinist in his psychology: "the mind of man first of itself is as a clean and pure table"—and will is as opinion is. He advances the anarchic postulate that for years men lived without a prince or a common council and that life was then more virtuous, more accordant with the dignity of human nature than it is under the existing social order. He prefers a country to a city life — "I had rather live in the wild forest." Lupset replies that civil life is grounded in man's better nature and is therefore truly natural; that cities are "stars upon earth" and that instead of abandoning them and returning to barbarism one should study how to remove their imperfections. Pole declares for elective monarchy: Lupset regards hereditary succession as a safeguard against civil war. The prince is the heart of the social order; from the heart all life and wisdom spring; and now is the time to labor for the state while we have "so noble a prince; never prince had more fervent love to the wealth of his subjects than hath he." True, in a sense not intended !

Starkey had a relish for proverbial philosophy: " Matters be ended as they be friended; many eyes see better than one; it is easier to spy two faults than amend one; he was never good master that never was scholar, nor never good captain that never was soldier," are some of the sayings embodied in the dialogue.

With so excellent a prince it is a marvel that the condition of society continued as bad as ever! Both disputants agree that England is in a bad way; castles and towns are dilapidated, lands lie waste, poverty is increasing and population declines while beggars grow more numerous. This gloomy picture is corroborated by Elyot: "What an infinite number of English men and women at this present time wander in all places throughout this realm as beasts brute and savage abandoning all occupation, service and honesty!" Starkey complains of the oppressive number of priests, canons, monks and friars; lawyers, those 'cormorants,' are out of all proportion to the number of artisans and farmers; bishops care only for the wool of their flock and ape the secular lords; commoners too seek to imitate lords in their expense and show. The conclusion arrived at is that a remedy for these ills is to be sought in encouraging marriage: priests should be allowed to marry, bachelors should be well taxed and poor men with five children exempted from taxation. For the due repair of decaying towns and the health of the citizens the old office of edile should be revived. The general idleness might be corrected by instruction in manual arts and more and better schools should be established.

The earnest mind of Sir Thomas Elyot was equally exercised over the political situation and he preceded Starkey in suggesting a better method of education as a specific. He was one of the most learned men of the reign, an ardent friend and admirer of More's and a servant of the king on diplomatic embassies. In 1531 appeared his "Governor"—an ideal of culture for an English youth destined to public office. From the unity of the supreme ruler Elyot, like Tyndale, derives his correspondent earthly monarchy: aristocracy and democracy,

he avers, are ever subject to division and discord : by examples
drawn from Scripture and the experience of Greece, Rome
and several Italian states he unfolds his philosophy of history.
In a single sentence he couches the apology of that revolutionary decade : "From God only proceedeth all honor and
neither noble progeny, succession nor election be of such
force that by them any estate or dignity may be so established
that God being stirred to vengeance shall not shortly resume
it and perchance translate it where it shall like him."

The "education of a gentleman" who is to serve his king
as a lesser "governor" or magistrate should begin in infancy.
He should hear no coarse word but only pure English and
Latin, which may be made familiar to him from his earliest
years. The refining influence of music is not to be forgotten;
it is a solace and a pleasant science and was so regarded by
the ancients. If the child is inclined to paint or form images
in stone or "tree," he should be encouraged — contempt of
art and artists suppresses genius and so we have to apply to
strangers when we would have anything painted or carved.
The boy's tutor should be selected with care, for an ignorant
and cruel master dulls wits as daily experience shows.
(Children suffered untold misery at their teachers' hands in
those days.) While learning Greek the little student is to converse in Latin, — and he should begin to read authors before
he gets wearied of the grammar, which should serve simply as
an introduction to literature. It is good to commit to memory
and to practise verse-composition. At fourteen years the lad
should have read Homer and Virgil, Ovid, Horace, Lucan,
Hesiod and selections from other classics ; he may then take
up logic and rhetoric, and geography as a preparation for
history which, with poetry, stimulates courage. Elyot defends
poetry; much may be learned, he says, even from comedies.
At seventeen years the youth should learn to restrain his ardor
by reason and philosophy — especially that branch called

moral: now he may study Aristotle, Cicero and above all Plato. To make the physical frame strong and supple, wrestling and running are recommended by the example of the ancients; swimming is good though it be not of much repute now; sword-play and battle-axe afford good exercise, hunting and hawking give one an appetite for supper. "All dancing is not repugnant unto virtue"; it may be a noble and virtuous pastime and should be turned to account in gentle education. The mixed dance signifies matrimony — and that is a sacrament. Among other amusements and exercises Elyot dissuades from dice as an invention of the devil; cards are not so bad but chess is best of all. "Shooting with the bow" is highly commended, but ten-pins, quoit-throwing and foot-ball are proscribed — the last because of the "beastly fury and violence" it excites and the danger of strain incurred.

So far the training of the youth; the second part of the work treats of the virtues which one in authority should practise, of his apparel and his dwelling. He should be affable, benevolent, liberal. A forcible sentence dissuades from anger — that hideous passion: "who, beholding a man by fury changed into an horrible figure, his face infarced [swollen] with rancor, his mouth foul and imbossed [frothy], his eyne wide staring, not speaking, but as a wild bull roaring and braying out words despiteful and venomous, forgetting his estate or condition, forgetting learning, yea, forgetting all reason, will not have such a passion in extreme detestation?" (Such a spectacle, one might suppose, should cure the beholder and the shame consequent on the exhibition the offender of any disposition to fly into a like rage or commit a repetition of such a scene.)

A magistrate's house should have its walls adorned with arras, painted panels and figures representing famous deeds and persons, and the board should be set out with plate and vessels engraved with histories or wise sentences. The duty of decorating churches inspired what is perhaps the most glowing sentence in the work; "These material churches whereunto repaireth the congregation of Christian people, in the which is the corporal presence of the Son of God and very God, ought to be pure, clean and well adorned, as the heaven visible is most pleasantly garnished with planets and stars resplendishing in the most pure firmament of azure color."

Elyot was the type of a cultivated, Catholic humanist of the latter half of the reign of Henry VIII. He was overpowered by the wealth and authority of classic literature; among his numberless examples drawn therefrom, his constant reference to ancient authors, we long for more nervous, original thought. He remains nevertheless (perhaps we ought to say therefore) a typical Englishman of the Renascence.

At the court John Heywood made merriment by his witty talk and song, epigrams and light dramatic pieces. He had been recommended by Sir Thomas More to the young princess Mary. In his dialogue of "The Pardoner and the Friar" written before the breach with Rome we are transported even to Chaucer's day; the atmosphere is still mediaeval. The two sinners strive to outdo each other in popular favor; the pardoner vaunts his power to absolve from every sin and the miraculous efficacy of his relics, while the friar celebrates the good deeds of his order; they preach at each other in alternate lines, work themselves into a passion and finally come to blows. In "John the Husband, Tyb the Wife, and Sir John the Priest" the woes of a henpecked husband are set forth, the ill usage he sustains at the hands of a faithless wife and a profligate priest, — but the brightest of Heywood's pieces is "The Four P's." A palmer, a pardoner, a 'pothecary and a pedlar rival each other in telling monstrous stories: at the last the palmer avers that he never saw a woman out of patience in his life: the others, agape, profess that he has won, for that is the greatest lie of all.

John Bale, a zealous partisan of the Reformation, composed mysteries and interludes, — but for the best dramatic relic of the day — the best morality, perhaps, ever written in Britain — we have to cross once more the Scottish border. Owing to the treaty with France there was relative peace between England and Scotland, and at the court of the young king, James V, we discern a transient blush of letters and arts, a touch of renascent scholarship, a freedom of thought and speech, a moment of gayety that recall the palmier time before Flodden. Among the scholars at the court was John Bellenden, whose version of Boece's Latin history of Scotland so pleased the king that he commissioned him to turn the work of Livy into the popular dialect. In 1537 James concluded a romantic courtship by bringing home from France the delicate young princess Madeleine as his bride — and in her train there came a page named Pierre Ronsard. The poor girl lived only a few weeks after her arrival in the north, dying before she could be crowned — and Sir David Lindsay gave expression to the general sorrow in a poetical lament. He had been the king's preceptor and it was he who wrote the moral-play mentioned above. It is entitled " A pleasant Satire of the Three Estates " — the spiritual and temporal lords, that is, and the burgesses — but the first of these had to bear the brunt of the satire which can hardly have been " pleasant " to them : and the first part of the play was designed as a lesson for the king — a warning and rebuke of his sensual propensities. King Humanity desires to rule his realm well but is tempted by Wantonness to yield to Sensuality ; good Counsel comes to recover him, to the alarm of Flattery and Falsehood, who disguise themselves as friars, change their names to Devotion and Wisdom, beguile the king and drive Counsel away. Now Truth appears — and is accused to the bishops of having an English Testament in her hand : an abbot advises a charge of heresy and summary banishment, but for the present she is put in the stocks. Chastity next seeks to save the king but Sensuality bids him choose between them and he banishes Chastity on pain of death. But now Correction who has been reforming the rest of Christendom arrives in Scotland: Flattery robs the king and runs away: Correction looses and recalls Counsel, Truth and Chastity and drives away Sensuality who takes refuge with the bishops and abbots.

The play was enacted before the court at Linlithgow palace in the year 1540. Lindsay used a plainness of speech that is an extraordinary revelation of the manners of the day. It speaks well for the king that he took his old tutor's remonstrances in good part: and without his protection Lindsay could hardly have ventured upon such bold criticism of the higher clergy. He illumines for us the ghastly abyss of corruption the surface of which the common histories skim with euphemistic, deceptive propriety. The gross sensuality of the decaying church is his dominant theme: "the Roman church is the lamp of lechery: the cardinals and bishops have banished chastity from Rome. Most of the prelates of this nation have concubines — some have three. The marriage of the clergy is criminal, is irksome, but a change of concubines innocent and pleasant." And the biting satire was irrefutable, so extreme was the moral dissolution finally induced by monastic restraint upon natural instinct and a canonical impediment to a lawful connection. And his clerical associates, counsellors and conscience-keepers connived at if they did not actually encourage the young king in his loose way of life. Such were the morals of the parties that combined to suppress the reformation in Scotland — and the corruption and tyranny of the Scottish episcopate is the sufficient explanation of the force that presbyterianism there acquired.

In the latter part of the satire which recounts the oppression of John Commonweal whose money is drained Romeward occur some quaint touches: a pardoner just from Rome finds his traffic diminishing and curses the New Testament, Luther and St. Paul as the cause; and the spiritual lords agree that "it had been good that Paul had ne'er been born!"

Among Lindsay's shorter poems is a remorseless exposure of the immoral suggestions of the confessional and the frivolous and mercenary nature of the penances prescribed. In his "Answer to the King's Flyting" he scores his royal pupil's profligacy in downright terms. In other coarse but clever verses he ridicules a passing fashion in ladies' dress and his "Justing between Watson and Barbour" is a satire with a double edge; it is a lampoon upon the professors of medicine and a Rabelaisian caricature of the courtly entertainment of the tournament — and when a once honored institution becomes a subject for jest and burlesque its end is near.

The best known by far, the most read and loved to-day of all the writers of the reign of Henry VIII are the poet friends Wyatt and Surrey; to them belongs the credit of having introduced the sonnet and blank verse into English literature. Wyatt was of the more masculine genius. Of his sonnets the octave is correct, Petrarchian; the sestet is composed of an ordinary or inverted quatrain and a couplet. In one experiment there are only three rhymes, two running alternately through twelve lines, the third forming the terminal couplet. He also composed rondeaux, songs, epigrams etc. in a single Chaucerian stanza or Boccaccian octave, and satires in the rhyming system of Dante's Divine Comedy. So deeply was his genius swayed by Italian influence, though French too was not wanting. His verse is analytical, reflective, — its subject is the passion of love. One pretty sonnet — the crystalline form is singularly adapted to contain distilled emotion — tells of the signs of love; another, of a dream that he had his love in possession; another describes the lover's woful state, now freezing, now burning — his life is compared to a ship tossed at sea and again to the Alps. There is scant observation of external nature in these poems: love is compared to a tiger, a stream, fire, wind, the sea, — but there is no landscape, no picture; external objects are introduced in a frigid, merely decorative way. He complains of his mistress' cruelty and his own lack of liberty; yet again though beloved by her he loves he suffers still and makes the discovery that there is pain even in love's fruition. He continues to analyze his feelings, his doubts: "by love hell may be felt ere death assail." (Perhaps it was in this mood that he took to translating the seven penitential psalms!) At last by an effort of will he breaks his bonds and adopts a manlier strain, rejoicing that he has regained his freedom, having broken the snares of love like a bird.

His satires are in similar vein: he exults that he has escaped from the court where speech is not free, where one must speak fair to wealth and rank, where life is no life but flattery and slavery: now he is free "in Kent and Christendom," — and there he invites a friend to join him.

He sums up his experience of life for his young reader's:

> " If thou wilt mighty be flee from the rage
> Of cruel will and see thou keep thee free
> From the foul yoke of sensual bondage . . .
> For He that hath each star in heaven fixed . . .
> Alike hath made thee noble in his working,
> So that wretched no way may thou be
> Except foul lust and vice do conquer thee."

Stars and the moral law! They are a young man's poems, self-conscious, introspective, aspiring; in them we perceive the soul turning in upon itself, studying its own workings; here is the personal element, self-analysis, contrast of outer and inner, — the note is distinctly modern, — the age is growing metaphysical, psychological, ethical.

Nature enters largely into Surrey's sonnets; one of them is a pretty description of spring — and in truth his was the springtime of modern poetry. " The sun, when he hath spread his rays " reveals a wide landscape :

> "The mountains high and how they stand,
> The valleys and the great mainland,
> The trees, the herbs, the towers strong,
> The castles and the rivers long."

Roaming about the streets of London one night with frolicsome companions, Surrey broke the big glass windows of some of the staid citizens — and was speedily lodged in the Fleet prison ; but there, instead of using the time for repentance, he penned a satire upon the city, the modern Babylon, and the vices of its inhabitants, — whose windows he broke to mind them of God's judgment !

He wrote many quatrains, versified several chapters of the book Ecclesiastes and several psalms — but his chief contribution to his country's literature was a translation of the second and fourth books of the Æneid in blank verse. We note that his caesura usually falls after the fourth syllable — the second foot, — rarely after the fifth ; on an average one line in seven begins with an accented syllable ; an alexandrine sometimes intrudes itself ; and the lines, of which only one in six runs on into the following, never end with a redundant syllable. So formal and mechanical at its introduction was that most plastic and ductile form of verse.

It is interesting to learn that at this very epoch the sonnet was introduced into French literature by Mellin de Saint Gelais. The fashion of psalm-translating was exemplified with eminent success by Clément Marot — a protégé of the queen of Navarre. He was an expert beside of polished taste in all kinds of mediaeval measures. His version of the psalms was widely popular and for thus abetting the religious movement and for his liberal opinions he was forced to flee into Italy. Another of Margaret's protégés — Bonaventure des Périers — was a satirist of all religions : he was no doubt a collaborator with his royal patroness in her famous Heptameron or "tales of the seven days" with which a supposed party of fashionable visitors to the springs of Cauteretz beguiled an enforced delay on their return. Genuine mediaeval license marks many of their tales.

The traits just slightly touched on are sufficient to indicate the fatal weakness in faith and morals by reason of which the French after many noble efforts surrendered themselves to the remodelled church of Rome. Deeply significant in this regard is the huge satire, the grotesque allegory, "Gargantua and Pantagruel"—the chief literary landmark of that time, and a cloaca, as it would seem, for all the ordure of the Middle Ages. Rabelais has ever been a problematical character; he was a monk, but a monk out of his cloister, a student of medicine and of the new learning; he was sincere in his uncouth satire upon the monastic and scholastic systems and for the latter he propounded a natural and sensible substitute,—yet he was not a Protestant, hardly a man of the Renascence; his eye was fixed upon the animal part of our nature and though he had glimpses of higher things he contented himself with mockery. So it was with his countrymen: France laughed with Rabelais and abandoned the ideal.

Sonnets had been written in Spanish, it will be remembered, long since, but the form was now fairly naturalized in Castilian literature by the poetic pair Juan Boscan and Garcilasso de la Vega, who afford a pleasing and forcible comparison with their English contemporaries Wyatt and Surrey. Their sonnets are tuned to the same pure and meditative strain and the young Garcilasso's are of even superior grace. They also experimented with blank verse, Boscan in a long tale, his friend in a poetic epistle. Boscan's best production is an allegory of love in Boccaccio's octave.

A sample of Spanish prose and of the politico-didactic interest of the period is the "Dial of Princes" by Antonio de

Guevara, historiographer to the emperor Charles V. It was widely read and translated. And a class of writings characteristic of Spanish literature, thence imported and made popular in many languages, was headed by Diego de Mendoza with his comic history, written during his student days at Salamanca, of the clever rogue and lackey, " Lazarillo de Tormès."

An interesting literary reaction against the late poetic movement under Italian tutelage was led by Christoval de Castillejo from about the year 1540. He advocated with all his might a return to old-time modes of verse.

The date is memorable for it was signalized by a strenuous ecclesiastical reaction whose capital expression was the institution of the Jesuit order. In 1541 the conciliatory conference at Regensburg in which a basis of agreement was sought for both Catholics and Protestants broke up in failure. In 1543 a Spanish Testament was suppressed and the Inquisition was introduced into Italy; the following year a Spaniard was burnt for Lutheran heresy; and in 1545 the great reactionary Council of Trent was convened. Its objects were a reformation of the church and suppression of heresy — but the former point though pressed by the French bishops was by Spanish and Italian influence postponed to the latter, and the decrees on the Scriptures and justification were carefully worded so as to exclude the reformers' views. The Roman church had at last awakened to the necessity of repressive measures and disciplinary reform if it would save itself from dissolution — and that awakening connotes the close of mediaevalism proper in southern Europe and the collapse of Italian humanism. The sack of Rome had scattered the humanists thence, Medicean tyranny had exiled others from Florence and numbers of scholars and artists wandered into France to enjoy the protection and patronage of its munificent king. Conspicuous among these and one of the first was the Florentine Luigi Alamanni, author of a didactic poem on agriculture patterned after Virgil's Georgics, in blank verse. The sculptor Cellini, the painter Bordone, the novelist Bandello followed — and the last was gratified by the gift of a bishopric. The Jesuit reaction was the finishing blow to declining humanism in Italy, — and perhaps it came none too soon. It was merited; for the indecencies of Pietro Aretino, the egotism, extravagance and license of Cellini, were indicative of the degeneration of genius and demanded a curb. In the tales of Matteo Bandello — the Boccaccio of this later Renascence — concupiscence moves the characters about like pawns on a chess board. They are not worthy of the name of characters: change of name and incident alone give variety — the intrigue is ever the same.

The conversion of the aged Bembo is symbolical of the change that came over the spirit of Italy: he was made a cardinal in 1539 and forthwith forswore the cultivation of classic literature as profane.

In 1542 Andrea Palladio began his careful measurements of old Roman buildings, published erelong a set of plans and restored elevations and elaborated for the builders of the reaction a congenial architectural style, ornate, mechanical, new Roman: of round arches, round or gabled window-heads, superimposed tiers of pilasters of different orders, and balustraded eaves.

During those years Giorgio Vasari, Angelo's pupil, occupied himself in collecting, before it was too late, information concerning the artists of past time which he digested in his incomparable " Lives." It was a last effort of the mediaeval memory, summing up the results of a long day of creative activity.

We remark finally a glowing Italian version by Bernardo Tasso of a romance long popular in the Spanish peninsula — the Amadis of Gaul.

In the realm of natural science the overthrow of outworn authority went on — for of investigations in the sphere of matter the powers that be are rarely apprehensive. Under and through the alchemy of the Middle Ages modern chemistry was working and protruding like the thumb of Ptah through his swathing-bands. In 1541 the troubled career of Paracelsus closed at Salzburg. He first made science stammer in the German tongue and though beset by teeming, mystical fancies struck into original and practicable paths of research. In token of his breach with past authority he gave the works of Galen to the flames.

The supremacy of the great Roman anatomist was more cautiously and surely undermined by the Fleming, Vesalius, whose discoveries also superseded Mondini's; he was the father of modern anatomy.

Shortly before his death in 1543 Nicholas Copernicus published his "Revolutions of the Heavenly Bodies," relegating the Ptolemaic system to the past; but strange to say that momentous work that wrought a revolution in astronomy only to be compared with Luther's in religion or with the discoveries of Columbus and da Gama remained without effect until the ensuing century.

The same year the first great botanic garden was laid out at Padua. And through the decade the young Swiss naturalist, Conrad Gesner, was travelling far and wide, studying plants, which he aimed to classify according to a natural system, gathering materials for his epoch-making work on animals.

The reactionary spirit of the decade was not without its influence on the temper of Luther; as he aged he grew harder, his opinions crystallized, he waxed ever more bitter against the Calvinists, more intolerant of all variations from his standard. Sebastian Franck's protest was especially irritating to him. Franck was a theologian of mystical tendency who made appeal from Luther's growing dogmatism to a higher spiritual court — that of conscience and inward conviction of religious truth. He was the spokesman of much secret dis-

content among Germans with some of the results and principles of the Lutheran reformation.

The sympathetic attitude of Dürer and Cranach, however,
reminds us that Luther never made the breach with art that
Zwingli and Calvin made. Indeed, he composed a series of
forcible sermons against iconoclasts that are beside good
specimens of his German style. He had the wisdom to set his
hymns to popular melodies and thus they enjoyed immense
vogue. Popular literature too was ever his ally; Hans Sachs,
the rhyming shoemaker of Nuremberg, in countless songs and
homely satires and narratives helped to advance his cause.

In England the late spring-tide of reform began to ebb.
Henry felt that the religious and intellectual movement had
gone far enough and needed a check — which he proceeded to
apply through the notorious Six Articles that he caused his
parliament to pass in the year 1539. Though it be hard to
recollect these in detail it is easy to remember that their pivot
was the mass. The first declared that the doctrine of transubstantiation was that of the church of England; this was
followed by assertions of the sufficiency of communion in one
kind and the efficacy of private masses; confession to a priest
was declared to be a pre-requisite to communion; and in
remaining articles the condition of celebrants was touched on:
sacerdotal celibacy was enforced and the binding nature of the
second monastic vow was set forth. This last was a peculiarly arbitrary provision; it was levelled at the hosts of monks
that wandered up and down the land, many of whom after
their ruthless ejection from their old homes were seeking to
make new ones by entering the marriage relation; by this
article they were forbidden to become thus merged in general
society.

For an attempt he made to attach the king to the protestant
interest in Germany Thomas Cromwell paid the forfeit with
his head. After the death of Jane Seymour, his third queen

— doubly endeared to him as the mother of his son Edward — his minister pressed upon Henry an alliance with the princess Anne of Cleves.   A portrait of her taken by Holbein — to whom we are indebted for likenesses of many distinguished personages of the reign — so attracted the king that the match was arranged — but when Anne appeared his disappointment was grievous : the cunning painter had flattered her, and she could speak nothing but German, of which he understood not a word.   He offered therefore to become her affectionate brother ; she was to receive a pension and take precedence next after his queen and daughter.   Anne was complaisant, agreed to a divorce and assumed her singular position at the English court.   But Cromwell went to the block on a charge of heresy, — and the very day of his execution the king wedded a second Catherine, of the great Catholic house of Howard.

The familiar political combinations of the past now repeated themselves as by an inner necessity ; Henry became estranged from his late ally of France, drew toward his imperial friend of former times and the partition agreement of twenty years before was reverted to.   Francis thereupon renewed his alliance with Suleiman II — and we behold again the familiar groups, the king of France, German Protestants, and Turks against emperor and king of England — who has now also perforce a war with Scotland on his hands.   From 1543 to 1545 the European war dragged on ; it was not pressed with energy by either party ; Europe was exhausted by the tremendous conflicts of the past half-century ; and more than all Francis himself desired reconciliation with the church and the emperor, — he too would become a prominent representative of the reaction.   The three great sovereigns now grown old were ready and willing to sustain as best they could authority and the old order, — so in 1545 peace was made between them, — a peace that Francis made haste to solemnize by a ferocious massacre of the Vaudois — the Protestants of the south of

France. Henry wielded over England his "whip with six strings," sending Protestants to the stake for infringing his articles while Catholics went to the block for denying his ecclesiastical jurisdiction; the land was overawed by his capricious, inscrutable policy; his closing years were a true reign of terror. His minister now was Stephen Gardiner, bishop of Winchester — a rigid sacramentarian, who made desperate efforts to bring Cranmer into discredit, instigating against him charges of heresy. Hugh Latimer, who had resigned his bishopric of Worcester upon the passage of the Six Articles, was sent to the tower. Yet ever and anon the reformers were heartened by some act like that which directed that copies of the Bible in English (Tyndale's version as revised by Coverdale and others) should be exhibited in parish churches, or that which provided for the publication of part of the service in the mother tongue. Henry's marriage to his last queen, Catherine Parr, was regarded as auspicious to their cause toward which she was well inclined, — but in conversations with the king on doctrinal subjects she gave too free expression to her views, was for an instant in grave peril and only extricated herself by a prudent submission.

Among the victims offered up to the dogma of transubstantiation none engaged deeper sympathy than the gentle, devoted and long-suffering Anne Askew, who was burnt at Smithfield in 1546. The height of the reaction headed in Scotland by the evil Cardinal Beaton was marked that year by the burning of George Wishart, a distinguished evangelical preacher.

The domestic condition of England continued unprosperous. The king's necessities led him to commit one of the gravest injuries a government can inflict on its people; he debased the coinage, — and workers found their wages shrivel in their hands they understood not why. The discontent and suffering were grievous. In consequence partly of the industrial depression, partly of the suppression of the monasteries where relief has been dispensed of old, vagabondage and pauperism attained dimensions so alarming that the rudiment of a poor-law had to be devised : "sturdy vagabonds " — voluntary paupers — were to be repressed and the deserving poor to be relieved from funds dispensed by episcopal almoners. The defect of the measure was that public charity alone was relied on to supply the funds which were hence uncertain and in bad times quite inadequate.

The literature of the end of the reign was scant and scarce worth mentioning ; indeed, none could flourish in that atmosphere of fear and suspicion ; in his determination to suppress all opposition to his arbitrary will Henry would seem to have been animated by a desire to annihilate literature. One by one its foremost representatives were killed off. Tyndale and More had been extinguished ; upon the fall of Cromwell Wyatt was committed to the Tower, and having been commanded to join the king at Falmouth died on the journey of a fever contracted in his anxious haste ; and a crowning injustice was the execution of Surrey because there coursed in his veins a strain of royal blood.

The king even brought legislation to bear upon literature and the drama, his object being the suppression of all publications in English upon the subject of religion. By an act of the year 1542 he put a stop to the performance of the old mysteries and forbade all religious plays, ballads and songs (of which many satirical specimens were current) as " noisome to the peace of the church."

Before his decease in 1546 Sir Thomas Elyot had the satisfaction of seeing his hints on archery expanded into an elaborate treatise, the " Toxophilus " or " School of Shooting," by his young friend Roger Ascham. It is in the form of a dialogue. Archery is pronounced a most honest pastime, indulged in by the ancients, wholesome for princes and students ; cards are condemned as devoid of exercise and honesty; and music of the new school "so nicely fingered, so sweetly tuned" is discountenanced as too nearly resembling the Lydian mode: beside, Galen has said that "much music marreth men's manners." An exception is made as to old-fashioned plain-song which is declining and should be encouraged. Here accordingly we have a quaint musical corollary to the doctrinal reaction!

By that time John Leland, who held the unique office of king's antiquary, had finished his great tour over England in the course of which he visited every city, manor-house, castle and monastery in the kingdom — if we may believe his declaration, — and saved as many manuscripts as he could from the wreck, distressing to his honest soul, of the monastic libraries. That archaeological survey at the moment when the Middle Ages were expiring was like memory, recapitulating at eventide the toils and triumphs of the day. It testified to the rise of national sentiment and an historic sense, — uncritical though it might be: in Leland the Arthurian legends found a last defender: he published a Latin assertion of their genuineness.

Now it was that written sermons began to supersede the old fashion of free and familiar delivery. Precision of statement and literary finish might thus be attained — but it was at the expense of the energy, picturesqueness and directness of appeal of the extemporaneous style.

Luther died in 1546, none too soon for him — he just escaped witnessing a seeming obliteration of German Protestantism. The year 1547 was the low-water mark of the reaction; the protestant leaders were divided among themselves and paralyzed by doubt and treachery; their wholly inadequate force melted away before the emperor at Mühlberg and Germany was at his feet. But the same year Henry and Francis passed away leaving the stage clear for new characters — Cardinal Beaton had paid for his tyranny with his life, — and western

Europe breathed more freely.   Slowly the tide began to turn
and a fifth chapter in Reformation history opened — a fresh
and even more vigorous forward movement than the last.   In
the course of a few years Charles lost the magnificent position
he had gained by his victory at Mühlberg; the new king of
France allied himself with the protestant princes to undo its
results and received from them a bit of territory on the bank
of the Rhine with the title "Protector of the Liberties of Germany"; in 1552 the Turks took Temesvar; and the emperor
was constrained to conclude with the Protestants what was to
him the humiliating truce of Passau, granting them freedom of
worship according to the terms of that early decree of Speyer.
In 1555 this was made the basis of the general and lasting
religious pacification of Augsburg; the labor of his life seemed
thrown away and the unhappy old emperor, bitterly repenting
that he had let Luther escape him, conscious that his whole long
career was a failure, abdicated and went into a monastery
where he soon after died.

Henry's attempt to graft a reformed, national polity upon the
old system of faith and worship had proved impracticable and
in his son's reign the latter went by the board.   The boy-king
Edward was a zealous little Protestant ; his maternal uncle and
guardian, the duke of Somerset, was hand and glove with the
reforming party ; Cranmer's star was in the ascendant, Latimer
was released from the Tower where he had spent the years of
reaction, and radical changes in the mode of worship were consummated; in fact the existing ecclesiastical system of England
was then fully inaugurated.   The Six Articles were rescinded;
with the doctrine of the corporal presence of Christ in the
eucharist private masses ceased, both elements were administered to the laity, and the clergy were allowed to wed.   The
liturgy was done into English ; in the year 1548 the Book of
Common Prayer appeared — the famous "First Book of King
Edward VI."   These sweeping changes seemed revolutionary

to Bishop Gardiner and his compeer Bonner of London; they remonstrated, were cast into prison and shortly deprived of their sees. Ridley was appointed in Bonner's room and Hooper to be bishop of Gloucester: his scruples about wearing the episcopal vestments, which he called idolatrous and impious, delayed the latter's installation. In Hooper the lineaments of the Puritan can be plainly discerned. To minds of his stamp it seemed that the church was not yet reduced to the just evangelical model; the agitation went on; after the crushing defeat of Mühlberg several eminent continental reformers took refuge in England and pointed out defects in the prayer-book which permitted quite too many of the old ceremonies for their taste. More statues and pictures were removed from the churches; the ancient stone altars gave place to communion tables and candles were no longer seen; in the year 1552 the Second Book of Edward VI registered the further rise of the tide. Objectionable practices allowed by the former book were dropped; the sentences used when administering the elements were altered to accord with the merely commemorative view; and worship became in outward form and in inward spirit evangelical.

It is interesting to observe how Wyclif's fame after its long eclipse came out now in full lustre: indeed, through the varying phases of doctrine that we have been studying, what men thought of him was a ready gauge of their position. Cranmer took issue with Gardiner about him: "John Wyclif was a singular instrument of God in his time to set forth the truth of Christ's Gospel, but Antichrist that sitteth in God's temple boasting himself as God hath by God's sufferance prevailed against many holy men and sucked the blood of martyrs these late years." The passage occurs in the archbishop's "Answer to a Crafty and Sophistical Cavillation" of his old enemy "against the true and godly doctrine" of the sacrament. The treatise is not agreeable either in temper or style — it could scarcely be expected to be, — but it defines clearly its author's position. He believed that "the very body of the tree or rather the root of the weeds — beads, pardons, pilgrimages, indulgences, service in Latin etc. — is the popish doctrine of transubstantiation." He appealed to Christ's institution : none of his apostles were so "fond" as not to know that the bread was not his body nor the wine his blood. Our opponents "teach that Christ is in the bread and wine. But we say according to the truth that he is in them that worthily eat and drink the bread and wine. My meaning is that the force, the grace, the virtue and benefit of Christ's body that was crucified for us and of his blood that was shed for us be really and effectually present with all them that duly receive the sacraments — but all this I understand of his spiritual presence. . . . Nor no more truly is he corporally or really present in the due ministration of the Lord's Supper than he is in the due ministration of baptism." Bread, wine and water are signs and tokens, not to be worshipped; yet Christ is in them as he is in his Word "when he worketh mightily by the same in the hearts of the hearers"; he is not present in the voice of the speaker but uses it as he does his sacraments.

The noblest figure in the English reformation was without question that of Bishop Latimer, — a brave man, earnest, large-hearted, buoyant of spirit — of all the reformers of the island-kingdom he most resembled Luther. In his youth as he himself testified he was as "obstinate a papist as any in the kingdom, — zealous without knowledge" like Saul the persecutor; when he was converted he became a sturdy pillar of evangelic faith. He was much the most popular preacher of the day and he magnified his office. His famous "Sermon on the Plough," conceived in the quaint, allegorical style that the people loved, enforced the duty of preaching. It was delivered at St. Paul's in the winter of 1549. Taking a passage out of St. Luke's gospel as his starting-point, — "the Seed is the

Word of God" — he proceeded to draw a parallel between the ploughman and a preacher. Erelong he rose into a prophetic strain, denouncing the pride and wickedness of London, calling upon its people to repent, — "but London cannot abide to be rebuked, such is the nature of man; they will not amend their faults and they will not be ill spoken of." Nevertheless he hesitated not fearlessly to expose its sins and to score those "unpreaching prelates" whom he held to be largely responsible for the wide-spread ignorance and wrong-doing. We can divine the hush that fell upon the great congregation as the orator engaged closer attention by the sudden question, "Who is the most diligent bishop and prelate in all England that passeth all the rest in doing his office? I can tell for I know him well. But now I think I see you listening and harkening that I should name him. Will ye know who it is? I will tell you; it is the Devil. He is the most diligent preacher of all other, he is never out of his diocese, ye shall never find him unoccupied, he keepeth residence at all times, he is ever at his plough."

The ensuing Lent, Latimer delivered a series of six sermons before the boy king and on one occasion in the following year preached to him both in the morning and afternoon of the same day. Still in prophetic vein he chose as his subject avarice and lust and their connection, which he illustrated by the adulteries that follow marriages for money. He returned to his charge against London — as wicked a city as Nineveh, equally in need of repentance.

An example of his homiletic allegorizing almost as good as his sermon on the plough was that "on the Card," in which he drew a moral from the popular pastime: in the game of life "hearts is trumps, as I said."

"If thou build a hundred churches, give as much as thou canst make to the gilding of saints and honoring of the church and offer as great candles as oaks, if thou leave the works of mercy and the commandments undone these works shall nothing avail thee,"—yet of themselves they are good. Latimer was not an iconoclast.

In 1549 appeared a metrical version of parts of the psalter —the work of Thomas Sternhold, who died that year. The collection was subsequently enlarged by John Hopkins and enjoyed for generations an extraordinary popularity.

A single dramatic effort is extant of the reign of Edward VI —the comedy of "Ralph Roister Doister" by Nicholas Udall, formerly master of Eton College. Other plays that he composed have been lost. Ralph is a brainless, rakish fellow of the town who is beguiled by a cunning parasite called Merygreek—an English Lazarillo—and is helped and hindered by him in a vain but persistent suit he pays to a well-to-do widow. The rhyme, metre and diction of the play are those of the homely popular tales of former times, the dialogue is easy and familiar, and the action progresses through well-defined acts and scenes.

The date of its appearance is fixed by a reference made to it by Thomas Wilson, the rhetorician, who published a treatise on rhetoric and logic in the year 1553. His object was the purification of the spoken language from the classic and foreign terms with which scholars, travellers and the fashionable delighted to encrust it. There is much sensible advice in the book: "Never affect inkhorn terms or be over-fine. Only the foolish fantastical *Latin* their tongues; journeyed gentlemen, for show, talk a French or Italianate English and the fine courtier talks nothing but Chaucer." Men were still half-ashamed of their native tongue which was then just emerging from its state of immaturity; it is evident that it was undergoing that expansion of vocabulary that was to make it the great medium of expression for the coming generation; but many in their half-culture, their would-be elegance, were making mistakes in taste and selection. Against such Wilson's was a manly and useful protest.

Sir John Cheke, the most eminent classical scholar in the kingdom and Edward's tutor in Greek, who had in the last reign had a sharp controversy with bishop Gardiner as to the proper pronunciation of that language, was equally jealous of the purity of his native speech and sought to expunge from its vocabulary words and phrases that had crept into it from foreign languages. He also suggested a simplification of its spelling.

We note elsewhere interest in the vernacular; Sir David Lindsay penned a vigorous defence of his in the opening of his " Dialogue concerning the Monarchy," — a long metrical account of ancient empires that winds up with an attack upon the papal monarchy in the style with which we are already familiar. It was the last monument of the old northern or mediaeval Scottish dialect, the literary history of which we have traced for two hundred years; its author died soon after.

A highly interesting parallel to these efforts for the extended use, enrichment and purification of the vernacular is offered by a school of French writers that rose at this very era. Its programme was set forth in an enthusiastic " Defence of the French language " published in the year 1549, — the maiden essay of a young poet named Joachim du Bellay whose dawning talent had been marked by king Francis and the queen of Navarre. After the fashion of the Renascence he was dubbed "the French Ovid." His defence of his mother tongue consisted in a word in the proposition that it was quite capable of appropriating spoil from Latin and Greek. A favorite analogy was the practice of the Latin authors who, though profoundly versed in Greek, did not therefore discard their own language but applied their scholarship to its enrichment and regulation. For the attainment of these ends du Bellay and his followers accordingly introduced into the language shoals of classic terms and to give it exquisite polish cultivated the sonnet with especial zeal.

After the appearance of his treatise which was the literary sensation of the hour, du Bellay visited Rome where he spent some years.   He exemplified his theory in a set of over a hundred sonnets "To Olive" and returned in the year 1552 with forty-five more on "The Ruins of Rome."   He was henceforth a particular star at the court of Henry II.   His contemporary, Pierre Ronsard, coöperated powerfully in the movement and erelong eclipsed his fame, winning from the admiring court the title "Prince of Poets."   He applied himself to composing French odes in imitation of Horace.   His preceptor in the classics, Jean Dorat — "the French Pindar" — was the Nestor of the movement, which progressed in spite of the ridicule of Rabelais — now approaching his end.

The year that du Bellay returned from Rome a disciple of his, Étienne Jodelle, then but twenty years of age, made himself the pioneer of an important form — classic tragedy — by his play "Cleopatra."   It was characterized by the mingled weakness and extravagance, the frigid, imitative rendering of heroic passions common to first efforts in this line, — but it was hailed by Ronsard the arbiter as equal to anything of Sophocles and it furnished a model of its kind for coming centuries.

The four poets just mentioned made up with some lights of less magnitude the celebrated group of the Pléiade.   One of the latter, Baïf by name, translated two of Euripides' tragedies and became an exemplar of the tendency of the school to degenerate into mere academic correctness.

While the affairs of the Protestants were prospering in Germany the death of Edward VI in the summer of 1553 opened the way for a third Catholic reaction, the most vehement of all, proportioned to the thoroughness of the late reform.   It was the sixth and last chapter in the long contest between mediaeval and modern ideas.   The princess Mary came to the throne at the mature age of thirty-six, her nature embittered by many injuries and by the thought of the ill-usage endured by a mother whom she deeply loved and whose memory it was her dearest consolation to defend. She inherited her father's tenacity of will but she was more than half her mother's daughter; her affections were fixed upon her mother's land of Spain. Hence from the first her whole heart was engaged in the project broached by the emperor of a marriage with his son Philip. Her devotion to her mother's faith was absolute: to restore it in its integrity was the object of her reign. She passed over therefore the latter part of her father's reign, aiming not only to maintain as he had done Catholic doctrine but also to restore the ancient form of church government, and took as her ideal the system of his earlier years, of her mother's time.

Gardiner's star was now in the ascendant; he was restored to his see and was appointed chancellor. Hooper and Coverdale were incarcerated in the Fleet, Ridley and Latimer in the Tower where they were soon followed by Cranmer; other prominent reformers fled to the continent. Bonner was reinstated in his bishopric of London and straightway the old crucifixes reappeared in the churches of his diocese and the texts with which the reformers had decorated their walls were blotted out.

Proceedings were hastened to reconcile England with the see of Rome. The queen's obsequious parliament declared that the marriage of Henry and Catherine had been valid and reversed Cranmer's sentence of divorce; every act of the late reign touching religion was revoked; and Mary's kinsman, Cardinal Pole, came sailing up the Thames in his barge to receive as papal legate the submission of the kingdom through its representatives. Parliament bent the knee, was absolved by him from the sins of heresy and schism, and renewed the act for burning heretics.

The sacrament became afresh the subject of impassioned controversy; the advocates of transubstantiation, flushed with triumph, balked not at its ultimate absurdity, asserting that at the Last Supper Jesus ate his own body.   The celibacy of the clergy was enforced, married ministrants were ejected from their livings.   The queen's forwardness was yet too slow for the ungrateful pope : he demanded restitution of all the old church lands ; but here Mary's hands were tied.   Of her own means however she managed to found anew a few abbeys.

There is something pathetic in this half heart-sick attempt to stay a vanishing ideal.

That the mediaeval revival might be whole and entire the old-time culture was brought into fashion again ; the literature, amusements and popular customs of past centuries were revived by authority.   The mystery-plays lately forbidden were sanctioned once more, the May-games and dances ; again on the Feast of Fools boys played the bishop or abbot and mimicked the solemn ceremonies of the church.   By such strange pastimes an outlet had been provided for the latent skepticism of the mediaeval populace — lest its mocking mood should flash into something more serious.

In 1554 a fine edition of Gower's " Confessio Amantis " was gotten out, in 1555 a like one of Lydgate's Troy-book; and the same year (a symbolic act) Chaucer's bones were reinterred in a Gothic tomb, — the first of poets in the since famous corner of England's historic abbey.   That year too the legend of the Sangreal appeared in a Spanish dress — a romantic emblem of the alliance subsisting between the two countries.

In 1557 a certain Richard Tottell got out a collection of poems by various hands — Surrey's and Wyatt's among the number — from which we single out two for particular mention because they were written in blank verse.   Their subjects were the deaths of Cicero and Zoroas (an Egyptian astrologer of Alexander's day), — their author was one Nicholas Grimald (of Italian descent, as his name implies).   These new specimens of English blank verse are marked by more variable caesura than Surrey's and are altogether more flexible than his ; run-on lines are frequent and light endings even appear. In the last reign Grimald had been Bishop Ridley's chaplain but under Mary he made little difficulty about conforming to the reëstablished mode of worship.

The jocund John Heywood was among the contributors to Tottell's " Miscellany." He had suffered some shrewd turns in the late inconstant times ; toward the end of Henry's reign he had been taxed with treasonable views touching the king's ecclesiastical supremacy and had made unconditional surrender ; under Edward it is said, perhaps jocosely, that his droll wit alone saved him from hanging. The accession of his former patroness was hailed by him with joy ; it promised a safe covert from such reverses for his sentiments accorded entirely with hers ; the years of her reign were fulfilled of halcyon days for him. He greeted her upon her coronation with a congratulatory address in Latin, and celebrated her union with Philip in a song. His humor was grateful to her and often lightened her melancholy moods. In 1556 he produced a lengthy allegorical poem in his quaint vein, "The Spider and the Fly," — the Protestants being figured by the ruthless spiders, the Catholics by the innocent flies: the heroine of this epic fable was of course the queen, who appeared in the character of a house-maid, wielding the broom of her temporal power at the bidding of her Lord and sovereign Lady, the church.

The laureateship of the reign was about evenly divided between Heywood and William Forrest — the queen's chaplain. In Edward's time he had been forced to conform sorely against his will to the reformed worship. He addressed to the young king a long didactic effort bearing the sounding alliterative title "A Pleasant Poesy of Princely Practice" in which he enlarged upon the unhappy condition of the laboring poor and the duty of a prince in such an exigency. Only a few months before Mary's death he finished and presented to her in manuscript his metrical vindication of her mother's memory, containing his interpretation of recent history. Catherine of Aragon in the character of the Second Griselda gave title to the work, which was couched in the Chaucerian stanza. Ere the exemplary queen was deposed the land flourished in plenty, God's service was maintained and the rich helped the poor — Griselda in special was kind to them. She attended matins at Greenwich priory and had an image of Christ's passion made — "not of idolatrous intent as certain miserable men hold." The rhymer is severe on Wolsey, who was no friend to Griselda; "yet he had an edifying end — God shield his soul from the infernal flame!" With the divorce began the affliction of both church and realm; schisms, sects and heresies of Satan's own raising entered in; the king — "expressed by the name of Walter — was led somewhat by light persons"; bad counsellors and agents took the place of good, self-will was the chief ruler, truth was set aside, the saints were slandered, the blessed Virgin Mary was no better esteemed than any other woman and any dunghill was as good as the sanctuary:

> "These mischiefs with hundredfold moe began
> At the incoming of this new Queen Anne."

Now the realm rapidly decayed, the poor suffered penury, rents were raised and there was dearth; fasting was made a jest, down went crosses, churches and monasteries. But Griselda's life was a pattern of piety and she made a good end, receiving extreme unction. "Now she prays for us — though wretched men seduced by Satan say that saints' prayers profit nothing: through hers I firmly believe we have been called back of late from the damnable race we were running."

The leading representative of the new learning fell a sacrifice to the violent ecclesiastical rebound. Men of the old school were thoroughly convinced that Greek letters had been largely responsible for the late religious upheaval: and in Sir John

Cheke a conspicuous victim was found. His heart was wholly in the cause of the reform; but now in age and weakness, in prison, trembling at the threat of torture, he sent in his recantation and was released — only to die of shame and distress of spirit for his betrayal of the truth.

The queen's Spanish match was generally unpopular and was made the pretext for a rising which was speedily put down but which involved the execution of the sweet and hapless Lady Jane Grey, a gentle representative of the new learning and the reformed faith. The princess Elizabeth even was in danger: she was suspected of complicity in the insurrection and was lodged for a time in the Tower.

The inmost nature of the desperate doctrinal reaction, the madness of a failing cause, had to be revealed, the connection of papal supremacy, the mass and persecution to be plainly exhibited. Squibs and satires upon the mass were many and were a vexation of spirit to Mary and her counsellors as similar ones had been to her father in his age. Under the lately revived statute for the punishment of heretics the burning of protestant martyrs began. The design was by a few single examples to intimidate the whole body. So early in 1555 Hooper was burnt at Gloucester and Bishop Farrar of St. David's at Carmarthen; in the autumn Ridley and Latimer were sacrificed at Oxford, the latter crying out as the fagots were heaped around them, "Be of good cheer, Master Ridley, and play the man, for we shall this day light such a candle in England as I trust shall never be put out." Gardiner died a few weeks after in remorse of soul and dismay at the magnitude of the odious task to which he was committed: the number of victims greatly surpassed his expectations. The following spring Archbishop Cranmer also perished in the flames at Oxford. He had shown little of the spirit of the hero, but his case was pitiable in the extreme and excited general commiseration. Cardinal Pole was now invested with the primacy.

In the course of this oppressive reign about three hundred persons suffered an excruciating death. Kent — the scene of the late insurrection — the city of London and the eastern midland furnished most of the victims. In its frenzy the reaction destroyed itself; evangelical faith received its baptism of blood and fire and evinced its truth and power by the fortitude of its martyrs.

In 1557 the queen's infatuation for her Spanish partner involved her in a disastrous war with France in the course of which Calais and Guisnes, last remnants of once broad possessions, were lost to the English crown.

Worn out with ill health and depression of spirits, full of misgivings as to the impending failure of her whole policy and repining at Philip's continued absence, Mary died, a disappointed woman, in the month of November, 1558. The tidings of her death were brought to her sister Elizabeth as she was walking under the autumn oaks at Hatfield. The Middle Ages were over forever.

www.ingramcontent.com/pod-product-compliance
Lightning Source LLC
Chambersburg PA
CBHW060615030726
47498CB00005B/1681